ALL THE RIGHT PLACES

BRAD
NEWSHAM

VILLARD BOOKS
NEW YORK 1989

Library of Congress Cataloging-in-Publication Data

Newsham, Brad.
  All the right places.

  1. Newsham, Brad—Journeys.   2. Voyages and
travels—1981–   . I. Title.
G490.N5   1988   910.4   88-27794
ISBN 0-394-57410-9

Design: Blackpool Design, New York

Manufactured in the United States of America
9 8 7 6 5 4 3 2
First Edition

Grateful acknowledgment is made to the following for permission to reprint previously published material:

APPLESEED MUSIC INC.: Excerpt from the lyrics to "Alice's Restaurant" by Arlo Guthrie. Copyright © 1966, 1967 by Appleseed Music Inc. All rights reserved. Used by permission.

CORAL REEFER MUSIC: Excerpt from the lyrics to "Somewhere Over China," words and music by Jimmy Buffett. Copyright © 1981 by Coral Reefer Music. Used by permission. All rights reserved.

FRANK MUSIC CORP.: Excerpt from the lyrics to "On a Slow Boat to China" by Frank Loesser. Copyright 1948 by Frank Music Corp. Copyright renewed 1976 by Frank Music Corp. International copyright secured. All rights reserved. Used by permission.

HARCOURT BRACE JOVANOVICH, INC.: Excerpt from *Hour of Gold, Hour of Lead* by Anne Morrow Lindbergh. Copyright © 1973 by Anne Morrow Lindbergh. Reprinted by permission of Harcourt Brace Jovanovich, Inc.

Grateful acknowledgment is made to the following for permission to reprint excerpts from letters: William M. Crute, Daniel Davidson, Shiori Kaku, and Russell Toevs.

With Love:

In memoriam, to Dad, who repeatedly turned my eyes toward the horizon.

To Mom, who at the train station in 1960 handed me a pen and a green spiral notebook.

And, especially, to Beverly.

ACKNOWLEDGMENTS

WITHOUT THE PATIENCE AND ENCOURAGEMENT of Donna Levin-Bernick and all the members of her writing workshop, Draft One would still be stored behind the hiking boots in my closet. Without Marvin Cohen's enthusiasm for Draft Two, the terrifying search for a publisher would have been unthinkable. Without Bonnie Nadell's and Waimea Williams's industrial-strength criticism of Draft Three, Robert Stricker would have had a wicked time getting Draft Four to market. And without the market; without the support and indulgence of my parents, siblings, and friends; without my special relationships with Sharon Bennett, Rhonda Gillenwaters, Blake Rodman, and Jon Van Vleck; and without you, the people who read, what would be the point?

SPECIAL THANKS TO ALL THE PEOPLE who provided me with food, shelter, transport, company, and entertainment along the way (some of you may not recognize your names, but your stories will have a familiar ring); also to Chris Adams, Mary Anker, Robert Dunham, Werner Erhard, Don Etzbach, Peter Gethers, Marsha Gillespie, Heather Lehr, Joan Marlow, Chris Newsham, Bird Nietmann, Jim and Mary Jo Nietmann, J. P. Nietmann, Garnet Weekes, and Richie Wiener, for their vital contributions to me and to this book.

1
TO
ASIA

Your land and home and pleasant wife must be left behind.

—HORACE
Odes

"DIVORCE," she whispered.
"No way," I told her.
This went on for months.

"I need my own place," she said.
"We need another trip," I told her.
This went on for weeks.

"I'm seeing someone," she said.
"C'mon. Let's go to Asia again."
This went on for days.

"I found a studio," she said, "with a view of the Golden Gate Bridge."

2
GAIJIN

There's a date that you can assign to all places. Maybe in Malaysia it's 1956. In Afghanistan it might be 1910 . . . It's a hundred years ago in Burundi, and perhaps it'll always be that; it's tomorrow morning in Japan . . . The future has already arrived . . . in Japan.

—PAUL THEROUX
Quoted in GEO magazine, November 1983

A VERY DIM LIGHT was coming from somewhere, and slowly my eyes opened and adjusted to the surroundings. On the floor, four feet from my bed, were two red backpacks propped against another bed. I saw black hair on a white pillow, twisted blankets covering a human form, and beside the bed, a ladder. Oh, yes: Okubo House— the cheap inn recommended by a friend back home, a friend who hadn't warned about short beds. Now I'd awakened feeling cramped, unrested, while my seven roommates buzzed gently in slumber. I swung my legs to the floor and pulled on my clothes. *But where are my shoes? Someone's stolen them!*

Then I remembered: my shoes were with all the others—in a rack in the lobby. I'd been given slippers on arrival. I found them under my bed, tiptoed out of the room, traded them for my shoes, and slipped out of Okubo House, sliding the wafer-thin door behind me. My watch said a few minutes before six. May 17. Start of the rainy season. Dark clouds flecked with purple by an invisible rising sun hung low overhead.

Okubo House was hidden in a small alley lined with gloomy structures connected by miles of crisscrossed wire. In the morning's vague light I saw two uniformed Japanese men trying to coax a response from another who wore a three-piece suit and lay sprawled in the gutter in front of a bar.

Just two years earlier, on our first morning in India, my wife and I had seen a cow sitting on our hotel steps.

As I passed, the drunk slurred something; the policemen scolded him. Otherwise, the streets were quiet. I had Tokyo to myself. Stoplights flashed their three colors at deserted crosswalks, the occasional car hummed past, and in the distance, always a few empty blocks ahead of me, I sometimes spied a fellow pedestrian. I meandered for a while, several blocks in one direction, several in another, trying to get an impression of the culture. It wasn't easy; ancient Tokyo had suffered the ravages of a 1923 earthquake and then World War II's firebombs, and during the hurried days of reconstruction little time or money was wasted on aesthetics. I walked through block after cloned block of dreary concrete structures, two and three stories high, wrapped and double-wrapped in electrical wires, labeled in the tangled algebra of Japanese, and featuring exteriors that offered no clue as to function.

I cursed myself for not having researched Japan, for having come on the spur of the moment armed only with a budget travelers' guidebook and a half-read copy of *Shogun*. Criminally unprepared, I was now reduced to studying the self-explanatory.

The religious shrines were obvious—dark pagodas with sloping roof lines that ended in elephant tusks. But were they Buddhist or Shinto? In the windows of restaurants, all closed at this hour, I found life-sized plastic replicas of the meals available inside, and their prices. I stood at one window and studied the food, recognizing the pink 8-ounce steak ($44) and the huge bowl of noodle soup ($2.20), but finding most of it as unfamiliar as the gaunt image staring back from the window.

"Oh, she'll change her mind," I promised a friend over lunch the day after preliminary papers were filed. "The court says to wait six months, and if we still want it, we mail in the final papers and that's it. But she'll change her mind. You can't get divorced without a good reason."

"Wake *up*," my friend said. "It's the eighties—'Life's a bitch, then you die.'"

"Well, I won't die working in a bank. Seventeen months—I gave notice this morning."

"Really! Gonna try journalism again?"

"No, Asia. We gave notice on the apartment last week, too."

"You've got money?"

"Six thousand. Yesterday I bought a one-way ticket to Tokyo and then Hong Kong. From there I can do whatever I feel like."

"Whatever you feel like, you look like hell. You sure this is smart?"

"They say travelers heal the world; I'm going to see if it works in reverse."

"Um-hhhhh."

"And who knows? Maybe she'll change her mind and join me halfway."

"Um-hhhh."

I f the future had preceded me to Tokyo, I didn't quite know where to look for it. Maybe it was in the omnipresent sidewalk vending machines, along with nearly everything else. During my walk that first morning I saw drinks of all kinds—beer, wine, whiskey, and a score of sodas. I wasn't sure what Tokyo would feed me, but it was clear I would never lack for liquids, batteries, ice cream, comic books, newspapers, magazines, or soft pornography. One machine was even filled with sex toys—dildos, handcuffs, a brassiere with nipple cutouts.

From a row of shops on a gaudy, neon-lit street came the ping-beep-beep of a video arcade. I poked my head into several doors; young men in three-piece suits were hunched over the flashing machines. Six-thirty A.M.

I came across an all-night diner. Instead of plastic meals, the window had English lettering: COFFEE SHOP. The inside was crowded with boisterous Japanese men coming off a factory night shift. I spotted an empty seat at the counter and elbowed myself in between two men nursing soupy bowls of noodles and fish. My knees banged the counter wall.

"Ohayo." I said my guidebook greeting to one of the men next to me. He raised his eyebrows, grunted, and looked away as though he owed me money. I stared at the counter. A rotund, balding man wearing a grease-stained apron appeared before me, talking in Japanese.

"Do you speak English?" I asked.

He laughed, turned away, and called aloud to someone on the other side of the room. Several people snickered. Someone behind me laughed the word gaijin (foreigner, barbarian). The man next to me gagged on his soup. The counterman turned back around, wiping his hands, and spoke to me, again in Japanese. I was baffled, he was baffled. He held his hands out at his sides: Whaddayawant, Mac? I gotta busy place here!

"Menu?" I pantomimed turning pages. "Menu?"

He yelled across the room again. More snickers. I pretended to crack an egg and drop it into a skillet. Blank face, laughter, snickers. I tucked my hands in my armpits, made the low cluck noise that had gone over so well in Afghanistan. Now, ten years later, it prompted only the derisive hoots of young hecklers. The man in the apron looked at me in astonishment. I felt my cheeks flush.

And then I remembered something from the guidebook glossary.

"Ko-hi," I said confidently.

Blank face.

"Ko-hi," I repeated.

Nothing.

"Ka-hi?" Now, I was guessing.

Still nothing.

"Coffee." I pointed at the English lettering in the window. "Caw-feee!"

The counterman looked out at the empty street, the winking streetlights, and then back at me. He spat in a gruff voice to the rest of the room; there was a volcano of laughter.

"Coffee ..." The cracking voice sounded like somebody else's. I wished that it were.

The counterman twitched his eyebrows. He waved his hand at the room and disappeared. The giggling stopped. The coffee shop became very quiet. Some ingredient in my neighbor's soup had started my eyes watering. I stared at the counter and made a point of not wiping my face. In a moment a cup of green tea with twigs floating in it was plunked down in front of me. I stood, ordered my legs into motion, and studied the progress of my feet across the tiled floor. Shortly it turned to concrete, then asphalt.

Two blocks away, a McDonald's was opening for breakfast.

3

WRONG PLANET

*As long as [Yabu] could remember he had hated
barbarians, their stench and filthiness and disgusting
meat-eating habits, their stupid religion and
arrogance and detestable manner.*

—JAMES CLAVELL
Shogun

HAVING MASTERED THE ART of ordering in Japanese ("Two Egg Mc-
Muffins and coffee, please"), I was ready to unravel the rest of the
country. I consulted the guidebook: "The Tourist Information Center in downtown Tokyo has free maps and English-speaking hosts."
I rode the world-famous subway—a single pale-faced blemish on
the face of Japan. Rush hour had passed, so the white-gloved at-
tendants known for stuffing commuters into already full cars weren't around.
All was calm, orderly, Zenlike—not quite laboratory standards, but at least
as clean as the McDonald's.

"Go nine stops"—the guidebook said—"climb the stairs, cross the street,
look for the office with the large sign: TOURIST INFORMATION CENTER." The
book might have said: "Follow any *gaijin*. They're all going to the same
place." Inside there were Arabs, Indians, Europeans, a Brazilian, a handful of
Africans, an Australian couple, and several North Americans. All come to
glimpse the future.

Behind the counter stood a tall, cool dark-eyed beauty with a sheaf of
straight black hair that swept across her face and dropped dazzlingly down
her back.

"You are very lucky," she assured me in an English monotone. "The sumo
tournament starts tonight. The wrestlers come to Tokyo only three times all
year. You should go. All tourists like sumo. If you can understand sumo, you
can understand Japan."

"Do you understand sumo?" I asked her.

She blushed, and for the first time smiled. "Just so-so," she said.

spent the day wandering—starting in the center of the city at the Imperial Palace, a stone fortress surrounded by a wide, black-watered moat. According to an Imperial Household Agency brochure, the very same Emperor Hirohito who had led Japan during World War II was now inside pursuing his interest in marine biology, a subject on which he had written several books. Once each year he and the Imperial family open their home to the public, Japanese only, but this was not that day. Outside, busloads of Japanese tourists and students were busily arranging themselves for group pictures, dropping bread crumbs to the moat's fat golden fishes, or silently watching the palace walls. Every face looked the same to me, reserved and cautious, and even though no one stared, I had the sense of being constantly watched. I caught a few eyes, but even as I found them, they were darting away.

I roamed the palace's oasislike outer grounds, sniffing fragrant bushes and pausing on different benches to make notes. *How will I get to know these people?* I asked my notebook. And: *What did they do before cameras?*

Near the palace was the Ginza—a district of wide avenues lined by prestige department stores, twenty-story office buildings, and hordes of shoppers. Inside each store a kimono-wrapped hostess performed an elaborate, to-the-ground bow for each new customer. After the first of these greetings I had to resist the impulse to yank the poor woman to her feet and explain that I, the most marginal consumer, was unworthy of her bow. Indeed, my only acquisition took place in a basement grocery store where a free sample of something slick and brown slid across my tongue and fell down my throat. *Fish?* I did look for an umbrella, the morning's clouds a reminder that my wife had our only good one, but I passed on the cheapest—nineteen dollars.

I rode the train in a huge one-hour loop around Tokyo; located the American Express office and two English bookstores; wasted a dollar in a pachinko (Japanese pinball) parlor; obtained a schedule of Tokyo Giants home baseball games; and once stopped on a busy sidewalk to count a thousand people pass by—noting that this took exactly eight minutes and that seven of them wore gas masks. The only person who spoke to me all afternoon was a Japanese waitress who followed me out the front door of an Indian restaurant where I'd eaten chicken curry. "So-dee," she said, and handed me the two-hundred-yen (one dollar) note I'd left on my table. "We no tip."

As the day wore on and my sightseeing legs wore out, I grew melancholy. When a late-afternoon drizzle began rinsing the exhaust-laden sky, I took refuge in a bus-stop shelter and tried reading *Shogun,* but the moment I stopped moving, I was ambushed by self-doubt. I was in Japan, but who cared? Around me several Japanese stood waiting for the bus. The lady nearest me was perched on black, open-toed high heels, knees locked, calves clenched, staring into the rain and the street traffic without a flicker of anything registering on her powdered face.

What was I doing here, posing as a carefree traveler? I was an impostor. No friends. No family. Thirty-two years old and no career. If I had any sense, I would go back to my own country this afternoon, find a decent job and a new wife. Travel might heal, but whatever it took I no longer had.

It was time to write affirmations, a practice I had adopted in San Francisco, hoping to still the resident voice in my head: "You're going to run out of money. Your body is falling apart. Nobody likes you. You've got the wrong planet."

In my bus-stop hideout I wrote out my favorite affirmation—*I am in exactly the right place, thinking, doing, and feeling exactly the right things*—ten times.

Encouraged, my pen took over. *The world will rejuvenate you,* it promised. *Trust it. There are 4.7 billion people here. That one of them wants a break after ten years of living with you doesn't necessarily mean anything. You've got money and credit cards and no obligations. Billions of people would trade places with you. Quit whining. Go to a sumo match.*

4
SUMO

*We must respect the other fellow's religion, but
only in the sense and to the extent that we respect
his theory that his wife is beautiful and his children
smart.*

—H. L. Mencken
Minority Report

GENERAL ADMISSION WAS THIRTEEN DOLLARS, but I managed to find a
standing room ticket for just over two dollars—a prudent move,
as Kukugikan Sumo Hall had plenty of empty seats. I picked one
midway in the upper deck, settled in, and began scouting the crowd
through my binoculars. There were only three other *gaijin,* all
seated in the very front row. A yellow-haired young woman with a
long-lensed camera was scooting around the wrestling platform lining up
shots, occasionally returning to sit between two men. I counted forty-seven
rows between my seat and hers.

I had arrived with the usual *gaijin* impression of sumo—fat men with thick
jockstraps butting bellies—and the evening's several hours of matches did
little to change that impression. By Western standards the sport is painfully
long on ceremony and short on action—the chorister's view of church. As
I arrived, two groups of sumos were impassively—no preening, no flexing—
parading their formidable stuff around the arena.

By any standard sumo wrestlers are fat, their fleshy arms carried at 45-
degree angles to their bodies, propped there by the sort of medicine-ball
bellies that horrify a tailor. This shape is neither accidental nor hereditary,
a sumo's full-time job being the acquisition and maintenance of bulk. He
adds height by growing his hair long and wearing it in a knob atop his head;
after meals he visits a masseur who manipulates his intestines, packing the
food in, freeing up room for more consumption. In Japan, the citadel of
sameness, this unorthodox life-style and appearance are widely respected.
The best sumos earn enviable sums. Retirement must come reluctantly, since
wisdom dictates massive weight loss, and custom demands a standard haircut and return to anonymity.

The parade's end was marked by a flurry of bowing—all the sumos hinging toward each other, toward the five black-robed judges seated at ringside, and toward the *gyoji,* a slight but all-powerful black-robed wizard who refereed from ring center. The *gyoji* had a ceremonial fan tucked into his belt in the same spot where his ancient counterparts (sumo dates from A.D. 200) carried daggers, prepared to self-disembowel should they err in judgment.

Bowing completed, the teams squatted on opposite sides of the wrestling platform like twin rows of inflated lifeboats stood on end for storage. The blond woman, slim and nearly as pretty as my wife, must have used half a roll of film on this shot. She had plenty of time, as the *gyoji* filled the next half hour with a droning list of announcements, during which the people around me slept, drank beer, read, and munched snacks. Waiters in kimonos and slippers shuffled back and forth to the concession stands, like ballpark hot-dog vendors, only quiet.

Finally, after the announcements and the introduction of each wrestler, the first match began. Two wrestlers approached the platform, climbed the steps to their own corners, and shed silk kimonos to reveal the simplest of outfits—a wide sash fed through the crotch and anchored at either end to a thick leather belt girdling the waist.

Properly undressed, each of the bulbous giants began a slow limbering-up routine: stamping their feet to scare off demons; squatting to test knee joints and jockstraps; shaking the kinks from each leg; sipping water from a ceremonial dipper and then spitting it out. Each performed this ritual with sly attention on his opponent, so as to get neither too far ahead nor too far behind. At last each grabbed a handful of salt from a container at ringside and turned to face the other. Carelessly, almost disdainfully, they tossed the salt into the ring, ritually purifying it, and stepped in. With the speed of upright turtles, both waddled to the center of the circle, toed their respective lines, and went into a slow squat, a yard apart, face to glowering face, preparing to spring when the time was right.

But in sumo the time is almost never right. First one wrestler backed off, easing away, not breaking eye contact, and the other was obliged to do the same. They retreated to their salt bowls and their ceremonial dippers, slapping their thighs, each trying to convey the impression that *he'd* been ready, but the *other* guy flinched. More stretching, more salt, another mouth rinse, and they tottered back into the ring, deliberately toed their lines, and lowered back down.

Amid small groans from the crowd, they repeated this backing-away process four times. Finally, on their fifth squat, the sumos lunged for each other; chests collided, fannies shook, feet clawed the clay floor; one of the men bullied the other backward to the edge of the ring and threw him across the line. Two frenzied seconds. The match was over.

There was no wild victory celebration. The loser picked himself up and moved to his corner; at a signal from the *gyoji* he waded off through the crowd, followed a moment later by the winner. The only person who paid them any attention was the *gaijin* woman snapping pictures. The spectators, sipping beer, browsing right-to-left newspapers, might have been at home watching TV in their living rooms.

The thirty-some matches that followed were much like the first one—long, slow buildups, instant endings. Only once did the sumos lunge for each other on the first face-off, and rarely did the actual wrestling last more than ten seconds. It didn't take long to see that the point of these contests was to match one's opponent ceremony for ceremony, politeness for politeness, pretense for pretense, and then—with all formalities evenly settled—throw his wobbly ass out of the ring. "If you understand sumo," the girl at the Tourist Information Center had told me, "you understand Japan."

Toward the end of the evening I felt a wave of the odd, lovely loneliness that haunts and soothes the solo traveler. Maybe it was better that my wife was at home. Were she with me, she'd have been jealous of my note taking, would long ago have suggested, and then *demanded,* that we leave, and would have spent too many yen on snacks. *She'd not tolerate three hours of sumo,* I told my notebook.

While jotting, I felt a soft tugging at my shoulder, and turned around. It wasn't my wife as I suddenly feared, or the *gaijin* photographer as I stupidly hoped, but a Japanese man from the row behind. He had a drink can in one hand, and was using his other to brush away a few clear beads of beer that he'd spilled on my down vest.

"Bzz bzz bzzai," he murmured, rocking forward, smiling.

"It's okay," I said, waving him off. "It's okay."

He apologized some more, bowing, buzzing; excessive remorse, I thought, for something so small.

"It's okay. Okay." I turned back to the ring, hoping that was the end of that.

Below, the most exciting match of the evening was beginning. Two of the largest wrestlers were stomping through their warm-up rituals and actually showing anger!—slapping thighs, growling, snapping their heads back and forth at each other. Instead of carelessly lofting their salt into the ring, they hurled it; the crowd ooohed and aaahed as though some taboo were being broken. The sumos squatted in front of each other and then broke away repeatedly, fourteen times I counted, glaring for long moments, smacking thighs and chests furiously, and stomping back to their corners through swirling clouds of salt and bluster.

When finally they did leap at each other, I was surprised by their agility. They careened around the ring like runaway trucks—tiny feet pummeling the floor in staccato bursts unexpected from figures so sloppy. Suddenly the *gyoji* signaled them to stop in their tracks: One of the men was losing his diaper! While they clenched each other's shoulders—reminding me of an amorous bull I once saw mounting a cow in an Illinois pasture—the *gyoji* matter-of-factly arranged a new knot.

Three minutes into the match, there was a surprise ending. At the same instant, both men flew from the ring in separate directions and appeared, to my untrained eye, to thud to the platform simultaneously. With his fan the *gyoji* waved them to their corners. The judges gathered at center ring; a long conference ensued.

Through my binoculars I was watching the judges and the *gyoji* and the photographer, who had crept to within six feet of their huddle (was that a ring on her finger, or part of her camera?), when my vision was abrubtly extinguished. I lowered the binoculars. Floating in front of my face was a can of Kirin beer, dangled there by the man behind me. He had slopped drink on a *gaijin:* amends were called for. Here was liquid apology.

I looked back at him and smiled. He smiled. Indeed, the whole row behind me was smiling, all teeth and crinkled cheeks.

"Arigato," I said, taking the can and popping the top. *Thank you.*

He lifted his can. "Sumo," he toasted. (He pronounced it "Smo.")

I hoisted my can—"Smo"—and sipped. Everyone in the row behind was tipped forward in their seats to watch me, one face staggered behind another like a poker hand. I grinned and ducked my head—setting off a chain re-action—and then turned away.

The three empty seats in the first row told me that the photographer had gotten what she wanted, and the judges scattering from the ring indicated that a verdict had been reached. The two wrestlers were silent, still squatting in their corners, and now they accepted the *gyoji's* announcement stoi-cally—no exhibitionism, no self-congratulation, no dancing in the ring, arms raised. But the noisy ovation that accompanied their departure, and the crowd members reaching out to thump the winner's back, said that a good fight stirs the Japanese the same way it stirs the rest of us.

It was dark outside and drizzling when the last match ended. Police had closed off the street in front of the auditorium, allowing the crowd to march unimpeded to the subway. I was surprised to find myself walking next to one of the sumos. He was several inches shorter than I, and outside the ring he didn't look so fierce. In fact—wearing slippers and a flowered blue kimono, and squinting through thick glasses—he looked docile, bewildered, maybe even lost. He was peering back over one shoulder as though hoping to meet someone.

That, I thought, is how I look.

5
THE MAN FIFTY-TWO STORIES UP

You may not believe this, but there is a man stationed 100 miles above the earth whose job is to pick people to go traveling in outer space. He's got just a few openings to fill, five billion people to choose from, and no computer, so he has to go by what he sees people doing.

When this man was the guest on a radio talk show last year, a woman caller asked how to improve her chances of being selected. His answer: "I look for people who are already in their own low orbit. Start circling the earth on your own as often and continuously as possible and don't worry—you'll be noticed."

—LANCE FREE
The Art of Tripping

T HE SUN WAS SHINING the next morning, its first appearance since my arrival. The early air was damp, and curlicues of steam were peeling off the streets as I left Okubo House. Shinjuku, an area of modern skyscrapers dominating the city's western skyline, is Tokyo's new business and entertainment district, and my room-mates had recommended the view from the fifty-two story Sumitomo Building, which towers over earthquake-nervous Tokyo like a sumo wrestler visiting a kindergarten.

I joined the rush-hour crowd surging to work, taller than all except one gangly teenager, whose head poked above the throng. We locked eyes—two horses fording a deep river in opposite directions—until he passed. It seemed the ultimate luxury to not have to hurry with this crowd, but to be free to amble at a comfortable pace in its frantic midst. I recalled my own recent morning scurries through downtown San Francisco, racing the clock on the ferry building at the end of Market Street. Now I relaxed. If you don't *have* to be there, downtowns are okay.

On a pedestrian overpass in Shinjuku I stopped to watch the traffic and the people below. The men marching head-down on the jam-packed sidewalks were identical blurs: blue suits, white shirts. The women showed more variety, but only slight—here and there a flamboyant blouse or colorful dress, sometimes a business suit, always high heels. Students—blue below the waist, white above—surged along in polite gangs, clutching at one another. Tokyo was starting to remind me of a giant Catholic school on lunch break.

Three "homeless" people (two men, one woman) carrying bedrolls and wearing tattered clothes were slumped against the wall of a public rest room, as unhurried and as conspicuous as I was. I watched them for a few minutes, wondering about their lives: Were they divorced? Was this a good country to be homeless in? (During five weeks in Japan I would see exactly six homeless people, all in Tokyo.)

I descended the steps of the overpass and followed my map in the direction of the Sumitomo Building. Several McDonald's and one Computerland store caught my eye. A sweet pastry smell wafted from a bakery. Rows of bicycles were parked—unlocked, unwatched, unbothered—on the sidewalks in front of department stores. As the eight-thirty cutoff approached, people jostled past on either side of me, no less intense than their American counterparts. Women were at a distinct disadvantage in this race, tight skirts and high heels forcing their chopped, awkward steps. I thought: Next year they'll commute in running shoes, like women across the Pacific.

I followed the crowds through the front door of the Sumitomo Building. The security guards in the lobby looked at me curiously, but said nothing. I strolled past a *ko-hi* shop, several restaurants, a travel agency (VISIT BEAUTIFUL OKINAWA!), a swimming pool, and stopped at a gymnasium to watch leotarded women dance aerobics and lunging men swat a volleyball. In my office people moved that vigorously only at quitting time.

A crowd of small, hard-faced people in full business regalia stood staring at a bank of elevator doors, silently willing them to open. I eased in among them—too tall, and dressed for Colorado (down vest, hiking shoes, day pack)—but my presence was elaborately ignored.

The elevator doors slid back. A group of us filed inside. The doors shut. The numbers on the panel only reached forty-eight. A young lady was looking at me out of the corner of her eye.

"Do you speak English?" I asked.

Her eyes widened in panic. *The* gaijin's *speaking to ME!* She swallowed. "A ree-tu bit." Her voice barely carried across the three feet separating us. I moved to her side.

"Can I go to the top?" Our "conversation" was the only sound in the car.

"At forty-eight you ... ummm ..."—she rolled her eyes up to scan the inside of her forehead—"... change era-vatuh."

"Thank you."

She smiled once and looked away. The elevator stopped, several people got off.

"Where hah you fum?" she asked quietly.

"San Francisco."

Her eyes jumped. "I was in San Jose."

"Really? When?"

"Three weeks."

"Three weeks *ago?*"

"No ..." She studied her inner skull again, and sagged. "My office ... forty-six froor. Preese come."

"May I?"

"At tin o'crock," she said.

The door hissed open, she disappeared, the door closed.

At tin o'crock? My watch said 8:50. Alone in the elevator, I laughed.

I was dating again.

The fifty-second floor was deserted. My rubber soles squeaked on the linoleum as I walked an inner corridor looking for an outside window. Finally I saw a man moving around in the darkness of a closed restaurant. When he saw me, I pretended, hand to forehead, to scout an imaginary horizon. Doors in India had opened only because of my wife, but the man came and unlocked this one.

"Preese," he said, and ushered me inside.

He motioned to the window, and with a bow disappeared into the shadows. I walked across the room, stifled a wave of vertigo, pressed my nose to the glass, and, hovering fifty-two stories up, I gaped. With its population of 14 million, I knew Tokyo was big, but it sprawled ten times further than I'd imagined: block after block, mile after mile, of buildings, parks, roads, neighborhoods. One glimpse was more education than the whole previous day.

And then I realized I was seeing, at best, only half of the whole. I looked at my Tokyo map. What I was seeing wasn't even shown. Shinjuku was on the map's very western edge, and I was on the western side of the building, looking even further west. All of the miles I had covered the day before were on the building's other side, blocked from my view. The Imperial Palace,

Ginza, downtown Tokyo—not one of these was visible. Nor was Mount Fuji, yet I knew it was only sixty miles away. Old paintings show the perfect peak looming in a crystalline sky just beyond ancient Tokyo; its last eruption, in 1707, had dumped a thick black soot on the city's street. But today a purple-gray dome of pollution and rainy-season haze was clamped above me. No volcano.

"Preese."

I turned around. On the counter behind me was a tall glass of orange juice. The man bowed.

"Domo arigato," I said, and drank. *Thank you very much.* It was the real thing, cold and fresh-squeezed! "Hey, that's great!"

He gurgled in Japanese.

"If my wife were here, you'd fix us breakfast."

We both laughed. The man took a jar from behind the counter, poured a refill, and then bowed out, leaving me alone again to drink orange juice and watch Tokyo's miniature citizens go about their day.

6

HALLELUJAH

It is the test of a good religion whether you can joke about it.

—G. K. CHESTERTON
All Things Considered

THE EVENING RUSH HOUR found me back across town in the Ginza district, sitting on a ledge, studying my map, and considering a trip to the baseball park. I was feeling better about myself and about the trip—it always takes a few days to get the hang of traveling.

The sun had finally dodged the clouds, and the day had turned out to be a really good one. There had been the tremendous view from the Sumitomo Building. And even if my "date" did wind up a disaster (we talked in very broken English for fifteen minutes about her three weeks, five years ago, in San Jose), it had nonetheless been a cultural exchange, of sorts. Today I'd ridden the subway with confidence, and I'd found a quiet wooded park where I could stretch, meditate, affirmate (*I am in exactly the right place . . .*), and read *Shogun*. And without setting foot in a McDonald's I'd had two authentic meals. My traveling legs were under me once again; my feet were pawing the ground. Japan was easy, a real piece of cake, nothing like India or Iran or Morocco . . .

"Ex-quuse me," said a voice. Sit down in any city for five minutes, and you forfeit privacy rights.

I looked up. A smiling Japanese man, very thin, with a bony face and glasses, was leaning over me.

"Do you have a lee-tu time?"

I laughed. Rarely had my time seemed so infinite.

"I would like you to visit my church. Receive a bressing."

Well, wasn't that kind!—an invitation into a Japanese temple. I had been intending to see some temples, maybe spend a night or two, meditate with a Zen master. This might be just the thing. It's amazing: When you let it, the world will lead you. When the student is ready, the teacher will appear.

"What's the blessing like?" I asked.

19

"People come to meet holy man, do some chanting, go in pool together."

I saw a heated pool in an underground grotto, naked bodies obscured by rising steam. And I knew a little something about chanting; in India, at Swami Muktananda's ashram, my wife and I had done three days' worth.

"What day would you like me to come?"

"Today. Now."

"Now?"

He nodded. "Now."

Suddenly my time was more finite. I wasn't sure I could, or wanted to, switch quickly into a church frame of mind. "How long does a blessing take?"

"Maybe thirty minutes."

Mental objections flared up: What about the ball game? You know you'll end up spending a lot more than thirty minutes with this guy!

"You really mean, 'right now'?"

"Huh-dite now." He was still smiling.

I brushed my objections aside. "Okay."

"Puh-deese, fah-doh me."

We walked quickly down the street to the nearest subway entrance. He bought a ticket at the machine, but when I started to buy one, he stopped me.

"This for you. I have pass."

We boarded a subway train—I didn't see which one—and sat down. I laughed to myself: at home I would never go to church with someone who approached me on the street, but Tokyo puts even the wary at ease. In three days I had seen nothing even remotely forbidding. Flecks of spilled beer bring a diplomatic apology. Bikes are left unlocked all day long. Even the drunks wandering in the wee hours wear three-piece suits and do nothing more threatening than grin and bark, "Ha-ro!"

"Where are we going?" I asked my new friend.

"To other part of Tokyo."

"How far?"

"Not far."

"Well, how long will we be on the subway?"

"Not rong. We make one change." He smiled.

"What kind of church is it?" I asked, thinking: Buddhist, Shinto, some exotic splinter sect. Then: Moonies?

"Lee-tu church."

"What's the name?"

"You not know it."

"How many members?"

"Very smaw. Maybe three-hundred thousand pee-pu in whole world."

That counted out Moonies, Buddhists, Moslems, Catholics, Jews—just about everyone. Relax, I told myself. Be surprised. This is the sort of thing you came to Japan for. Go with it. Learn something.

His name, I found out, was Hirotake; he was twenty-eight years old, his profession: "wholesaler." He had been born in "another prefecture" but lived now in Tokyo. His English was good, his questions mostly about my parents and siblings. Leave America, and your family becomes very important.

"When does the service start?"

"When we arrive, service start. You seem not scared."

I looked at Hirotake's face. The corners of his mouth were pulled back in a soft, even smile. Behind the glasses his eyes were shiny, almost watery. Whatever his beliefs, I guessed he was sincere about them.

"Why would I be scared?" I asked him.

"I was scared. Many pee-pu come with me are scared."

"Many people?"

"I invite many foreign pee-pu to my church. Once a week maybe. I have many foreign friends now."

"Do most people come easily, like me?"

He laughed. "No. You very easy. I more scared than you, I think. Always I am scared to invite pee-pu, but after pee-pu receive bressing, they very happy. Write me many letters."

"Does everyone like the blessing?"

"No, not everyone. Bressing very pow-a-foo, but some pee-pu not understand. Like me. First time, nothing happen. So I come again. Get another bressing. Then everything happen. My life become like magic. I much happier now. I not worry about things."

s Hirotake had said, when we arrived, the service started. The church, a clean, simple stone structure, was located in a quiet residential area. I checked for a sign outside, but there was none; had I been wandering by on my own, I might have guessed it was an elementary school.

Inside the front door we were greeted by a Japanese man in a blue suit. He recognized Hirotake, spoke to him in Japanese, and welcomed me in English. There were "inside slippers" at the door; we surrendered our shoes and were escorted to a table in a carpeted area the size of a classroom. We sat down; cups of tea were brought. We sipped, and grinned at each other for a few moments. The hum of distant chanting was barely audible.

A Japanese woman in a white robe, like a judo outfit, approached our table. "Ah," said Hirotake. "Holy man is woman today."

She was young—maybe twenty-five—energetic, high strung, and spoke the typical broken Engrish. She asked me several quick questions—What country? How long Japan?, etc.—and then described the procedure. "We say prayers, a chant, very fast. Then go to pool for bressing. Okay?"

She was standing, we were seated. She laid her left hand on my right shoulder and said, "Now, close ears."

I closed my eyes.

"Say *'Ha-du.'* "

I said *ha-du.*

"Faster. *Ha-du-du-du-du. Ha-du-du-du-du-du-du-du-du-du.*"

It was as though we each had a mouthful of tacks and were in a contest to see who could be the first to spit them out, one by one. They fired from our lips, about five per second, but no matter how many we spit, we somehow still had mouthfuls.

"Ha-du-du-du-du-du-du-du-du-du." The sounds blended together into a broken buzz. *"Ha-du-du-du-du-du-du-du-du-du."*

This seemed curious to me, almost comical, but what the hell? It was their country, their religion. I *ha-du-du*'d right along. Hirotake was saying it, too. *"Ha-du-du-du-du-du-du-du. Ha-du-du-du-du-du-du-du-du."*

This was not like the other chanting I had done. This was more like a joke. *"Ha-du-du-du. Ha-du-du-du-du-du-du-du-du."* We went along like this for several minutes, gulping breaths and sputtering; sometimes we speeded up so quickly that my tongue fluttered on the roof of my mouth like the beating wing of a hummingbird. *"Ha-du-du-du-du-du. Ha-du-du-du-du-du-du-du."*

And then we stopped. I opened my eyes. Hirotake and the holy lady were looking at me with smiles of anticipation. Keeping a straight face was going to be a challenge.

"Did you like it?" the holy lady asked.

"It was fun," I managed. Don't laugh, I told myself. Be polite. Already I was becoming Japanese.

We were joined by another white-robed person—a young brown man who did not look Japanese. "This is Ringo," said the holy lady. Even though I was seated and Ringo was standing, our eyes met on the same level. "He will help you get ready. Preese, come with us."

At the door the four of us changed into "outdoor slippers," then marched single file into a garden of fragrant green bushes. Snowball-like blossoms hung overhead, and high above I noticed the sky turning pink with sunset. The steaming grotto and naked women I'd hoped for were certainly not going to appear, but there was a dreamy quality about the whole thing that I found equally fantastic: a secret ritual, my own escort of earnest white-robed midgets.

We came to a door at the back of the building. The holy lady said Ringo would get me a robe like hers, and I could change in the room behind the door. Then we would go to the pool, and she and I would get in it. "I say bressing, then underwater, then more bressing. That is all."

Inside the room Ringo showed me my robe and some new slippers. He spoke excellent English, and while I changed, he asked several questions:

"You are American?"

Yes.

"What is your religion?"

I said I didn't have one.

"Are you a Christian?"

I told him I wasn't "a" anything.

"Isn't America a Christian country?"

I said that was more or less true. Christmas *is* the biggest holiday.

"Are your parents alive?"

Yes.

"Are your grandparents alive?"

No.

"What were your grandparents' names?" He had pencil and paper now. I told him my four grandparents' names, first and last. He wrote them down.

"Did you ever have any close friends die?"

I lied and told him no.

Ringo said he was from Indonesia; he was nineteen years old. When I asked what this robe-and-pool stuff was all about, he smiled at me. "You will see," he said gently. "It is okay."

Hirotake and the holy lady were waiting for us outside the door. Hirotake—still in street clothes—was the only one without a white outfit. My robe and loose white pants were seductively comfortable, much more sensible than my Western clothes.

Beslippered, and dressed in clean, flowing linens, I felt refreshed as we single-filed back through the perfumed garden to a small concrete pool I hadn't noticed earlier. It was overhung by the branches of lilac bushes blooming purple. The sky was aflame now. Birds were chirping; all else was silent. I thought: So *this* is Japan.

"Follow me," said the holy lady. She walked down the steps into the waist-deep pool. The water was cold—not freezing, but definitely a jolt. My groin shrieked and shrank up as I waded in beside her. Nothing about this scenario was what I'd pictured.

"Preese crose hands."

I made fists.

7

WHERE'S
THE CHEAPEST
PLACE TO STAY?

"Home is the place where, when you have to go there
*   They have to take you in."*

—ROBERT FROST
"The Death of the Hired Man"

HE NEXT MORNING I headed for the subway, thinking I'd go downtown toward, oh, say, the Telephone and Telegraph Office, from where, should I happen to feel like it, I might just call my wife; strictly as a courtesy, of course—to let her know I'd arrived and was having a terrific time.

"Hey, Brad!" Walter, an Okubo House roommate, caught me at the subway entrance. "Where you going?"

"Nowhere special."

"Wanna hit a few baseballs?"

It doesn't take a visitor to Japan long to confirm that the Japanese are wild about baseball, and have been ever since their first professional league began in 1936. Every neighborhood has a batting range; every park of any size has at least a couple of fields occupied by teams from grade-school level on up; and no major city is without a pro team. The Japanese are considered world-class fielders, bunters, and base runners, and take great pride in the fact that Oh Sadaharu—"the Babe Ruth of Japan"—hit more home runs during his career than any professional player in the world, but for day-to-day slugging power they've been importing *gaijin*. Each team has a limit of two Americans—usually older players in career eclipse, or younger ones with contract disputes back home.

A game on TV at Okubo House the previous night had left the Japanese in an uproar: first an umpire reversed his call to go against the Tokyo Giants (a microphone behind home plate allows an umpire to confess publicly

26

before changing a decision); then, with the score tied, bases loaded, and one out in the ninth, the television station switched to the news. The baseball game had used up its time slot; anyone interested could buy the morning paper.

As we walked toward a Shinjuku batting range, and as Walter began describing himself at great length, it occurred to me that it would be helpful for travelers to draw up one-page résumés: age, hometown, months on the road, financial shape, countries visited, last job, last love relationship, last diarrhea bout. Without a résumé it took Walter half an hour to deliver his basics: twenty-eight, Philadelphia via Alaska, fourteen months "this time," "down to my last thou," fifty-three countries (Europe, all of Asia and the South Pacific), electrical engineer, currently dating a Japanese woman but girlfriends scattered everywhere, lost twenty pounds in China.

My basics were more basic: "... but it's not final for six months and I'm expecting it to work out."

"Now you can't tell me that you're going to be gone all these months and you're not going to meet ladies out here."

"That's not why I'm out here. I just want to get some air—give my wife a chance to miss me. And maybe see a few new places."

"You really think she'll change her mind?"

"I don't see why not. For a long time she thought I was pretty great."

"Now what's her gripe?"

"She says she just doesn't like being married."

"There's gotta be more to it. Were you sleeping around?"

"Nope."

"Did you fight a lot?"

"Hardly ever."

"Well, what didn't she like about you?"

"She only had one complaint—I'm not *spiritual* enough."

"Oh, boy, that's a good one. What's it mean?"

"I'm not exactly sure."

We were in Shinjuku now, jostling with the crowds. "Hey, see those girls over there?" Three teenagers were lined up at a Coca-Cola vending machine. "They could help you."

"How?"

"They're Christians."

"How do you know?"

"One of the guys in our room. That geek from Texas. They invited him to their temple. Nearly had him baptized before he figured out what was going on."

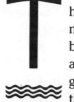

The batting range was an outdoor affair with a bowling-alley format. Spectators sat in a rear gallery to watch a row of twelve batters duel against a row of twelve distant robots with steel arms and endless supplies of white rubber baseballs. Nets draped ground-to-ceiling separated the batters; balls ricocheted inside the wire enclosure, rolling underfoot, or lodging in the nets like Christmas-tree ornaments.

Walter and I were the only *gaijin*. We selected bats and paid $3 apiece for 100 swings—fast, slow, or medium. "We've gotta do the fast ones," Walter said. "They think all Americans are pros, and we can't let 'em down." Indeed, a small crowd gathered in the gallery behind us.

Walter smashed a line drive that bounced off his batting machine. I fouled my first pitch into the netting. "Maybe you're not spiritual enough," Walter teased. "Come on—it's easy." WHACK! "Pretend this next one's your wife. . . ."

"You don't get it." WHIFF! "I don't want to hit her—I just want to understand. Two years ago today she and I were on Crete. . . ."

"Hey, I spent two weeks on Crete with this Yugoslav lawyer lady." WHACK! "Great time."

"We were at the end of a six-month trip around the world ..." WHIFF! "We'd been together eight years, and every day on the whole trip, we woke up giddy we were so glad to be with each other. . . ." WHIFF!

"Hey, I was just kidding, man. . . ." WHACK!

"Well, I'm not. I wanna know how that disappears so fast. Where's it go? I can't get used to her not being here. . . ." WHIFF!

"Sorry, man. Didn't mean to set you off. . . ." WHACK!

"I know there're people on this planet with real problems. . . ." WHIFF! "Diseases, poverty, starvation ..."

"Impotence ..." WHACK!

"And that an American out traveling doesn't deserve any sympathy. . . ." WHIFF! "But dammit!—emotions, relationships, those are real problems, too! And they're *my* problems." WHACK!

A smattering of applause came from behind us.

"Nice rip," Walter said. "Look, prove you can smile, and I'll get you a date with my girlfriend's sister."

I proved myself, but said I'd pass. "Give me a break. Four mornings ago I was still in San Francisco living with my wife." WHACK!

"Just wait. As soon as you get used to Japanese women, you're gonna love 'em." WHACK! "It's okay for 'em to act like little girls over here." WHACK! "Have you seen the way they put their hands up in front of their faces and giggle? They're so cute." WHACK! "They don't have to put on that macho act like American women ..." WHACK! ". . . trying to outmuscle the men for jobs and careers." WHIFF! "Crap! And here it's okay for a man to act like a man. Go ahead, have some fun." WHACK!

I didn't make it to the Telephone and Telegraph that day. Or the next, or the next. Instead, I flung lines to my new peers, the residents of Okubo House. The place was full every night, two floors of thin-walled cubicles occupied generally by people similar to myself—people floating from one side of the world to the other. There were several Asians, one black, and a handful of Japanese, but mostly Europeans and North Americans going to or coming from China.

Gradually I came to know who had been at Okubo House a while and who was just arriving, who was on the way "home," who had a birthday, who was single, which were couples, who wanted a mate or a used Walkman, who had lots of money, who was broke and trying to sell a backpack. In times of distress, other people's problems are a great comfort.

There was a Japanese-American man who couldn't speak any more Japanese than I could; he'd been born in Michigan to Japanese parents who spoke only English, a mix that confused every situation he was in. The Japanese would endure a blue-eyed blond who couldn't speak their language, but a person as obviously Japanese as this fellow was another matter. The immigration people at the airport wanted him to speak Japanese; bus and subway operators were similarly intolerant. The people running Okubo House considered him a mutant.

Strict tabs were kept on the Asians staying there, but as long as we Westerners paid our $5.60 a night, our hosts didn't give a damn what we did. If an Asian man and woman wanted a private room in Okubo House, they were required to prove they were married; *gaijin* were not. The Japanese found us at least as unfathomable as we found them, and then some. *Gaijin* were big, clumsy, rude; whatever we did didn't count and never would. But Okubo's Asian visitors—especially any Japanese—had to obey a strict code of behavior.

Many of the residents intended to live in Tokyo indefinitely, and many were already working. Some had found highly coveted work as movie extras or models, but most taught English—tutoring privately or working for a language school. Others were translators, proofreaders, and editors.

"If you ever really get desperate," said Mary Jane, an exuberant Canadian from Montreal, "there are several bars where the owner will pay you twenty-five hundred yen [twelve dollars] just to sit for four hours and talk English with anyone who comes in. Heck, it's not the greatest, but you can live and eat for a day on twenty-five-hundred yen."

The "greatest" were the jobs that belonged to Pat and Glenn, two tall, blond twenty-year-old Canadians who had come to Japan to improve their low rankings on Canada's national judo team. They had been spotted working out with a Tokyo judo club and were offered acting jobs in a television series about the Japanese-Americans thrown into California's World War II detention camps—a hot topic in the Japanese media. Pat and Glenn earned between one hundred and two hundred dollars a day for their work, which consisted of wearing U.S. Marine uniforms, carrying fake rifles, looking surly, and tossing a Japanese person around the set once in a while. After all-night shooting sessions they were delivered to Okubo House by taxi early in the morning, something that inspired envy among the English teachers, many of whom earned two hundred dollars for a full week of often tedious tutoring: "Base-ball. Not 'base-a-boro'—base-*ball*!"

Still, the general consensus regarded it a miracle that, with no greater skill than having learned to speak their own native tongue, so many foreigners could come to Japan and make a decent living. Each morning two pages of ads in *Japan Today* begged for English teachers: "North American accent preferred, no experience necessary." Virtually everyone who could speak even a little English was in demand—Australians with thick accents, Swiss with twisted grammar and tiny vocabularies, even several natives of New Delhi who chirped their English in the singsong Indian manner. Many of these people claimed to be unemployable in their own countries, and laughed ironically at life's sweet gift of travel and prestige across the seas.

The black man was from San Francisco, and regarded me as a recent arrival from the promised land. One night we were standing in the hall, wearing the kimonos supplied by Okubo House, and waiting for space to open up in the men's bath.

"San Francisco! Oh, man, that's home! Hey, how is it? Is Feinstein still mayor? Are the gays still running the place?"

"Feinstein's still mayor," I said. "I don't know about the gays running the place. I'm not gay myself. . . ."

"Hey, me either," he cut in, winking. "San Francisco's great if you're not gay. All the pussy you want." And then his résumé: thirty-six, an "entertainer" with a degree in dance from UCLA, in Tokyo on a six-month nightclub contract. He now hated the Japanese—"biggest racists in the world; you'll see"—and couldn't wait to go back to his home in San Francisco's Tenderloin. "Two more weeks and I'm outa here."

I was always heartened to see people older than I was out traveling. Their existence told me that not everyone had taken a job in a corporation and intended to gut it out there forever. It gave me hope and validation: if there were others out wandering, and if their lives seemed to be working, maybe it really was an okay thing for me to be doing.

There was Don Schermetzler from Madison, Wisconsin, who blamed the air force for his wandering. They had trained him as a linguist and assigned him, at age eighteen, to a secret listening post on the Turkey-Russia border. "Since then I've had a bunch of jobs, but mostly I'm a graduate linguistics student. Semipro. Professors call me up every spring and say, 'Look, we've got this scholarship nobody's going to use next year unless you do. It's a special program in New Delhi or Kuala Lumpur or Ouagadougou and it pays this much money—why don't you take it?' Now I speak Russian, Chinese, Malay, Hindi, Urdu, French, Spanish, English, and American."

Don was thirty-eight and, after six months in China and India, down to his last couple of hundred bucks and a plane ticket back to Chicago. "I'll probably come back to Asia in another year," he grumbled, "but I'm getting too old for this shit. Going around asking people, 'Where's the cheapest place to stay?' Who needs that shit? I never see anyone older than me out here unless it's some grisly old fucker."

Don spent a lot of whatever money he had left on beer—I often saw him in the café down the street, hands cradling a tall brown bottle of Kirin or Saporro while he watched the Tokyo Giants on television. He was a voracious baseball fan and knew the major-league standings by breakfast each morning. "These Japanese teams are for shit," he told me. "Can't wait to get home and drive down to Milwaukee to see the Brewers."

David and Heidi—Canadians, thirty-three and thirty-six years old—were also headed home. They had spent a dreamy year in a small seaside village where only one other foreigner was living; they made pottery, learned Japanese, toured the country in a van. With "absolutely no regrets," they had spent twenty thousand dollars, and now had to go back home and find work. Their finale had been a six-hundred-kilometer bicycle ride over the Japanese Alps, from Kyoto to Tokyo.

Me: "My wife and I once rode bikes over the Cascades, from Seattle to Idaho."

Heidi: "Where's your wife now?"

David: "Want to buy a bike?"

8
ZEX WISS YU

A man marries to have a home, but also because he doesn't want to be bothered with sex and all that sort of thing.

—SOMERSET MAUGHAM
The Circle

N THE SAME ALLEY AS OKUBO HOUSE there was a Japanese café where many of us went for breakfast—eggs, coffee, bacon, toast, $2. One morning Walter was there talking about his women. He raved about the Japanese lady he was dating—she'd taken him to a sex show the night before ("Well, two of 'em, actually")—but it seemed he had women all over the place. Each one he talked about was "a doll" or "real sweet" or "a real nice girl."

Like Annie. "I was hitchhiking along a road in New Zealand—which is a real must, by the way—when Annie blew past on a bicycle. She gave me this real big American 'hi!' and a great big smile. I waved her back to me. We just stood there in a drizzle, talking for a while. We ended up traveling together for four months. She stored her bike and we hitched."

Then there was the Swedish girl he toured the Philippines with: "I thought she was gonna kill me sometimes—she was so moody. You know, women in general are much moodier than men."

And the girl from Phoenix whom he met in the Sydney airport. And the British girl he "did two months with" in China, and another lady in Alaska—a naturalist—and one in Iowa.

After describing each one, he would tell me, "Now I could really see you two together"—or some cousin of that statement. "You'd make a great pair." Or: "Remember my Yugoslav lawyer friend? I should give you her address."

I told him that all I was interested in today was finding the nearest post office.

"Hey, I'm going there right after I finish this coffee. Hang on a sec. I'll go with you."

A sign on the post-office door said 0900; we were fifteen minutes early. "I'm waiting," said Walter. We stood next to a mailbox on the sidewalk, talked about life and women, and watched the Japanese whizzing to work.

A continuous low growl emerged from the throng of shuffling feet, beeping taxis, packed buses. Commuter trains on an overpass—stuffed tubes of human salami—thundered toward the downtown shopping and business districts. Near us, shop owners were beginning to roll up their storefronts and build sidewalk displays of their goods: fruit from California; plastic souvenirs from Taiwan and Hong Kong; shirts from mainland China; Japanese cameras, watches, tape decks.

It occurred to me that Japan was the perfect communist society—everyone working in close quarters without rioting, with no visible loafers and none of the overt disciplinary machinery of the totalitarian countries. All the social wiring was either internal or invisible. The Japanese went to work as though it were the most natural thing in the world, hidden magnets drawing them from their houses in the morning and propelling them home at night. Nobody had to force them to do it; it never occurred to them not to.

Suddenly there was a smiling Japanese woman in front of me, only six inches away, talking an unfamiliar stream of sounds. She was thirty to thirty-five years old, neither particularly attractive nor unattractive; the top of her head reached almost to my chin, making her tall for a Japanese. Ignoring the dumbfounded look on my face, she babbled on—smiling, talking softly, almost cooing—and while she did so, she reached up and gently stroked my right shoulder.

After several days of studying the unexpressive faces of the marching millions on Tokyo sidewalks, people peering at me from the corner of a narrowed eye if they looked at all, I was now unprepared for this full frontal assault. I looked at Walter—he'd been here six weeks, women were his favorite subject—maybe he could help. No such luck; face stiff and colorless, Walter was gaping at my admirer in disbelief.

And in front of me nothing was changing—the continuous clang and shuffle of Tokyo rush hour, the smiling woman happily smoothing my shirt, caressing my chest now. Was she drunk? I looked closely. No, she was clear-eyed. Crazy? Not that either. Whatever she was, I wanted her to disappear.

Instead, she leaned close, stretching on tiptoe up to my ear, and murmured another gush of sound at the end of which I thought I heard "... zex wiss yu."

"What?"

She stretched back up to me, hand still on my chest. The same stream of sounds, the same ending: "Zex wiss yu."

At any hour prostitutes are hard to figure—at 9:00 A.M., impossible.

"Please, go away!" I said this directly into her face, but she did not get it.

People were stepping around us on either side now. Her fingers were kneading my right biceps.

I shook my head. She didn't get that either.

"... zex wiss yu," she said, and giggled.

Walter and I exchanged glances; he shrugged and rolled his eyes. I reached out my left hand and put gentle pressure on the woman's right shoulder, easing her in the direction she'd been going before she stopped. This brought a quick reaction: she dropped her arms and stepped back half a pace. Her body stiffened, and her voice dropped three notches. She delivered another quick burst of Japanese, no longer a lullaby but an unmistakable rebuke.

She spun on her heel and strutted defiantly away, but not before her right hand shot out and said a quick hello—somewhat more than a brush and, thankfully, less than a punch—to my privates. I flinched and gasped and, mouth ajar, watched her swish off into the crowd—rust-colored sweater, short black skirt, milky legs showing from midthigh down. The flow of people on the sidewalk, oblivious to our thirty-second drama, had swept onward. Now it whisked her away.

"I wouldn't have believed that if I hadn't seen it," Walter finally said, releasing a fat sigh—seemingly the first breath he'd taken since the woman's arrival.

"The hookers sure get up early here."

"That was no hooker—just a horny housewife. They really go for tall, blond foreigners." Walter was dark-haired. "You're in big demand, kid."

It started to sink in. She hadn't mentioned money—at least not in any way I could understand. She had simply expressed interest and offered herself. Now I felt foolish. Maybe this was the way of Japan. Maybe the culture had been around long enough to develop a naturalness toward sex. In America nothing corrodes a relationship so mercilessly as the acid of an extracurricular affair, but maybe this was not the case everywhere. Why had I reacted so stiffly? No wonder *gaijin* were seen as coarse, crude, clumsy, rude. Stay open, I chided myself. That's what traveling's all about.

After the post office, Walter went right back to the café—"Wait till Pat and Glenn hear about this!"—and I headed for Okubo House. The woman's face, the pressure of her hand on my chest, kept coming back to me. Casual sex was an option I'd switched off when I got married. Maybe my whole attitude toward sex, marriage, people, needed reevaluation, a global adjustment. Would the Man 100 Miles Up look favorably on someone crouched timidly behind a shell of marriage? Maybe the woman had been a message from this world I claimed to trust.

But hell, I thought, I didn't want to sleep with that woman—not for a price, not for free. If the world wanted zex wiss me, it was going to have to upgrade the offer. I could do whatever I wanted, and not do whatever I didn't. I was in exactly the right place, thinking, doing, and feeling exactly the right things.

Just a few doors from Okubo House I noticed three Japanese men walking in front of me, looking back and smiling shyly. Eager to patch up my foreign relations, I picked one and grinned at him.

"Okubo House?" he asked.

"Yes. Okubo House."

"Ah, Okubo House," they all said in unison.

There was a brief silence as we walked.

"American-u?" one asked.

"Yes." I nodded. "American."

"Ah, American-u!"

Another silence.

Now we were at my door. They looked nervously at one another. Finally, in a whisper, one of them popped the question:

"Hah yu homosex-u-oo?"

9

THE SPECKLED DICK EXPRESS

What was important then was not that the beggar was drunk and reeling, but that he was mounted on his horse, and, however unsteadily, was going somewhere.

—THOMAS WOLFE
You Can't Go Home Again

I COULDN'T STAY IN TOKYO FOREVER. I was doing nothing there: wandering around each day, browsing in English bookstores; going to batting ranges, baseball games, sumo matches; meditating and stretching and writing affirmations in the park. I walked and rode the trains and subway all over the city, directionless, eating in sushi shops and gulping smog. After eight days, I'd had my fill.

From David and Heidi, the heading-home Canadians, I bought a bicycle for three thousand yen (thirteen dollars), and one morning told my friends at the café that I was leaving after breakfast to ride the six hundred kilometers to Kyoto. Everyone but David and Heidi said I was foolish. Walter: "In May? Didn't anyone tell you about rainy season? Buckets of water all day, all night. It's already overdue."

I told him I'd survive. My wife and I had weathered torrential rains in the Cascades. And besides, I was in exactly the right place, thinking, doing, and feeling exactly the right things.

"Whatever you say, screwball."

I used the Okubo House bathroom one last time, and was shocked to discover tiny brown spots in an extremely sensitive place. Although painless, they were frightening. I had not thought about physical breakdown, nor was "doctor" in my budget. Furthermore, I'd just announced my departure—I had to leave, spots or no spots. I pondered for a while my personal interpretation—a little mangled—of the Christian Science I was taught growing up, and resolved to just ignore them until they disappeared or started to hurt.

I strapped my sleeping bag and a change of clothes to my new three-speed, shook a few hands, exchanged a few addresses, and pedaled away from the comfort and safety of Okubo House. *The Speckled Dick Express is on the roll.* In a park a block away I saw a familiar figure sitting on a bench, hunched over a book. It was the black guy from San Francisco.

"Hey, where'd you get the bike?"

I told him where I'd gotten it and what I hoped to do.

"You're gonna get awful wet. Rainy season's any day now."

The sky above us was gray and low and threatened to rip open momentarily. I shrugged bravely. And then I noticed a sleeping bag on the ground. I asked, joking, if he was camping in the park.

"Well, I did last night, and unless I get some money in the mail today, I'll be here again tonight."

No kidding?

"No kidding. My girlfriend is in Kyoto, and she's supposed to send it, but she's awfully slow."

Before he could hit me up for a loan, I wished him luck and rode off in the direction of Mount Fuji. Somehow his situation made my own seem downright bearable. Better brokenhearted than just plain broke.

avid and Heidi had given me maps, which I kept in the handlebar basket. They showed a major national road, paralleling the expressway toll road, and leading west out of Tokyo.

"Fuji's two easy days of riding or one hard one," David had said.

"Real hard," said Heidi.

I raised the seat as high as it would go and began pedaling. My plan was to take it easy—ride at whatever speed felt comfortable until Kyoto appeared or something went terribly wrong. The bike was a three-speed ladies' model, with a basket in front and a rack in back—no tools, spare parts, or tires. If it was going to fail me, I would just as soon have it happen near Tokyo, so I would have at least a slim chance of finding a mechanic who spoke English. Also, my body was issuing no guarantees; wandering around Tokyo for a week hadn't been a particularly effective training regimen. And the spots—who knew how long they could be ignored? And the rainy season. *I am in exactly the right place . . .*

As each neighborhood gave way to the next, it occurred to me that this was the same area I had viewed from the fifty-second floor of the Sumitomo Building, several mornings prior. It now seemed a planet away. Who was up there today? Were they looking my way? Only eight days earlier, Tokyo had seemed forbidding. Now, Tokyo was home, and it was the land ahead that threatened me. I was no less scared of leaving this city than I had been of leaving San Francisco. Never underestimate the ability of a human being to find a rut and fall in love with it.

I clawed my way out of Tokyo, riding on the sidewalks, ringing my bell to clear Japanese pedestrians off their own turf, and taking final note of those things that had seemed so unusual on Day One, but which were now commonplace: a Japanese man frozen in the act of dropping a coin into a vending machine, gaping slack-jawed at me, uncertain whether it was okay to smile; a wide-eyed woman breathing through a surgical mask, standing aside to let me pass; dishes of plastic food filling the windows of a nearby restaurant; a stack of sex comic books sticking out of a trash can in front of a neon-lit pachinko parlor; the ubiquitous sign—MITSUBISHI BANK. These scenes repeated over and over for several miles until I suspected Tokyo was a backdrop on rollers and my bike was on a treadmill.

But slowly the city yielded. Green areas became more common, and several times I found myself riding under leaf canopies. English signs disappeared. Except in an occasional reflection, I saw no more white faces. Just a few miles from downtown Tokyo, all evidence of any civilization but the Japanese one was gone.

10
LAUGH.
CRY.
KEEP PEDALING.

*The thought of suicide is a great consolation;
with its help you can get through many a bad
night.*

—FRIEDRICH NIETZSCHE
Beyond Good and Evil

T HE FARTHER THE BIKE WENT, the more it charmed me. It was slow
and clunky and creaked under its load, but it just kept going; the
sky or my body seemed more likely to break first. Yet my body
seemed to be enjoying the work, saddle soreness its only complaint.

Around one o'clock I bought a half-dozen bananas at a roadside
stand and ate three of them immediately. At a grocery store I bought a
package of rice crackers and put them in the handlebar basket, where I could
munch them at will. In making these purchases, I hit upon a useful shopping
technique: I would make my selections and go to the register with a pile of
yen in my extended palm—lunacy in most of the world, perfectly appropriate
in Japan. The shopkeepers would take the correct amount, make change,
bow, and say, *"Domo arigato."*

Having been warned that finding an English-speaking Japanese outside the
major cities would be as difficult as getting a Berliner to admit to a Nazi
past, I had copied down fifteen Japanese phrases: Which way?, how much?,
I understand, I don't understand, the names of certain foods.

The "police boxes" were another aid. I recalled that San Francisco's mayor,
Diane Feinstein, had once come here to inspect Tokyo's one- and two-man
neighborhood stations. Now I stopped frequently to look at the wall maps
and to say one of my favorite new words.

"Fuji, *massugu?*" *Straight ahead.*
"*Hai, hai,*" the police always replied. "*Massugu.*"

I passed the western outskirts of Tokyo in midafternoon. At Fuchu, the map showed a small side road, about a mile away, which paralleled the busy national road; to get to it I had to turn south and cross a long bridge over a wide, mostly dry riverbed. From the bridge I could see the Tokyo skyline, twenty miles back on the receding horizon; around me the land was much less developed. To the west, pale green mountain ranges lurked in the rainy-season haze; on the banks of the river were low apartment buildings and business districts separated by long stretches of overgrowth.

Halfway across, I paused to watch a forty-person film crew creating a drama in the gravel bed beneath the bridge. They were mostly kids; the star was a young lady dressed in a shiny gown who chased off several kung-fu attackers with a stick. While I watched, they did several takes, shifting lights, adjusting makeup, and changing the choreography. I looked for Pat and Glenn, the Canadian actors from Okubo House, but they weren't there.

As late afternoon approached and my body grew tired, the thrill of having begun something bold was swallowed by the uncertainty of not knowing where I would sleep. Traveling raises more questions than insights: What was I doing here? What contribution was my trip making to the human race? What sense was there in riding a beat-up bicycle across the mountains to Kyoto? Why didn't I just go back home and get a job in a corporation that would care for me until death? And why bother waiting? Why not die this afternoon?

That last thought seemed attractive. Death would relieve me of the responsibility of having to find a place to spend the night. It would still the voices in my head. And my wife would collect forty thousand dollars from the accidental-death insurance policy I had taken out three weeks earlier. And what better place than Japan, where suicide was an acceptable, even expected, response to failure?

I have a theory that men often die the way they play sports—a theory I developed mainly by observing one particular football player at the college I went to. As a freshman running back trying to make his mark with the varsity, he was five yards from a touchdown one fall Saturday when he fumbled a pitchout. Instead of falling on the loose ball, he tried picking it up, but booted it accidentally, again and again, until he was swarmed under by a wall of tacklers who rushed him from behind. Years later he died in a freak accident. He was standing in the bed of a moving pickup truck, taking footage of the road behind him for—of all things—a traffic-safety film, when he was smacked in the back of the head by a low overpass. As with the gang of tacklers, he never saw it coming.

In college I spent a good deal of time on the basketball court "taking the charge." I would plant myself in front of an oncoming opponent and try to convince the referee that the ensuing collision was not my fault. I now contemplated "taking the charge" from a train or a bus—materializing in front of it when it no longer had a chance of stopping. Let the ref call it an accident. I would (presumably) get a respite from my anxieties, my wife would get the forty thousand dollars. Then she'd appreciate me.

I n the distance was a range of mountains. Ahead, the map showed a national park surrounding Mount Takao, a good bet for a place to camp; this became my goal for the night. I pedaled for two hours, snacking on rice crackers, hugging the left shoulder, and stopping at the police boxes (less frequent now) to consult the maps. Eventually the roads led me back to the busy national road.

Motion tends to self-justify. People going forward discover or create things that validate their movement; immobile people atrophy. Laugh, cry, I told myself, but keep pedaling.

At dusk I reached the end of the Tokyo plain. The road narrowed, and was lined on both sides by the village of Takao, the "last chance" for motorists before the climb into the mountains. A hotel was advertising rooms for fifteen dollars; I considered taking one, but didn't want to set an expensive precedent. The money should be saved for a rainy night or spent on food.

I found a diner where noisy Japanese were eating plates of food and drinking beer. I sat alone at an empty table, sweaty and ragged-looking after a sixty-five-kilometer day. The waitresses had a small debate over who would serve me.

"*Kon-ban-wa,*" I said to the losing waitress. *Good evening.*

"*Kon-ban-wa.*"

"*Niwatori?*" *Chicken.*

"*Ramen?*" she said. *Noodles.*

"*Niwatori.*"

"*Ramen.*"

People at nearby tables had bowls of noodles and vegetables, and one person had a whole fish on his plate. None of it looked very appetizing.

"*Niwatori,*" I begged.

"*Ramen.*" She had a one-track ear.

"Butaniku?" Pork.
"Ramen."
"No *butaniku?"*
"Ramen."
"Okay. *Ramen."*

T he light had faded from the sky by the time I got my fill of noodles. I headed into the mountains—alternately pushing and riding my bike—with an eye out for a place to sleep. The road became an upgrade of sharp curves through a wedge of valley. All of the flat spots were taken up by small homes or planted with crops. Nothing seemed quite right: either the area was too exposed, a dog was barking, a house was too nearby, or the traffic too close.

I was exhausted, numb and yawning. My legs wobbled. I pushed for a few kilometers, hoping for something good around each new curve. Always there were houses, yapping dogs, rice paddies, and more curves. *Come on, God! How 'bout a break? I've been baptized, you know!*

Finally there was a turnout and a chain across an entrance to a wide field, dry and unplanted. I lifted my bike over the chain and pushed it to the back of the clearing, a hundred yards from the highway. I stomped down some weeds, tossed away a few rocks, spread a poncho and a foam cushion. With my flashlight I checked for speckles: still there. I ate a chocolate bar and a banana, brushed my teeth, and wiggled into my sleeping bag.

Stars were twinkling overhead; a dry night seemed imminent. The dark shapes of mountains loomed up on all sides; flat on my back, I fantasized I was in the bottom of an empty tuna-fish can, gazing upward. Lying on the ground a few yards from a rice paddy, with thick jungle covering the knifelike ridges around me, I felt much closer to an older Japan. The future may have arrived in Tokyo, but forty miles away it's still 1950.

Traffic sounds intruded from the highway. Crickets clacked; a bird was calling; something rattled in the nearby bushes. Not a person in the world knew where I was. My mind glided down the mountain, breezed past the noodle shop, crossed the river, and slipped back into Tokyo; avoided the black guy camped in the park, stopped at Okubo House for my backpack, dodged the Pentecostals on the streetcorner; goosed the lady wiss zex on her mind, took a rain check on sumo, caught the train to the airport, and flew back to San Francisco. According to my calculations, the sun would right now be rising over the bay. She would be sitting at the dressing table, tilted forward, arm raised, sketching eyeliner onto a drooping lid. I fell asleep, half hoping that during the night nothing would eat me, half hoping that something would.

11
A SERIES
OF
UNMARKED FORKS

*Macon wondered if even this moment would
become, one day, something he looked back upon
wistfully. He couldn't imagine it; he couldn't think
of any period bleaker than this in all his life, but
he noticed how time had a way of coloring things.*

—ANNE TYLER
The Accidental Tourist

IT WAS TEN MINUTES UNTIL FIVE in the morning when the mosquitoes
woke me. The stars were gone now, obscured by a predawn mist. I
got up and packed my bike. A good start would get me to the youth
hostel in Fuji-Yoshida, the town at the base of Mount Fuji, by noon—
it was only fifty kilometers away.

I wolfed my last two bananas and wheeled my bike back to the road.
With a full load, I found it impossible to ride up steep grades; after five
minutes of pedaling I got off and pushed. Before long, I was clammy with
sweat. The road was narrow and challenged on either side by heavy vege-
tation. Often the white line marking the shoulder disappeared completely
and I was forced to move as far to the side (the *left* side) as possible. Even
at that early hour, a few trucks, cars, and motorcycles were out. Whenever
a vehicle passed, noxious exhaust fumes lingered in the air, gritty on my
throat and nose, stinging my eyes. But when the traffic faded away, all was
serene. I was alone with the mystical sounds of the forest creaking to life,
and the rich smell of damp air, fragrant with honeysuckle.

For half an hour I pushed uphill, stopping once to gulp water from my
canteen. How long would this upgrade continue? All morning? All day? There
was nothing else on my schedule; if pushing my bike to Fuji was what life
was offering, well, so be it.

Finally, the summit; the grade leveled off and then dropped away. I threw a leg up over my bike and coasted down into a short tunnel, popping out at the other end into a panoramic, vapor-streaked valley stretching below and beyond. Here was the Japan I had imagined in pretrip dreams: gentle, fog-shrouded hills outlining the course of a wide, dark river; the folds of several formidable mountain ridges jutting in the background; an occasional building, but mostly a landscape of greenery and mist solidifying in the morning light. And a spiraling ten-kilometer free-fall down an asphalted chute through the jungle ...

On the valley floor a black iron bridge spanning the river caught my attention; older, narrow, about 150 yards long and just wide enough for one car. I turned off the main road, pedaled to the bridge's middle, and stopped. Tree branches overhung the river's edge, begging for rope swings. A chain of rowboats extended from a shoreside dock, wagging in the current like a lazy kite tail. When looking for a nation's soul or for your own, try the countryside early in the morning.

The map indicated a secondary road on the far side of the river. It would be quieter than the national road, no doubt, and would also lead to Fuji; furthermore, it appeared to be a shortcut. I forsook the level national road and began climbing again, into the mountains. On bluffs above the river were the well-spaced homes of rural Japanese, always with a garden or a rice paddy, and a small stone shrine in the yard. The houses were not flamboyant but simple—fragile and delicate and colored brown or gray or the shade of slate. Much of the time I had to stand on the pedals and grind away, or dismount and push. But the quiet and peace were sufficient compensation. I relaxed and drew the deep, clean breaths that had been unthinkable in Tokyo.

I came to a series of unmarked forks in the road and made my best guess each time. But several towns shown on the map did not appear; the mountain roads were getting steeper, the valleys narrower; I was nearly always pushing up a hill or coasting down one with the wind whipping my hair. Towns grew smaller, farther apart, and the few road signs were always in Japanese.

This pattern continued well into the morning. Having eaten only the two bananas, and having now drained my canteen, I was famished and thirsty and feeling somewhat faint. In one small village I tried asking directions from a lady walking along the roadside, but she seemed afraid of me, staring at the ground and refusing to look up.

And then, rounding a curve high in the mountains, I saw something that broke my mood. On the side of the road, at the foot of a driveway, was a vending machine. I stopped and deposited some coins; an orange drink slithered into the trough at the bottom. It was cold and tasty and I took it, and the second one, too, as an omen.

Half an hour later I came to a three-pronged fork in the road. A small store located at the junction was not yet opened for business, but when I clomped onto the front porch, an elderly woman appeared inside.

"*Ohayo,*" she said through the screen door.

"*Ohayo.*" I pulled out my map. "*Map-u,*" I told her.

She turned and called to the back room. A surprised-looking man twice my age shuffled forward in slippers, beckoned me inside and unfolded a pair of glasses. He took my *map-u,* spread it on the counter, and began chattering.

Through a sliding screen I saw teacups and noodle bowls laid on a low table in the next room. *Maybe they will invite me to breakfast.* But they didn't. A flurry of clucking sounds indicated that my benefactor had located our position. He pointed to a spot in a range of mountains at least fifteen kilometers off my shortcut road to Fuji.

I shook my head in disbelief. "No."

"*Hai, hai!*" he insisted, double-checking.

Oh, well . . . I dropped my head and thought for a moment. If I backtracked all the way to the river and followed the national road, I'd still reach Fuji-Yoshida by nightfall. Or maybe there was a different way to go? I motioned the little man to the door, and pointed at the intersection where the three roads met.

"Fuji, *do-chi*?" *Which way.*

He pointed in the direction I had been riding when I arrived, and outlined a route on the map. I would not have to backtrack after all; but ridge after ridge of mountains loomed ahead.

"Steep?" I asked, drawing sea-serpent humps in the air.

The man and his wife, shoulder to shoulder on the front steps, wrinkled their foreheads.

I pointed at my bicycle and made up-and-down roller-coaster motions with my hand. They nodded and laughed. *Silly* gaijin.

"*Ikura* kilometer?" *How much kilometer?* I was butchering their language.

The man barked at his wife. She brought pen and paper. He wrote: *40k.* In three hours of hacking through the mountains, I'd drawn closer to Mount Fuji by ten kilometers. Technically this was progress.

In their tiny, poorly stocked store I found a small loaf of bread (it turned out to be filled with a slimy gray pastry), and held out my money. After the lady made change and filled my canteen, I bowed profusely, said "*Arigato, arigato, arigato,*" and then rode off while they stood in the doorway, smiling broadly. They seemed to be thinking: "Doesn't that beat all?"

Around the next curve I came upon a larger grocery. Inside I found orange juice and bananas, a box of chocolate-covered almonds, and a bag of peanuts. The lady who ran this store said "*Ohayo,*" and nothing more. She sorted through my change, took what she needed, and studied her toes.

While mounting my bike, I heard her call from the store's doorway. In her arms was a blond melon the size of a basketball.

"Present-u." She was smiling.

I pedaled down the road, the heavy melon wobbling precariously in my handlebar basket. At the earliest opportunity I stopped and ate; the slime-filled pastry and three-fourths of the melon sailed noiselessly over a cliff.

T he day was customarily hazy, as though a forest fire were burning out of control several ridges away. The view from the Sumitomo Building had introduced me to Tokyo, and now this ride-and-push through the mountains was my introduction to a different Japan. Cars were rare. A clear stream bounced from pool to pool down the middle of the narrow valley; fishermen squatting on smooth house-sized boulders held bamboo poles over the deeper holes. Groups of peasants, pajamas rolled up over knees, stood calf deep in flooded rice paddies, stooping to pull weeds or plug in new seedlings. High on the valley walls an occasional skinned patch indicated the presence of a logging in-dustry, but generally the slopes were covered with thick stands of pine.

A building in one small town had a polished red fire engine in the garage. I stopped—partly out of curiosity, partly to verify my location. The ground floor was deserted, but television sounds came from the top of a staircase. I climbed it and came to an open door. Four young men seated with their backs to me were watching a soap opera. One of them sensed my presence and turned around; he leaped to his feet, squawking in Japanese, and the others followed. Someone hurried across the room and turned off the TV. I'm not sure who was more embarrassed—me or them. I spread my *map-u,* asked some easy questions, and left as quickly as possible.

How did these people in the countryside view me? I wondered. Looking at me, what would they see? A man-boy—competent, purposeful, intrepid? They could not read my thoughts, knew nothing of my marital woes or the spots in my shorts. They would have to be impressed. I liked sneaking up on them; unlike Tokyo's jaded sophisticates, they were not prepared for me. In the instant they spotted me, brows lifted, eyes widened, postures shifted, and they were helpless to prevent it. I imagined I was lifting a skirt, seeing a Japan not often seen, catching these locals before they could get their smiles up and their bows down. *Here are the faces I'll remember,* I told my notebook that night, *these shy, whiskered hillbillies, unable to comprehend what brings an apparition like me to their crease of mountains. That I don't know exactly what I'm seeing, that I can't speak the language, hardly bothers me. Reading* Shogun *was in fact exactly the right preparation. Better to know too little about a place than too much; better to go cold than wait until you know it all. Gather your data raw, soak up everything; interpret it later, some future night, around a fire somewhere in some mountains with your wife and kids.*

At eleven o'clock in the morning, six hours after breaking camp, I reached a notch at the top of the mountains. Except for the sound of wind frisking pines, all was quiet. I drank water and wished I hadn't eaten all the chocolate-covered almonds. Snaking behind me was the valley I had just labored through. Ahead was a narrow green trough with an asphalt track corkscrewing downward, toward Fuji. The youth hostel was only twenty-five kilometers away now, and from my vantage point everything was downhill.

12
SOFT SNOW, GATHERING HAZE

It serves you right!
You traveled with yourself.

—SOCRATES
To a man who complained
that he had received
no benefit from his travels, quoted in
Seneca, *Epistulae ad Lucilium*

 "FUJI-SAN," THEY CALL IT. Sacred mountain. Living symbol of Japan. A near-perfect volcanic cone over twelve thousand feet high and frosted with year-round snow.

During the post-rainy season months of July and August, when the snow has receded from Fuji's lower slopes and the haze has been scrubbed from the sky, pilgrims flock to it, a single glimpse being the nicest gift bestowable upon a Japanese soul. Hikers climb to the summit at a rate of nearly one thousand a day.

But May is a different story. On the afternoon of my arrival, visibility was down to a few murky kilometers. The weather and the regulation-conscious Japanese were doing their best to keep me off the mountain.

"Cannot crime. Crowst untu Jew-rye," said the young proprietress of Fuji-Yoshida's empty youth hostel. (For the three weeks prior to my visit, the guest book showed only ten names, including David's and Heidi's.) The Tourist Information Center in Tokyo had said the same thing—Fuji is open only during July and August. But word at Okubo House was that Fuji is always open, unofficially. "How do you close a mountain?" Don, the air-force linguist, pointed out.

But now all of this seemed irrelevant. The appropriate question would have been: "How can one crime what one cannot see?"

"View is bettah en mo-neen," the hostel manager said. "Maybe tu-mo-do you can see."

Further encouragement came from the hostel bulletin board, where several hikers had posted accounts of recent trips to the top. A note dated a week prior reported a pleasant climb with no difficulties, and gave this counsel:

> Anyone who comes here and doesn't climb Fuji once is
> a fool. Anyone who climbs it twice is also a fool. Allow
> four and a half to five hours round trip. Dress warm. Take
> sunglasses. Best to start at 3:00 A.M., when snow is firm.
> Amazing sunrise from summit!
>   Peace.
>
> Fred—Christchurch, New Zealand.

Peace—I'll take it. Three A.M.! No thanks, Fred. The previous night spent on the ground may have been spiritually rewarding (and free), but it had not been particularly restful. Nor had Okubo House been a sleeper's paradise. I decided to sleep in and take a feasibility reading when I awoke. On a futon in a five-dollar room of my own, I slept stonelike until 9:00 A.M.

Overnight the air had cleared enough so that from the window of my room, over the dark-tiled roofs of the town, I could see the immense Hershey Kiss shape of Fuji ruling the sky and dwarfing the town from a position that seemed, somehow, directly overhead. Suddenly Fuji-Yoshida shrank in stature, demoted from small city to insignificant village status. Awe and magic rang through my body like an alarm. A lien had been slapped on my consciousness. Soft snow and gathering haze be damned—I was going climbing.

A forty-kilometer road led from the edge of town to a tourist area near tree line, halfway up the side of Fuji. I pedaled to the beginning of that road, chained my bicycle to a light pole, and stuck out my left thumb. The third car, a mini-van, stopped for me.

"*Domo arigato,*" I said to the Japanese driver as I climbed into the passenger seat.

He nodded.

In the seats behind us were five women, employees of the tourist-area restaurants and souvenir shops. They stared silently; I turned and gazed back.

"*Ohayo.*"

They answered as one—"*Ohayo gazai-u-mas*"—then fell quiet, still staring.

I touched my chest: "American-u."

There was a murmur, followed by more silence.

"Sahn Frahnceesco." For foreign situations I have an all-purpose foreign accent.

There was another murmur; still the women's faces were drawn and guarded. I pointed at the mountain ahead, and made climbing motions with my fingers.

A lady in the back row clucked and mumbled something that sparked a convulsion of laughter. The five stiff faces cracked open, forming canyons of crooked or missing teeth and pronounced wrinkles.

The driver said something to the rearview mirror, prompting new laughter. One of the ladies addressed me in a questioning tone. I held my hands helplessly out to my sides and said, *"Skoshi Nihongo."* *Very little Japanese.* I ticked off my few words: *"Ohayo, domo arigato, sayonara, Mount Fuji . . ."* More laughter, then extended silence.

I sat back and watched the driver guide us steeply upward, through twisting 180-switchbacks, thick forests, patches of cloud, on toward the lusterless sun. The mountain put me in mind of the years I'd spent in Colorado: its lower slopes were smeared with a covering of pines and some birches whose lime-colored leaves shimmered like frail aspens; green and white highway signs identified the area, in English, as a national park; bicyclists were straining uphill on slim ten-speeds. But the sky—groggy with haze, and permitting a view that was rarely distant and seldom in focus—was very *un*like Colorado. It was more like . . . And then I caught myself. *Be here now. This is not Colorado—it's Japan.*

Forty-five minutes later we stopped in a three-acre parking lot full of tour buses. As our van emptied, I was assaulted by cold, stinging air and a barrage of bowing *Sayonara's.* My new friends disappeared into the cluster of stores.

After browsing the souvenir shops (Fuji rocks, Fuji ashtrays, Fuji candy), I found a path that led away from the commercial jumble, away from the excited tourists rubbing shirtsleeved arms, and into the surrounding woods. A quarter-mile later I found a wooden sign, as big as I am, jammed into the side of the mountain. It warned in English of deceptively slick ice banks, treacherous wind gusts. EVERY YEAR SEVERAL CLIMBERS ARE KILLED.

Wide, barren rock fields spread for hundreds of yards on either side of me; higher up were miles of empty snowfields. I thought: Fuji is much more impressive from a distance. Several thousand feet below, the town of Fuji-Yoshida was now a street map surrounded by quilted squares of green and brown and red. Other details of the view, including the ridges I'd bicycled the day before, were obscured by the woolen sky. The crowds of Tokyo seemed a brief hallucination. The only sound was my breath, searing my lungs with an energizing chill, and billowing out in steamy clouds.

In my Fuji fantasies I never dreamed I'd have the mountain virtually to myself. Through my binoculars I spotted only half a dozen other climbers, a group of dark specks creeping through the whiteness near the peak. Alone, I started up the hill, heading for the mountain's last grove of trees, ten tall pines a hundred yards ahead. The trail underfoot was well worn, veined with runoff gullies and exposed roots. In spots it was frozen. My mountaineering equipment consisted of scarf, gloves, long undershirt, sweater, down vest, and light hiking shoes. I strode ahead with springy steps and an expanded feeling in my chest. Life was good.

But the pines were booby-trapped; I took one whiff of their perfume—tangy needles and fresh-scuffed earth mixed in a base of thinned air—and burst uncontrollably into tears.

There'd been no warning. In the last day and a half I'd come to feel sufficiently together, blazing through the mountains of Japan, my traveler's credentials once again in order. With a cheap bike and some language scraps, I had fought from Tokyo to the slopes of Fuji. But now, in one thoughtless instant, this. Why? How much longer?

I crumpled onto a log, leaned my back against a tree, closed my eyes, and sobbed and sobbed and sobbed. The emotion of an entire lifetime, it seemed, had been hidden in my throat, awaiting some secret signal to storm the portholes of my face. I sobbed through grief, through sorrow and self-pity, right through fear, sobbed maniacally until two minutes?—five minutes? ten minutes?—later I had sobbed myself right to the door of insight. *My quaking chest, heaving shoulders, leaking eyes—they're mechanical. I'm a machine. A human machine sobbing atop an island in the Pacific. My wife wants a divorce. Big deal! So what! In ten years it won't mean a thing. It means nothing right this minute.*

I could have laughed, but I put it off, wanting to linger with my insight and with a not unpleasant dose of self-pity. I saw that the tears had been triggered by a single sniff of mountain pine, an aroma linked in my mind to Colorado, linked in my mind to my wife, linked in my mind to feeling left and alone and hurt. I wasn't crying about my marriage. Or about Colorado. I was simply a mass of memory and exposed nerve endings mechanically processing feelings—"A" plus "B" plus "C" equals tears.

With the haze congealing around me, I sat in that pine grove on the steep slopes of Fuji—sixty miles from Tokyo, an ocean away from San Francisco—and slowly saw the joke. I had convinced myself that life centered around a piece of paper in a file drawer in the office of the city clerk. But now the ill logic was obvious: you can not be striding along a mountain path feeling good about yourself one moment, break into tears the next, and still believe that it's somehow all the fault of a woman five thousand miles away. A boulder of truth bounded down the mountainside and struck me in the solar plexus: I was crying because I was crying—it was no more complicated than that. They were my own tears, it was my own life. I, too, had signed the papers. I'd bought my own airplane ticket, own bicycle, sought out this mountain all by myself.

I sobbed some more, just for insurance, until from somewhere deep within, a warm reminder, forced upward by the strength of thousands of repetitions, came bubbling gently to the surface: "You are in exactly the right place . . ."— a gust of wind tugged at my hair— ". . . thinking, doing, and feeling . . ."—a bead of sweat rolled into my moustache— ". . . exactly the right things." I expelled a sigh.

"Ahhhhhhhhyesss," I told myself, "I am in exactly the right place. I am, I am. And if she is back in San Francisco, trying to forget me, that is where she should be."

Our relationship, I saw, was intact. "Married," "divorced," "separated"— those words do not define relationships; they are but weather reports. *"This,"* I realized, "is our relationship: her there, me here, and the world spinning through space at who-knows-how-many miles an hour."

I opened my eyes and looked around. Fuji-san was still there, and I was still halfway up it, sitting wet-faced on a log. *"World traveler!"* Hah! *I'm not traveling—I'm a coolie, a slave of love toting a bale of misery around the planet.*

After drenching that grove with my tears, I now shook it dry with laughter, several gasping minutes of it. Cleansed, I wiped my eyes, got off my log, and marched up the mountain.

13

"SAKE!" HE BOOMED, A THIRD TIME.

The use of traveling is to regulate imagination by reality, and instead of thinking how things may be, to see them as they are.

—HESTER PIOZZI
Anecdotes of Samuel Johnson

"OH, YOU'VE GOT TO TRY the public baths," a friend told me before I left San Francisco. "They're the best thing about Japan."

Now, frazzled and exhilarated after my climb, I decided it was time. I took my bathing kit and strolled toward the neighborhood baths.

A honeycomb of narrow alleys and dusty, shop-lined streets surrounded the hostel; undulating through the middle of town was a canal lined with mature, leafy trees. I leaned on the railing of a wooden footbridge, and studied the gray shroud that was the evening sky. Fuji-san was again invisible, the evidence indicating it had never existed.

At a temple next to the canal, school kids played hide-and-seek, and a bent gray-haired man bowed to an outdoor shrine. The children eyed me cautiously at first, but soon abandoned their game to walk behind me, barking all the infinite variations of "Ha-ro!" They escorted me—no, they chased me—to the baths' entrance.

The inside presented me with a choice between two closed doors, a dilemma solved by the arrival of a teenage girl who looked straight through me before entering the door on the left; I went right. An elderly lady sat behind a raised desk at the end of a high screen separating the men's and women's sections—one leg, one arm, one eye on either side. I showed the hostel receipt that entitled me to free bathing. She took it, chortling, and poked a bloated finger at the fine print. Tiny English lettering said: HAIR WASHING—30 YEN EXTRA. I forked over the fifteen cents.

A half-dozen men in various stages of nudity were in the dressing room. They glanced at me quickly and then pretended I wasn't there. But news of my presence caused a stir in the women's section; three teenage girls peered around the screen, leering as I chose a locker and slowly unbuttoned my shirt. "Ha-ro!" they squealed. And: *"Gaijin! Gaijin!"* They were eager, I knew, to confirm the great-*gaijin*-penis legends the Japanese whisper among themselves, but they didn't get the chance. The lady attendant clucked and shooed them away. Before they could return, I quickly got naked and headed for the bath. In the mirror I saw everyone—attendant included—sneaking peeks at me. But after verifying that I was indeed on the correct side of the screen, they retreated into themselves, the men scrubbing their brown bodies, the lady building orderly stacks of change.

In the tub room was a row of knee-level faucets where I imitated the other men, squatting, dumping small buckets of water on my head, and washing away my grime. In the process I noticed the spots were gone. Vanished forever. Skin as clean and smooth as penis skin ever gets. No trace and no doctor bill. As I eased myself down into the scalding pool, I thought: Fuji-san. Sacred mountain. Hmmmmn . . .

About a quarter of the homes in Japan have no bathing facilities, hence the importance of the public ones. The neighborhood bath is an institution, a relaxed meeting place where people come to soak and scrub and visit with one another. Presumably these men all saw each other here regularly, but from my steamy vantage point I noticed a curious thing: when standing or walking about the room, they all held small washcloths in front of their loins. It did not matter that their genitals—wine corks anchored in beds of dark moss—were plainly visible, but it mattered greatly that each followed the pretense of concealing himself. Ritual modesty had replaced the real thing.

As I soaked, I pondered the data I'd gathered on the Japanese version of conformity. Sumo—the national game—was a birthday cake of ritual decorated with a single candle of action. Baseball had been similarly homogenized, the body mechanics of Japanese players nearly identical, as if the entire country had one coach. And—as several Japanese pointed out to me—the widespread reluctance to speak English, a compulsory school subject, is nothing more than the fear of making a mistake, violating form, looking un-Japanese. The absence of crime: even that, I supposed, could be a function of form—if stealing was bad form, then a Japanese would automatically work, or die, before stealing. Form takes precedence over life itself. *Japan Today* reported that the inquiry into a train derailment ended (between the lines I read: satisfactorily) with the gas-oven death of a certain employee. An American I met at Okubo House told of breaking off a love affair with a Japanese girl whose parents insisted that the shame brought on by this mixing of the races had but one antidote: suicide—mutual *seppuku*. Not for the two lovers, but for the girl and both parents. The American and his feelings were never considered: *gaijin,* it is known, have no shame.

Accordingly, when I had endured my limit of hot water, I did not cover myself for the trip back to my locker. I was American, required by my own culture to be shamelessly different.

And besides, I had no washcloth.

T hat night there was a festival in Fuji-Yoshida, an annual affair, and the whole town turned out. The main business thoroughfare was blocked off, lined with stalls and booths. Merchants had closed their shops and moved their wares into the narrow street now lit by festive lanterns and soft electric lights.

A mosaic of food awaited: skewers of pork, sushi rolls, rice and vegetables, pastry, ice cream, even live lobsters clawing blindly in tanks of green water. Midway contests were set up for the children: darts, a ring toss, a game of knock-a-bottle-down-with-a-cork-gun. Dream-faced little boys ogled junk prizes and shiny souvenirs, schoolgirls promenaded hand in hand.

There was even a freak show. Standing a head taller than everyone, and looking oh, so different, I was maybe the event's largest attraction. Parents pointed me out to their toddlers. Chuckling mothers lifted wide-eyed babies to search my face. Young boys in ambush barked, "Ha-ro," and then scampered away lest I test their English. Groups of teenage girls wearing saddle shoes and white ankle socks gawked, and giggled into their fists. I thought: A booth—*SEE GREAT GAIJIN PENIS: 100 YEN*—would pay for my trip.

Since Tokyo I had not seen another white face; my last words with a native English speaker had been with the fundless black guy camping in the park. Having Fuji-Yoshida "to myself" produced a borderline euphoria. No notes of danger intruded on the peaceful night: polite children running freely, young parents strolling, wizened elders with diamond eyes, vendors hawking wares. I ate pork kebabs, tuna sushi, and several ice-cream bars, paying in my here-take-what-you-need manner. If ever a future world is created by taking the best of each country, Japan's biggest contribution will be *no crime.* My passport and travelers' checks and three hundred dollars in cash lay loose in my unlocked hostel room, but I was unconcerned. This was the perfect society.

I stopped and jotted in my notebook:

> *We must have all been crazy to have fought a war so recently. What could possibly have gotten into us? They battle my father's generation, but forty years later completely welcome his son, who is surprised to find a people with nothing more in mind than living quiet lives of peace and prosperity in the shadow of a great mountain. I wonder: Were they confused in 1940 when their leaders, just over the hill in Tokyo, informed them they were at war?*

I was ambling back to the hostel, slurping nonchalantly at the last of an ice cream and mingling with the flow of people departing the fair, when a man stepped off the sidewalk and blocked my path. "Goo evereen. Ow hah yu?"

I stopped and said, "Fine, thank you." I suspected he wanted to practice his English, but then I noticed his eyes, slightly glazed, and his breath, slightly ripe.

He shook his head, rejecting my reply. "Japanese," he slurred. "No Engrish." The friendliness I had imagined in his voice was gone. I smiled politely, eased around him, and started slowly down the street; he followed right alongside.

Was he enjoying the night air? I asked, trying to get a reading on him.

He lurched and bumped me in the ribs. Accident or provocation?

"Japanese. No Engrish," he said, and bumped me again. He was a solid man, tall for a Japanese, with a square face, flattop, and thick forearms. A seaman, I imagined.

"Sake," he said.

I pretended ignorance. "Engrish. No Japanese."

He bumped me a third time.

I looked around for police. There had been several back at the festival, but now there were none. A steady flow of pedestrians passed by, ignoring us. A fisticuffs between this man and myself would be pretty even, I judged. Then I recalled some guidebook advice: "Avoid physical confrontations at all cost. When the police arrive, the first thing they do is arrest the *gaijin*." *Well, I could always outrun him.*

"Sake." He tugged at my arm. I stopped walking and faced him. He pointed down an alleyway lit with neon bar signs, demanding me to follow.

"NO," I said. *"Do-mo-ar-i-ga-to-*but-NO." I pointed in the direction of the hostel and pantomimed sleep—head tilted, palms pressed to cheek.

"Sake!" he boomed, a third time.

"NO!"

We were standing chest to chest now, staring. His black-pea eyes narrowed and burned. His jaw was set, chin pushed forward, and his hair stood straight up from his scalp. Almost imperceptibly he was growling, the guttural pre-bite sound a dog makes. He was so close that the pores on his nose, reflecting the neon, were grains of blue sand. And he stank—his breath fermented with sake or something stronger, and an animal odor surrounding him like a warning. *So* THIS *is who Dad fought.*

We stood like that for several moments, eyeballing each other, while people streamed around the small island we formed. Finally his growl faded. He wobbled slightly and his dark eyes blinked. He was not going to bite.

"Domo arigato," I said, and immediately wondered what I was thanking him for.

He looked at me with a hurt expression and then turned away, down his alley. I walked back to the hostel and wrote in my notebook until well past midnight.

14
SAME-SAME

. . . this is what travel can always do for you, whether it be travel by air or sea or cinema. You can take a trip, and if you are lucky you begin to know a stranger, who in turn helps you see yourself and your homeland with clearer eyes.

—JAMES D. HOUSTON
"Hawaii's Festival of International Cinema,"
San Francisco Examiner, November 8, 1987

HE JAPANESE ALPS were home for the next ten days. By day their ridges and valleys opened before my bicycle and closed behind it, lending me images of flat lakes, windless pine forests, and rugged river canyons. By night I snuggled in my sleeping bag in quiet woods, watching the stars, or else stayed in the larger towns' youth hostels. In one three-day stretch I spoke nothing but Japanese. When I arrived in Kyoto, twelve *rainless* days after leaving Tokyo, my first item of business was to find a café, buy a cold Asahi beer, and write a bragging aerogram to my wife, pronouncing myself better than new—tanned and fit and fearless. I told her I missed and loved her and that if she was obstinate enough not to join me, well, she sure was missing a good time.

Kyoto, Japan's old capital, was the only major Japanese city not turned to ash and rubble by World War II. Before the war the wife of an American general had visited Kyoto and been deeply smitten with its beauty, its old sections, its elaborate shrines and temples. Years later, when she learned that her husband was involved in deciding where to dump the Bomb, she had a warning for him: "Kyoto is their most sacred city. Destroy Kyoto, and the Japanese will never forgive you." The general listened and managed to steer the selection committee in the direction of Hiroshima and Nagasaki, cities less crucial to the Japanese self-image.

On my second afternoon in Kyoto I decided to pay my sightseeing dues. Ryoan-ji Temple, home of one of Japan's (and the world's) most famous Zen rock gardens, was only a few minutes' bike ride from my inn. In an inner courtyard of the rambling complex I found a rectangular expanse of white gravel, thirty yards long and meticulously raked. Placed among the gravel, apparently at random, was a string of fifteen rocks of assorted sizes, the biggest the size of an armchair, the smallest a deflated football.

Surprisingly, when I arrived, the garden was deserted—no one in sight but myself. I sat on a viewing porch adjacent to the garden, stared at the rocks and the gravel, and tried to think Japanese. Instead, the thoughts of a terrorist filled my mind: *How is it,* I asked my notebook, *that this national treasure is left unguarded? When one goes sightseeing, one expects—if not crowds—at least a policeman or two.*

But these thoughts were premature. My solitude was shortly punctured by an onslaught of Japanese tourists—swarming schoolchildren, dark-suited men, powder-faced women. A loud pod of blue-collar types were passing around a jug of Kirin beer. I felt trespassed upon. A loudspeaker screeched to life and explained—in Japanese and then in English—that different people envision very different things in the arrangement of rocks and combed gravel. Some see mountaintops poking through heavy cloud cover, others a concerned tigress leading her cubs across a foaming stream. My notebook: *I see Japanese tourists awash in a vat of Kirin beer.*

"You are student?"

The innocent introduction ... I looked up.

Standing over me was a smiling Japanese man, about fifty years old, wearing a fresh gray suit, matching tie, and starched white shirt. Gold glinted from a front tooth. "May I join you?"

I closed my notebook and invited him to sit. He opened a tourist brochure and spread it precisely on the porch.

"You are student?" he repeated, settling.

No.

"Ah, toodist!"

Yes. Toodist. Sahn Frahnceesco. Three weeks. Bicycle. Fuji. Etc.

"You saw Fuji-san?"

I boasted that I had *climbed* Fuji-san.

"You ah rucky," he said. "Fuji-san very spashu."

Yes, I agreed, very special.

The man was Mr. Mashahiro from Osaka, thirty miles away. For the last ten years he had been the owner of a small grocery.

"Getting more deefeecoot now," he said. "Competition. Big supa-mahket open in my nay-ba-huht. Two yiss ago, ten ree-tu grocery. Now, one big supa-mahket and five ree-tu grocery. I will be okay, but I don't know about my chiddren."

Children?

"I have five chiddren. Aww daughters. No gran-chiddren. Odest daughter is twenty-two. My father rivvs wiss us, too. He is eighty-faww!"

I asked if his father was born in 1900; Mr. Mashahiro's eyes widened in surprise. How had I known? And then he saw it.

"You are right," he laughed. "Nineteen hundred."

Was his father a soldier?

"No. My father ran an eight-story hoteww in Osaka, near the rayuro station. I was in primary sku during World War II. When it ended, I was in six grade." He enunciated carefully, partly for my benefit, but also for the eavesdroppers; several crew-cut boys sat nearby, watching and listening.

I asked Mr. Mashahiro if he remembered the day the atom bomb hit Hiroshima.

"Oh, yes," he said immediately. His brow hardened, and he grew solemn. He looked away toward the rock garden. "I rememba that bad thing."

As it turned out, he didn't actually remember that specific day—Osaka was 175 miles from the blast—but he had other war memories.

"I rememba every day Bee Twenty-eight bombers dropping things on us. One night I stood on hill outside my home, twenty kee-do-meter from Osaka. Many Bee Twenty-eight bombers came. The sky was red. There were . . . phdames. You know phdames?"

I knew flames.

"Osaka was on fie-yuh." He spread his arms as far as they would go, indicating the whole sky ablaze. "And the necks mawning, aww around ah house"—he looked at me after each phrase to make sure I understood—"there were things from Osaka, haff-burn, rying on the ground. Many books and papers, haff-burn. You undah-stan, haff-burn?"

I understood. Did Japan still resent America?

Mr. Mashahiro considered this for a moment. "No. I don't sink so. I sink we ah phdends now. Japan did a very bad thing to America."

Pearl Harbor?

He nodded. "Purr Habbuh. And America did a very bad thing to Japan. Japan Purr Habbuh, America atom bomb—same-same. Now we are even." He bumped his hands together in front of him. "Everybody phdends again."

I suggested that the world must have been out-of-whack for World War II to have happened. The day of our conversation was the fortieth anniversary of D-Day, and now Japan and America were close allies. How could this be?

Mr. Mashahiro's explanation was simple: "Pee-pu ah kdazy."

I related a strange experience I'd had in a Shakey's Pizza Parlor (ALL YOU CAN EAT—500 YEN) in Tokyo: four Europeans shared my table and, after some hemming and hawing, told me they were German technicians employed by the Japanese government to work on an American-designed nuclear reactor.

"Yes," said Mr. Mashahiro, nodding. "Time has changed. I have experienced two worlds. After War-War II we didn't even have a pen-su. Rearry. Not even a pen-su. And today . . ." He held out his hands to show his suit, his starched shirt, gleaming cuff links. His gold tooth winked at me. "Today is mira-cu," he said. "We have food. We have jobs. We are strong. We have many pen-su." He laughed. "And we have no enemy. Japan has no defense and no enemy."

Why did he think this was so? Why was Japan doing so well today when much of the world was having difficulties?

"Because Japan iss i-so-rated."

"Ah."

We were silent a moment. The boys around us looked at me curiously; one ventured a smile. I asked Mr. Mashahiro another question: What was it like when the Americans came?

"We were very sahprized. American sojers were very kind. Very kind." His voice became soft, sentimental; his head swiveled back and forth in amazement. "We were very afraid. Ah reeders toad us Americans bad pee-pu, very bad pee-pu. But GIs came and gave us food. And medicine. They were not bad pee-pu. They were very kind. We do not forget this."

It was the strongest unsolicited expression of thanks I've ever heard a foreigner address toward America. A swell of compassion rose in my chest; I wanted to hug this man. I told Mr. Mashahiro how glad I was to hear his words, and mentally I thanked my parents' generation for its mercy; a vision came to mind of smiling GIs with crew cuts and three-day beards passing out chocolate and bread and pencils.

"Very kind," Mr. Mashahiro echoed. "Very, very kind."

The loudspeaker rasped again, the woman's voice repeating the earlier announcement. It was a recording. My new friend looked at the garden.

"Do you see clouds and mountains?" he asked.

Yes.

"Do you see tigers?"

Well, maybe.

"She says one end is higher than the other end. I wonder if that means some-sing."

I guessed that it might be a Zen riddle meaning nothing more than that one end was higher than the other.

Mr. Mashahiro laughed. "You have been reading Zen."

I asked if he was Buddhist.

He stiffened and cocked an eyebrow at me: *Of course!* "I have Boot-hist ancestors. Automatically I am Boot-hist. Japan has many Boot-hists. Sometimes, in old days, some Boot-hists fight other Boot-hists. Kyoto Boot-hists used to fight Nara Boot-hists."

"Now they have baseball teams."

His face clouded over. "Base-a-boro?"

"I am making a joke," I told him, and tried to explain.

Mr. Mashahiro laughed politely, but I knew he didn't understand. The conversation faltered. Soon he rose to leave. To the boys around us he said,

"American-u." He pointed at me and shook my hand. "Americans and Japanese ah phdends." He was smiling. "Phdends."

One of the boys thrust his hand at me. "Ha-ro."

And then there was another, and another, and ...

By the time all the hands had been shaken, and the afternoon had been recorded in my notebook, long broomlike shadows had swept the sun from the garden.

15

RAIN
DROPPINGS

*Those who travel heedlessly from place to place,
observing only their distance from each other, and
attending only to their accommodation at the inn
at night, set out fools, and will certainly return so.*

—LORD CHESTERFIELD
Letters, October 30, 1747

T ANI HOUSE, THE INN WHERE I STAYED in Kyoto, was a dark, older two-story box with winged Japanese roof and a palisade of fifteen-foot bamboo trees surrounding it. Women guests slept on futons in a large room on the lower floor, men on an upper floor that also had three or four smaller rooms for couples or groups. Some nights more than forty people were shoehorned into the house, including latecomers that the owner, Mrs. Tani, let sleep on the second-floor porches. Her accommodating disposition (for fifty cents she'd do your laundry) was one reason for the inn's popularity. Other factors were price ($6 a night) and location, a quiet district half an hour by bus from the hooting rush of downtown.

The sprawling parklike grounds of Daitoku-ji Temple surrounded Tani House; from the inn's back porch I saw temple buildings and acres of gardens, and orange-robed monks pacing manicured, rock-lined paths. A graveyard of marble shrines and markers butted up to the back fence, and in the mornings the sound of chanting carried from the temples, floated over the headstones, and bothered Tani House's late sleepers.

But not everyone slept late. Many people were there for the novice Zen meditation classes offered next door. Six-thirty each morning brought a quiet rustling of fabrics as the meditators whispered each other awake, dressed, clomped down the wooden stairs and out the front door. They would return in a rowdy mood a couple hours later, just when the heathen were beginning to stir.

As the cast of lodgers changed every day, so did the cast of meditators.

During my first few days I noticed one older man serving as head meditator. The registration book identified him as Daniel Davidson, a forty-seven-year-old from Chicago who listed his occupation as "teacher." Indeed, he looked professorial—black-rimmed glasses, full beard gone gray, and hair headed the same direction. In conversations that were always lively but never broke down into argument, he discussed Zen with many of the other travelers. He had a good backlog of Zen lore and parables, talked engagingly about the different levels and stages of study, and described how Zen masters think and how they differ from the rest of us.

I had been meditating off and on for a few years, sitting quietly for twenty minutes once or twice a day, trying to observe the constant parade of thoughts through my consciousness without becoming seduced by them. Sometimes I've reached a mildly euphoric state of seeming transparency, relaxed and happy, with a rather pleasant "nothing" going on in my consciousness.

"That's probably the state of *reverie*," Daniel said, "something common to all novices, the same state one might experience in a cathedral under the influence of organ music. But a Zen master has attained the ability to go into a state far beyond reverie, beyond tranquillity, a state where he is completely conscious and aware of everything—the chirping of a bird, the closing of a distant door, the thoughts of the person next to him—without being attached to or affected by any of it. It's ungraspable to others, but accessible to a Zen master under all circumstances, not just the special conditions of church or temple."

I t was raining the next morning as Daniel and I and two other novice meditators shuffled beneath umbrellas toward the temple.

"The monk might hit you with his stick," Daniel said.

"What?"

"The monk might hit you with his stick. But don't worry. He knows how to do it so you'll feel it, but it won't injure you. You might even *ask* him to hit you—just for the experience. If he comes and stands in front of you with his stick, just bow your head and he'll whack you on the back of your shoulders. He canes someone every day."

The other two initiates were Steve, a freshman from Yale, and Rhonda, a married lady from New Zealand whose husband was still sleeping. "He's into volleyball," she said. "He stays out late in the gyms, I'm up early in the temples." Both Steve and Rhonda had been to the temple before, and both had been caned.

"It smarts at first," said Rhonda, "but it helps get my attention off my knees. After about twenty minutes of that half-lotus position, I feel like screaming."

The session's format was to be this: One forty-five-minute meditation, then a five-minute break for walking in a silent circle, another forty-five minute meditation, then ten minutes of chanting. Everything had an exact proscribed form. "But don't worry," said Daniel. "If you're doing something wrong, the monk will tell you."

Puddles were forming on the walkways, gray pebbles washed clean by the bouncing rain. Daniel led the way through a maze of bushes, buildings, and trees, through wooden archways and around corners. At one point he slid aside a bamboo gate and held it until the four of us were through. Finally we came to a series of flat stones placed a couple of feet apart on a green lawn; the path they formed brought us to a small gazebolike prayer building with steeply pitched roof.

"Take your shoes off," Daniel said, whispering now. We left shoes and umbrellas under an awning in front of the sanctuary, and stepped into the ever-present slippers. At the doorway Daniel stopped, pressed palms together breast high, and bowed deeply. On a table in the center of the room was a shrine of bells and a small Buddha. Along the right and left walls were two raised platforms where we would sit and meditate; two other Westerners were already there squatting on cushions, looking into space.

"Get lots of cushions," Rhonda whispered to me.

I grabbed four of them from a stack near the door and arranged them under my buttocks so that when I began crossing my legs I was a foot off the floor, easing the strain on my knees.

It was a building of windows. The roof was anchored in each corner by thick posts, but the walls were merely bamboo screens that slid back to allow a free flow of air through the room. I was the only one looking around; the others were sitting cross-legged, hands clasped in laps, staring at the floor with barely opened eyes. Across from me was an attractive woman my own age with the word *Windsurfing* arced across the front of her sweatshirt.

We sat for several moments, listening to the tick of rain on the roof, until there was a motion at the doorway. Out of the corner of my eye I saw "the Monk" changing from outdoor slippers to indoor ones. He straightened at the door, bowed to the Buddha, and strode effortlessly across the room without looking at any of us. His head was bald—shaved and gleaming. He wore a gray robe made of expensive material. His motions and gestures had obviously been practiced at great length, each one flawlessly smooth and connecting naturally with the next.

The others in the room adjusted noiselessly into the half-lotus—one foot twisted up onto the opposite thigh, the other pretzeled beneath them—a painful contortion, which I imitated. On a mat at the far end of the room the

Monk assumed the full-lotus position. He tapped on a high-pitched bell, three times, precisely spaced.

Pinggggg!

Pinggggg!

Pinggggg!

The first few moments passed unnoticed. I studied the rounded contours of "Windsurfing" several times and entered a mammareal reverie, comparing the docile, small-bosomed Japanese women with the busty, briefcase-toting ones back home. I thought about how long it had been since I'd hugged anyone, and I considered proposing marriage, or at least adultery. I watched my breathing for a while. In, out. In, out. In, out. And then I noticed my legs. How long before my ankles snapped? Was I doing this wrong? Was there something deficient about me? Hadn't there always been? Was I supposed to focus my eyes on a spot on the floor, or was I supposed to let them drift? Was there something particularly holy about this pagoda that I should try to pick up on? Was today the day that I would finally "get it"? Had some critical nugget of divine inspiration crept out of the Himalayas and into China several centuries ago, wound its way down the Yangtze, leaped the Japan Sea, and lodged at Daitoku-ji Temple, where today it would be gloriously revealed?

Would the Monk be insulted if I moved around a bit? Would he come over and beat me with his stick? Was there some suggested reading I should have done? Shouldn't I have asked all these questions before coming? What sort of thoughts were the others having? How long had it been? Ten minutes? Fifteen? Or only two? Oooh, my ankles ...

I tried to will the blood to circulate in my legs, tried mentally to heat my feet, but it did no good. My ankles and knees screamed to be moved. Around the room there was stillness and complete silence. I wiggled my toes, flexed an ankle, started to remind myself about being in the right place and all, but my body congress jeered and threatened impeachment. *I will never be Japanese,* it occurred to me. *Never be Buddhist. I've come to see the country, not convert.* Japan had granted me temporary asylum; that was all I could ask. Any understanding would be strictly a bonus.

Just as I was preparing to ease my foot off my thigh, the Monk rose to his feet. Without turning my head, I saw the rod in his hand. *He's read my thoughts. He's coming to cane me!*

Instead, he paced slowly in front of the three people across from me— Daniel, Windsurfing, and a Western man I didn't know. His back to me, the Monk stopped in front of Daniel and presented the cane. I raised my head to watch. Daniel leaned slowly forward. Using precise, choreographed motions, the Monk placed his stick flat against Daniel's left shoulder blade. Without hesitation, he lifted it high and slapped it down sharply. Four times.

Crack! Crack! Crack! Crack! The noise sounded and resounded through the room, the temple complex, the quivering universe. I thought: Rhonda was right. My blood-starved legs were long forgotten.

The Monk shifted slightly and placed his cane on Daniel's other shoulder blade. He showed no doubt, no indecision, and he did not look to see how Daniel was receiving his correction.

Crack! Crack! Crack! Crack!

Daniel straightened. The Monk bowed. Daniel bowed. The Monk moved away. I looked back at the floor, pretending not to have seen anything, pretending to be above it all, pretending to have been lifted to some other, loftier plane of being. But my legs were jeering again. It was hopeless; when the Monk came to me, I would ask for a rain check, beg permission to leave, promise to come back tomorrow. He was pacing my side of the room now; he stopped in front of Rhonda and Steve and punished both of them with the cane. Again the universe shook.

And then my time came. The Monk stopped in front of me, gray robe obscuring my field of vision. I kept my eyes lowered, pretending to meditate, and waited for something to happen. It was a very short wait.

I heard a gasp, and looked up. The Monk's eyeballs had inflated and the individual black hairs of his eyebrows were frozen into concerned arches. He was staring at my aching feet.

"Zzox!" he hissed in a whisper. *Was he expecting me to speak Japanese?* "No zzox!" He reached out and touched my socks.

"Oh."

"Teek zzox uff." He pointed toward the open doorway.

A miracle! A reprieve from the governor! I unkinked my legs and my pulsing ankles, slid down off the platform and into my slippers, and walked to the door, trying to imitate the Monk's graceful motions. Blood poured into my legs; my toes tingled. I took my time at the door, pulling off my zzox and tucking them into my zzhoes. I debated making a run for Tani House, but decided against it. With restored legs, I climbed back onto the meditating platform, but scaled my half-lotus down to about one-quarter.

The Monk had gone back to his mat, and for the rest of the session stayed there. "Teek zzox uff," turned out to be his only words of instruction.

When it was all finished, we novices stood quietly under the awning, pulling on footwear, claiming umbrellas. The Monk joined us, a blank expression on his smooth face. No one spoke. He stood there a moment watching us, then studied the leaking sky. He stretched a hand out from under the awning and caught several wet splats.

"Rain droppings." He stared at his palm.

"Yes," said Daniel, liaison for all of us. "Rain."

The Monk looked up, chuckling, his face now a network of wrinkles. "Not animal droppings." He smiled at his own play on words. Soon we were all smiling.

"Rain droppings," he said again, whimsically. "Not animal droppings." And then, still chuckling, the Monk shook open his umbrella and padded away, into the rain.

Droppings.

16
PHONY

The mask represents art. Behind it hides man.

—PAUL KLEE, diary entry
Quoted in *The Christian Science Monitor*
October 28, 1986

VER BREAKFAST DANIEL AND I played back the morning's meditation and talked about our lives. After telling about my marriage and my bicycle trip, I asked how he had come, at age forty-seven, to be staying in a six-dollar-a-night Japanese inn. I noted his sad, lens-distorted eyes, his laugh lines, the loose white skin of his forearms. Was this me in fifteen years? For the first time I saw that his beard was missing its moustache; the upper lip was shaved, creating the impression that his whiskers were the dime-store variety and would lift off with his glasses.

Like the Monk, Daniel laughed amicably, as though life were but a yarn spun by a Gypsy, full of rain droppings and the like—a possibility that his unlikely résumé seemed to bear out. He had been teaching English in Taiwan recently, but was actually a trained painter who had once gone reasonably far in the art world. During his twenties and thirties he had been a noted avant-garde artist who made a good living teaching art at a small college in upstate New York, and who was very respected, both at the school and in Manhattan, where he kept a loft and spent weekends.

"I was mentioned frequently in entertainment columns and art magazines and all that," he said. "I was married then, too. For six years." He lifted his eyebrows: *You're not the only one versed in heartbreak.* "She was one of my students. We became romantically involved and did all the things that young, romantically involved artists do. And that got me mentioned in the columns even more. The press started to cover things I did. My career was on an upward curve. I was on my way.

"The pinnacle was my own show—a one-man show at the most exclusive avant-garde gallery in New York. A couple of pieces sold—two, maybe three. Actually I was surprised that more didn't sell, but nonetheless it was widely acclaimed, as they say. More mention in the columns. People from other galleries came to look. The gallery owner was happy. Your typical success.

"But even before the show opened, somewhere around the time I was getting the pieces together—choosing which ones to put in the show, and then moving them to the city—somewhere around that time, I realized it was all phony."

"Phony?"

"Yeah, phony. All my life I had considered myself an artist. I was always talking art, art in general, *my* art in particular—'Yeah, my art is my expression of myself. If you want to understand me, you have to understand my art.' But now I began to see through that.

"I saw that all I'd really been doing for forty years was making art that I figured would be appropriate for an 'avant-garde artist' to be making. I was just doing what I thought people would like, painting things I figured would be appropriate for someone who—by his fortieth birthday—would be having one-man shows in New York City. Worst of all, I even realized that I'd been creating paintings so that I'd get a show *not just anywhere*—but in *that one* specific gallery!

"This was some jolt. My art wasn't a free expression of myself at all—it was a mask I was hiding behind. It had nothing to do with art. Oh, yeah, my art was good—if you believe what everybody said about it. Everybody loved it. But by the time of the show I was already beyond that. My life was still stuck on 'up-and-coming,' but my mind had moved ahead.

"I quit doing art. Only other painters—my 'competitors'—actually understood what I was trying to do. I wanted to break the cycle of doing what was expected—of going back to the studio to make more avant-garde art pieces so that I could have a second one-man show and then a third, so that I could charge incredible prices, and then have a fourth show, so that someday everyone would agree that I was a talented, even a *very* talented, painter. That wasn't being creative!

"I quit my teaching job, gave up tenure—my friends said I was crazy—and took odd jobs. For a while I was a curator in a museum. I call it my 'confused period.' My wife hung around for four years after the show, then left me. She decided she had actually picked a loser, a failure. Later she said she really wanted the image—it wasn't me she was interested in, but the thing I had fooled everyone into thinking I was. She felt she'd gotten damaged goods. Can't say I blame her. We got a divorce. That was four years ago. She married a banker.

"It was back then that I started studying Zen, and it sort of drew me to the East. For the last couple of years I've been teaching English. I had to leave Taiwan this month to get my visa renewed. I've always wanted to come to Japan—and I finally had the money—so I came."

I asked him this: "How do you know that forsaking your art and getting a divorce and coming to Japan to study Zen isn't just more of what an avant-garde artist should do? Are you sure you won't look back and think this is phony, too?"

He laughed.

"I'm *not* sure," he said. "In fact, it sounds pretty suspicious to me."

"And would it have made any difference if more pieces had sold? What if you'd sold fifteen pieces?"

Daniel stroked his beard. "That," he said, "is a good question."

seemed to aggravate her stiffness. She was running into
furniture when inside and constantly veered to the right.
    Dr. Ashley was out of town so I took her to Dr. Orcutt
down on the corner. He spayed her for fleas [malpractice?
misspelling?—I didn't know], gave her a cortisone shot
and two kinds of pills. She has perked up considerably the
last couple of days—eaten well and been more alert.
Thank goodness. I hope she will continue to be comfortable
until your return, but the thought of "ending her misery"
has been greatly on my mind. Do feel you would be o.k.
with that, but it's still a *big* decision.
    Please call or write.
    Enjoy!

Love,
Nancy Lynn

This barrel-scraping, your-slip-is-showing entertainment had one redeem-
ing quality: it was free. Having sensed that the mystery of the *real* Japan
would remain unsolved, I had become a model of frugality, dedicated to
running the cheapest possible investigation. My bicycle saved thousands of
yen in transportation costs, meals seldom ran more than three dollars, and
my only major indulgence was ice cream. For a while I kept my daily ex-
penses under fifteen dollars.

    And then, on my fifth day in Kyoto, I blew it all. In a mindless moment on
a wet afternoon I walked out of a downpour into the Telephone and Telegraph
Office and spent twenty minutes and fifty dollars cash talking to my wife. It
was midnight in San Francisco, clear and mild.

    "Oh, Brad!" she shrieked. "I knew it was you. I've been sending you mes-
sages."

    "I never got a one."

    "Yes! You did! They were mental messages!"

    She had been working for days, mentally instructing me to call. (I thought:
So who should pay?) She just wanted to talk, to tell me she missed me and
loved me. We cried about it all at $2.50 a minute, 50 cents a tear.

    She told of a recent dream: "It was more like a vision than a dream, it was
so clear. You were in Japan, getting out of a pool." (I thought: *Ha-du-du-du-
du . . .*) "It was the second or third night after you left. Were you in a pool?"

    "I'll tell you about it later."

    That got her curiosity up, but I managed to deflect it—to my bike ride,
her job, our families, to everything but the divorce papers. Toward the end
of the call I gulped and asked if she was seeing anyone these days.

    "No," she said. "Are you?"

18

TWO BARSE, ONE STRIKE

And Jacob was left alone; and there wrestled a man with him until the breaking of the day.

And he said, Let me go, for the day breaketh. And he said, I will not let thee go, except thou bless me.

And he said unto him, What is thy name? And he said, Jacob.

And he said, Thy name shall be called no more Jacob, but Israel: for as a prince hast thou power with God and with men, and hast prevailed.

—GENESIS 32:25–29

 T DUSK, THE DAY AFTER THE PHONE CALL, I was standing by the side of a highway in a narrow green valley near the town of Miyoshi, three hundred kilometers west of Kyoto. The sky had been gray and threatening, and now, for the first time all day, sprinkles of rain began to rasp against my down jacket. The only building in sight was a deserted restaurant a hundred yards away, and I was hoping someone would pick me up before the approaching storm drove me to seek cover there.

The previous evening Mrs. Tani had drawn the *kanji* characters for "Hiro" and "Shima" on a piece of paper, and I had imitated them in magic marker on a square of cardboard. Now, I held this sign over my head to keep dry. Staring down the empty road, I reminded myself, "I am in exactly the right place, thinking, doing, and feeling exactly the right things."

Japan is probably the best place in the world for a Westerner to "hitch-hik-u." It is unusual for a hitchhiker to be allowed to pay for anything—even his own meals; *gaijin* tell stories of drivers going a day or two out of their way to deliver them to a destination. And while nothing so lavish had been forced upon me that day, I had certainly been pleased with my rides.

The first was with a Japanese "hippie" driving a Toyota pickup truck with a sawhorse and red metal box full of construction tools in the back. His hair was a frizzy ponytail wadded together by a red rubber band, and he claimed to have been to India three times. "I also am world traveler, but not like most Japanese. Japanese and Americans are the worst travelers. They take big money"—he patted his trouser pocket—"and spend it all, then go home. I am like European traveler. Europeans trade things, make business. Last time I go to India, I take two video cameras. In Japan, very cheap; in India, very expensive. I make big money." Again he patted his trousers.

He went as far as Osaka (only thirty kilometers) and let me off at a rest area where I was sure to get a ride from a trucker. "Japanese truck drivers very nice."

I spent a depressing hour at the noisy rest area, with scores of big rigs thundering by. Finally a Japanese businessman in a Toyota sedan rescued me, bought me lunch, insisted on driving fifty kilometers out of his way to show me the famed "White Castle" in Himeji, and dropped me at another rest area halfway to Hiroshima.

I stood on the highway near this second rest area for a long time. Very few cars passed; the occupants stared at me, none slowed down. Clouds stacked up overhead. Seventy-five yards from me, the rest area had a tiny store. Every few minutes a man, the store's lone employee, came to the door to check on me. After half an hour he walked down to where I stood.

"Hitch-hik-u?"

"*Hai.* Hitch-hik-u. Hiroshima." I showed my sign.

He sucked air across his teeth. "Hitch-hik-u veddy deefeecoot. Nobodee stop. You go train. Train good. Hitch-hik-u no good. Japanese no hitch-hik-u—Japanese go train."

He walked back to his store, muttering, shaking his head.

I'm outa here, I told my notebook. *If one Japanese is worried about me, I'm a national problem. Somewhere in the control center of the Japanese mind a light is blinking: "Stray* gaijin *west of Himeji. Get him."*

As I finished jotting this sentence, a car pulled into the rest area. Four people got out to use the rest rooms. As they got back into their car, the muttering employee approached them. He pointed at me; all heads turned. Thirty seconds later I was loading my pack into a television commercial: gun-metal gray Hyundai mini-van with the model family—Mom, Dad, one boy, one girl, one ice chest full of Coca-Cola cans. They gave me a Coke and a package of rice crackers and they smiled, but no one spoke until we reached the Miyoshi train station, an hour and a half later. *"Sayonara,"* they chorused, pointing toward the ticket window.

When they were out of sight, I walked away from the station, toward Hiroshima, comparing the squiggles on the highway signs to those on my cardboard one. A car stopped. "Where hah you going?" The driver was a young Japanese man, an English teacher with a car full of students. I suspected he had seen me walking and quickly collected his class. As we drove into the countryside, they interviewed me shyly: "Hah you married? Pray base-a-boro?" The teacher stopped near the deserted restaurant and apologized profusely for not driving me the last hundred kilometers to Hiroshima. "Previous engagement," he said. As he turned and drove back toward Miyoshi, the pink of sunset was fading from the mountaintops, and the sprinkles were just beginning. "I am in exactly the right place ..."

A silver tanker truck with a Mobil Oil logo on the side was the first vehicle down the road. I held out my sign, the truck slowed to a stop right next to me. I stood on tiptoe to reach the door handle, opened it, and—over the chug-chug-chug of the engine—called up, "He-ro-she-mah See-tee?"

The driver smiled, nodded, and motioned me up into the cab. *"Arigato,"* I said, and swung myself and my pack upward. All of a sudden the road was ten feet below.

The driver was perhaps the friendliest-looking person I've ever seen, one of those rare gentle people who seem not to have a mean or aggressive vein in their entire being. A white sport shirt and tan skin gave him the relaxed air of a cruise-ship tennis pro. Of all the Japanese I met, this man, with lean face, high cheekbones, bright, perfect teeth, round eyes, and no glasses, would be the country's best representative.

We knew only a few words of one another's language, but we used them a lot. I was able to determine that he had two jobs; for every ten days he worked for "Mobil Company," he also served five in the navy. West of Hiroshima, at Iwakuni, the Japanese Navy and U.S. Marines share an air station. After delivering his load of gasoline to the Hiroshima airport, the driver would report for duty. He was thirty-two—my own age—married, with a girl, ten, and a boy, seven. His father was fifty-four years old, his mother dead. He had no brothers or sisters. He lived in Tokyo and his name was Kanemoto. Kanemoto said we would cover the ninety-seven kilometers to Hiroshima in two hours.

He learned that I was married, home was San Francisco, I used to work as a journalist, and that I was on a "vacation" that would last at least "one hundred days." (He whistled at this.) I told him, using my fingers, that this was my fifth ride since Kyoto, and that I was going to see the Peace Park in Hiroshima. His face lit up at that: the Japanese always seemed pleased when I mentioned visiting Hiroshima.

I told Kanemoto my first name.

"Bird?" he said, and wiggled his hand through the air.

I started to correct him, but changed my mnd. "Yes, Bird."

"English, Bird. Japanese, *Tori-ho-nay.*" Again his hand flew.

"Tori-ho-nay," I said, and repeated it a few times. I had been baptized; didn't I deserve a new name? I thumped my chest. *"Tori-ho-nay."* We looked

at each other and laughed. (Later I learned why Kanemoto was laughing so hard. He had named me, literally: *Birdbones.*)

For a while there was still enough light outside to see the fading country-side. The road climbed over darkening ridges, and twisted down into misty jungle valleys. Ghoulish fingers of fog and steam hung low over the streams and treetops; heavier clouds patrolled the ridgebacks. As dusk thickened, the rain fell harder, popping like frying-pan grease on the black highway ahead of us. I had found my exact right place not a moment too soon.

Kanemoto found a baseball game on the radio, the Tokyo Giants playing someone. Two Americans, ex-major leaguers, were playing for the Giants: Warren Cromartie from the Montreal Expos, and Reggie Smith of the San Francisco Giants. I told Kanemoto that I had seen Reggie Smith ("Smee-su" to the Japanese) play at Candlestick Park the year before.

He interpreted the play-by-play for me, something that wasn't absolutely necessary. The ball–strike count was given in English ("Two barse, one strike"), and many other words were familiar. The crowd's hum surged in the background, and in the announcer's excited chatter I heard the word "singa-ru."

Kanemoto turned to me and said, "Hit-o."

Later came: "Out-o." And: "Dub-ru pray."

In the fourth inning (I knew it was the fourth, because when I asked, *Ikura* inning? Kanemoto held up four fingers) Warren Cromartie and Tokyo's third baseman, Hara, hit back-to-back home-a-runs, giving the Giants a 5–3—*go–san*—lead. Kanemoto was pleased.

The two hours passed quickly. On the outskirts of Hiroshima Kanemoto detoured the big tanker to drop me off at a stoplight a quarter mile from the "use hoster-u." We threw just about every word we had in common into a long, friendly good-bye. Mentally I froze my last glimpse of him smiling down at me from the cab, hands relaxed on the huge steering wheel, a Japanese Robert Redford, lips parting over white, even teeth to mouth "*Sayonara,* Tori-ho-nay."

There was a convenience store at the stoplight; inside, an elderly Japanese cashier was watching the base-a-boro game on TV. While he was totaling up my milk, banana, ice cream, and a mystery sandwich, I had a little fun.

"Cromartie!" I said.

When the cashier looked up, I pantomimed Cromartie's home-a-run, cluck-ing my tongue and swatting an imaginary fastball over the ice-cream freezer. The man grinned.

"Hara!" I said, and sent another one downtown. The man yelped with delight.

"Tokyo Giants," I continued. *"Go–san."*

"Hai. *Go–san.* Tokyo Giants." He smiled and waved a clenched fist quickly by his side. "American-u?" He stuck his hand over the counter for a congratulatory shake, then walked to the fruit rack and wrenched a second banana from its stalk.

"Present-u."

"Domo arigato," I said, and bowed deeply.

The road up the hill to the use hoster-u was lined with apartment houses. As I walked through the sprinkles, gumming my banana, I noticed the blue-gray glow of a TV set in every window. Each one was tuned to the base-a-boro game.

19
HMPHF

[Hiroshima] had not been visited in strength by B-san, or Mr. B, as the Japanese, with a mixture of respect and unhappy familiarity, called the B-29 . . .

—JOHN HERSEY
Hiroshima

From my notebook:

MY ROOM IS ON A LOW HILL overlooking the city center. Hiroshima is stretched out below, horizon to horizon, two and a half kilometers away. Somewhere right in front of my eyes, thirty-nine years ago, IT happened. Three planes droned overhead, something fell from one of them. If I had been sitting here then, looking down, I might have been blinded, scarred for life, or dissolved in the Blast.

Now, a cluster of tall buildings surrounds the Spot. A Bullet Train zipping along an elevated railway horizontally bisects the view. The Scar has covered over as though IT were not really such a horrible thing, but a natural, evolutionary sort of event. Around the central cluster, life has sprung back with a vengeance. Development has filled all available lowland space and threatens to march right up the nearby hills.

In the thorny tree outside my window birds are peeping to one another. In the meeting hall one floor below my room, a small classical orchestra is practicing. The sounds of a flute, a piano, and an oboe drift through my open window.

"No more Hiroshimas!" Hmphf. From two and a half kilometers, on a drizzly gray morning, the real horror is that Hiroshima doesn't seem so bad. I had expected to feel shame, revulsion; maybe that will come, but right now I have a sense of peace I have not known for months, possibly ever. It is as though everyone is safe here. Nothing *that* bad could ever happen again. Hiroshima has been baptized, exorcised of demons once and for all. I feel clean, washed.

On the hill behind me the map shows a "Medical Care and Research Center for A-Bomb Survivors." I wonder if they are feeling as peaceful today as I am. A baseball team, the Hiroshima Carp, plays its home games these days in a stadium directly across the street from the monument marking the Spot. This morning at the airport another load of Mobil fuel has been delivered. Down the coast the U.S. Marines and Japanese Navy are coordinating maneuvers. At the corner grocery I joke with a man easily old enough to have seen the Blast. At the youth hostel's front desk a smiling boy, born here twenty years ago, bids me, "Welcome to Hiroshima." Has all truly been forgiven?

I must go and see.

20
SHRED
OF ASSURANCE

The fireball seen nine kilometers from the burst point was of bluish-white or pinkish-white hue and had a luminosity of about ten times that of the sun.

—From a Peace Park brochure

I N THE MIND OF EVERY HUMAN BEING there is a murky, bulb-shaped mental image of the first atom bomb going off. But a Hiroshima with no cloud seems somehow less believable, and before descending into the city I felt compelled to paint in one of my own. From the youth-hostel hilltop I identified the range of eastern hills over which B-san would have passed before dumping his ugly load; I spotted five of the seven rivers that flow out of the surrounding mountains, surveyed the delta fed and drained by these rivers, and directly overhead I put my cloud.

Thus oriented, I walked down the hill toward my cloud, crossed one of the rivers, the Enko, and came to the square hulk of Hiroshima Castle, the first structure rebuilt by the occupying Americans. Now, schools of lethargic carp and a dozen angry swans patrolled the moat, and a nearby group of teenage girls spun through baton routines with a nonchalance that was hard to imitate; once already I'd heard the buzz of a plane and jerked my head up, expecting to see a club-shaped speck falling toward me, growing larger and larger.

I made my way through the blocks of concrete apartment buildings that fill Hiroshima's central section, and arrived at the backside of the baseball stadium. People were milling about. A TV crew was stringing cables. A sign over the ticket window said the Carp would play at 1300 hours; cheapest seats, $3.

And there it was. Ground zero. The hypocenter. The spot. In a park across from the stadium, surrounded by beds of red and yellow flowers, stood the scarred remainder of what had once been Hiroshima's Industrial Promotion Hall. Of all the damaged buildings, this single ruin had not been razed.

I made my way to an empty bench and reflexively pulled out my notebook:

> This is the only place in all Japan that I remember an abundance of benches. The culture's work ethic encourages minimal public sitting. Even major parks are often bench-less.
> Oh, come on! You didn't come here to write about benches. Write a little something about "responsibility." Whose is it? Ours? Theirs? Or mine alone?

"Good-morning. How-are-you?" A Japanese woman, toddler in arms, was standing over me, speaking deliberately and smiling like the Goddess of Forgiveness. Did I look *that* guilty?

"I'm fine," I said, relieved to be talking to someone. "How are you?"

"I-am-fine." She held out a camera. "One-picture-please?"

"Sure, sure."

I took the camera and walked with her to a spot where the wrecked dome filled the background.

"Thank you," she said, when it was done.

"You're very welcome."

She stuck out her hand, an unusually forward gesture for a Japanese woman. But this was an unusually forward place. We shook. "American-u?"

"Yes."

"We-are-your-friends," she said.

"Yes. Thank you. We-are-your-friends, too." And then I touched her startled daughter's nose. The lady smiled, we bowed; I went back to my notes.

> Dome fenced in. Surprising how much still standing—five stories. Charred bricks. Warped steel. Why have the nearby trees grown back tall and healthy instead of mutant?

"Excuse me."

A man and his son wanted "one picture please." Next there was an entire family in need of photographer. Then two young sweethearts. These people could have asked each other to use their cameras, but they didn't. They, too, were tourists, and hadn't come all this way just to mingle with other Japanese. They wanted some tangible shred of assurance that people other than their own were unnerved by the fact of Hiroshima and the possibility of repetitions. They wanted personal contact with a Westerner—preferably an American—and I was the only *gaijin* in sight on this quiet Sunday morning.

A small footbridge across the Motoyasu River leads from the Hypocenter Dome to the main body of the Peace Park, thirty acres of what was once Hiroshima's business center and most densely populated neighborhood. Now, it is a flat sweep of green, wooded in spots, open in spots, and edged on two sides by rivers that meet at the Peace Bridge.

A line of polite young pilgrims was formed at the Peace Bell pavilion. There was no hurry, no touristy rush—that is for other parks. Here each person was allowed ample time to collect himself (no females were in line) and then slam the log clapper. Murmurs of "American-u" skitted through the crowd when my turn arrived. My best shot produced a low, mournful gong sound and a rustle of applause, an acknowledgment only of my foreignness.

A young boy ran up to me. His parents stood ten feet away, smiling. He sputtered and waved his arms, buying time to organize his English. "This ..." he said loudly, "... is *Jah-Pan!*"

21
THE VEGETABLES OF HIROSHIMA

*... every one of them seemed to be hurt in
some way ... Some were vomiting as they walked.
Many were naked or in shreds of clothing ... Almost
all had their heads bowed, looked straight ahead,
were silent, and showed no expression whatsoever.*

—JOHN HERSEY
Hiroshima

T HERE WAS A MOVIE TO SEE, a reality-bending documentary full of Can't-Be statistics and No-Way horror stories. The populace had been given the "all-clear" That Morning and most were on their way to work or school when the Bomb dropped. Approximately two hundred thousand people—half of Hiroshima—were killed by the bomb or the fire that followed. "What happened to the train approaching Hiroshima?" the film asked. "What happened to the group of schoolgirls crossing the bridge?"

The first ground-level photographs were taken three hours later, two kilometers away, and showed stunned survivors sprawled or groping in the wreckage. At that point no one had any idea what had hit them. There had been a flash followed instantly by a blast, and then hell arrived on earth. Families disintegrated. People near the hypocenter became sizzling puddles. Those farther away were slammed across courtyards, buried in rubble, or had their skin seared and torn away like rags. Hospitals were obliterated; ravaged people gathered at the edges of the disaster, moaning clusters of scorched flesh, hardly human. We were shown footage of a girl whose feet had been bubbled away by molten asphalt: "The doctor treating her died four years later from atomic disease."

The film made it clear that those who went in the first instant were the fortunate. A superheated fire enveloped the whole city, killing tens of thousands trapped in the rubble. Radiated "Black Rain" fell for two hours. Years of horrendous diseases followed.

When the room lights came on, there was a mushroom cloud of silence. The film had been in English, the dozen or so viewers were Westerners. No one spoke. Across the room I recognized Steve, the freshman from Yale who had been caned by the Zen monk back in Kyoto. The quiet tone of that earlier morning now seemed like wild jocularity. Steve tipped his head toward the door. We met outside.

"That was awful," he said. He looked pale.

We scuffed at the ground for a couple of moments. Words seemed ridiculous.

"Have you eaten anything here?" he asked me.

"Dinner, breakfast. Some ice cream ..."

"Any vegetables?"

"I suppose."

"Don't," he warned. "They're not safe yet." Grotesque pictures from the film flashed to mind. "It takes millions of years for that stuff to go away," Steve said. "It's in the soil."

I thought: "The Vegetables of Hiroshima"—a course for Yale freshmen? But I didn't say it. I was too woozy. We stood there for a moment, reeling.

"I'm getting out of here," Steve said. "I feel ... claustrophobic."

He hadn't been at the youth hostel; I asked where he was staying.

"Tani House," he said. "I came over on the Shinkansen [Bullet Train] this morning, and I'm getting the hell out of here right now. This is the most depressing thing I've seen in my life."

One of the museums had an exhibit of artwork, "The Unforgettable Fire," crude drawings done by blast survivors. For many, the drawings, done around 1980, were a first attempt to express their feelings about the Event. A large percentage said that in the intervening thirty-five years they had *not once* talked about it.

Several drawings included splashed visions of the Blast itself, and most included people: a man with rawly exposed ribs; another missing his jaw; a screaming lady—the artist's mother—trapped under a concrete block; a girl whose side had split open like a dropped avocado, and whose head spurted blood; naked people with liquefied skin wandering in the countryside, huddling in poisoned rivers.

By the time I left the exhibit, I felt like a survivor myself, numb and listless, straggling hopelessly from one abomination to the next. It was around one o'clock in the afternoon by now. The Carp game—which I had earlier considered attending—would be starting, but the thought of baseball now seemed vulgar.

Buses had been arriving all morning, carrying squadrons of blue-and-white-uniformed students and Japanese tour groups. The area around the museum had become quite crowded. In the distance I saw the Hypocenter Dome and the invisible cloud floating above it. In the foreground, near a white marble monument housing the eternal flame, I counted eighty-three people standing in a circle, holding hands. I heard music and faint singing and was tempted to join, but there was still one more museum—the last "must see" on my list.

Inside were pieces of the rubble: clocks that had stopped precisely at 8:15 A.M., a stack of coins fused together, iron beams bent double, tortured silverware. A section of granite steps from a bank building had been brought, intact, into the museum. Burned onto the steps was the shadow of a man who had been sitting there at the Instant. No explanation was needed, or provided, as to his fate. What, I wondered, was his last act? To smoke a cigarette? Read the morning news? Admire a passing woman?

A mob of grade schoolers were crowded around a life-sized wax replica of a horrified woman whose arms and hideous breasts were melting. Long stretches of skin drooped from her fingers like pulled taffy. She carried them ahead of her, afraid to touch anything lest the gummy flesh become attached, and lost. Directly in front of me were two boys. One elbowed the other in the ribs and motioned for him to look back over his shoulder. He turned and saw me standing two inches behind him, looming above. His mouth flew open, his knees buckled, and he grabbed at those around him for support. How he managed not to scream is a mystery. He moved away, cowering behind his friend and peering around at me in the most obvious dismay.

22
WE SHOULD NOT FORGET

"Today's average bomb is twenty-five hundred times bigger than those that fell on Hiroshima and Nagasaki."

—Closing words of film at Hiroshima Peace Park

N THE MUSEUM, I had seen only two other *gaijin*—a bespectacled gray-haired man, and a sharp-looking younger man wearing designer jeans, blue blazer, and gray shirt. On his lapel, a button: NUCLEAR FREE ZONE. There was something very watchable about him; he had the look of a movie star trying to go unnoticed, but in *that* crowd he didn't stand a chance.

Now, I found him sitting on the front steps, staring into the distance. The lobotomized look on his face was, I realized, probably the look on my own. Maybe talking would help.

"May I butt in on your thoughts?"

He looked up and shrugged. His eyes had a catlike emerald tinge about them.

"Did you come far out of your way to see this?" The sentence sounded contrived even as it drained from my mouth.

"What?"

"I just feel like talking with someone." I squatted alongside him. "Where are you from?"

"I'm British," he said, softening.

"Are you on holiday?"

He eyed me for a moment, sizing me up, then sighed, as though slinging down a heavy load. "Actually I'm a member of Parliament." *Ek-shu-a-lay.*

"Oh, really!" I eyed *him* for a moment. Was he for real? I quickly decided that he was. After the soul-shaking truth of the museum, it would have been incongruous to find an imposter on the front steps, pretending to be a member of Parliament. And the movie-star look—I now recognized it as the look of extreme electability, the Kennedy look.

"There're two of us here," he said. "Ted's still inside. You probably saw him—an older fellow. I had to get out."

"Are you on vacation?"

"This is a working trip. We're in Japan for ten days. Then we're on to your Washington. You're American, aren't you?" *Uh-medicun.*

I nodded.

"This is a once-in-a-lifetime thing for me," he said. "We're staying in Kyoto. Today's a day off for us, ekshualay. They had a trip to see the temples arranged for our group, but Ted and I decided to hop a train over here instead. This is what I'm really interested in."

"What sort of work is your group doing?"

"We're studying energy problems. In Japan we're looking at the nuclear industry."

"Is Japan heavily nuclear?"

"About twenty-eight percent right now, but they're gunning for fifty. Polls show seventy percent of all Japanese opposed to it, but half see no alternative. Personally, I don't think it's safe. And even if it were, it seems that nuclear power always leads to nuclear bombs, and I've been speaking out against nuclear bombs my entire career." He looked sideways at me. "You're against nuclear arms, I suppose?"

"Well, sure. Nobody could go through that museum and then come out here and say he was *for* nuclear arms!"

"Quite true! Ted and I were just saying that there should be a required course for world leaders, and this should be the first stop. Let them see the consequences their decisions can have."

I told him something I'd read in the news: President Reagan had turned down an invitation to visit Hiroshima when he was in Japan last week on his way to China. *No time,* he had said.

"Pity," said the member of Parliament. "Just coming here would change a lot of people's minds."

"Jimmy Carter came here two weeks ago. That was in the paper, too. He was the opposite of Reagan—Hiroshima wasn't on his itinerary, but he specifically had it changed to come here. Like you."

"Yes. We were really pleased to get a day off. It's turned out quite well."

It had. Even the weather had cleared—a royal blue pushing from the sky all clouds but the permanent one. We sat there chatting for a quarter of an hour; I found myself very fond of this man. "I hope you get reelected as many times as you want."

He asked where I was from and about my travels, and I heard envy in his voice ("Oh, I've always wanted to do that. . . .") when I said I hoped to ride the train from Beijing to Moscow. We talked travel and nuclear disarmament ("These things are just simply too dangerous to have lying about," the MP said) until Ted came out of the museum. "I'm sorry," my new friend said, "I haven't got your name. Mine's Kevin Barron."

We stood for a round of introductions.

"I understand you're a member of Parliament," I said to Ted, who looked less shaken than I'd expected, as though he'd just emerged from an hour in the Louvre.

"Yes, that's right, unless something terrible's happened."

We talked about the women protesters chaining themselves to the gates at Greenham Commons, and about Ted's son who had hitchhiked the United States and whom I reminded him of, until they said they had a train to catch. I commended both of them for having taken the time to come here.

"Someone's got to see this thing," Ted said. "If the Japanese are willing to forgive it, as it seems they have, it's only fair that the rest of us not simply forget about it. . . .

"Yes, that's it," he said. He'd spotted a slogan in his own words. *"They* should *forgive. We* should *not forget."*

23
CLICK

*Support your
local oddity*

—Bathroom graffito,
Chatanuga Cafe, Haight Street, San Francisco

MY NOTE-TAKING WAS INTERRUPTED by a cautious "Ha-ro." Two uni-formed schoolgirls were standing ten feet away, holding hands. I said hello. They looked nervously at each other: "You ask him!" "No, you ask him!" "No, you ...!"

"It's okay," I called.

They came closer: starched white blouses, light brown skin, gleaming black hair, happy, embarrassed eyes.

Finally: "What country?"

"America."

"Ohh!" They looked at each other. They giggled. They decided to play with me anyway.

"What see-tee?"

"Sahn Frahnceesco."

Suddenly, like pigeons chasing popcorn, a cooing flock of fifteen or twenty girls swirled around us. They were eighth graders from the island of Kyushu, classmates of the original pair. Several boys hovered a dozen paces away, while the girls formed a press conference around me.

"Wife-u?"

I showed my ring. They oohed.

"Where wife-u?"

I told them. They aahed.

"Bay-bee?"

I shook my head. They frowned.

I was the undisputed center of attention. The museum had been interest-ing, but I was better. Kyushu is an out-of-the-way place—blond hair and blue eyes an uncommon sight. When the girls ran out of questions, they just stood there simpering at me, then at each other, then back at me. Their faces filled my entire field of view, creating a scene with the surreal texture of a dream. I had strayed into a hall of mirrors, and strangely enough, on every mirror was the shy, smiling face of a Japanese schoolgirl. Sprouting from the head of the girl in the farthest mirror was the top of the dome. Above that was a glistening band of clear blue sky: the invisible cloud had dissolved.

One of the two original girls pointed to my hair, sun-bleached from the bike trip and in need of a trim, and gestured to touch it. A squeal went up when I nodded consent. Three or four joined in, groping at my bowed head with tentative hands.

"Pee-chur?" someone asked, brandishing a camera.

There was a flurry of movement as they rearranged around me, coming as close as possible without actually touching. I thought of hugging a couple of them to me, but I didn't. Too forward, I told myself, too *gaijin*. And then, at just the right moment, the two on either side slipped hands through my elbows.

Click.

24
HONK
HONK

People don't take trips—trips take people.

—JOHN STEINBECK
Travels with Charley

I T WAS A YEAR OF THE RAT, and that June the populace of Hong Kong indeed had an "Abandon ship!" look. After their 140-year stay, the British were planning the colony's return to China, a proposition that made the locals jittery. Hong Kong's roads and parks and buildings looked decidedly more ragged than they had two years earlier; real-estate prices were slipping, the Hong Kong dollar was tumbling, people were trying desperately to get themselves and their money out to some safer place.

By contrast, as I waded through the airport crowd and climbed aboard the bus to downtown, I was feeling pretty good about being there. In spite of the constant traffic noise that once led my wife to call it "Honk Honk," this was a city I liked. She and I had spent ten days here; I knew restaurants and parks, would not start from scratch. I would find a cheap place to stay, spend a few days visiting old haunts, gathering intelligence, and getting a feel for what direction to go next.

Echoing in my head was a phone call I'd made at the Tokyo airport: "I think we should just tear up the divorce papers," I heard. "I want you to come home now." It wasn't until I was on the airplane that I could organize a postcard reply:

> It was a lot of work getting to where I can look in the mirror without crying, and I'm in no rush to test my new confidence. It's better, I think, for both of us, that I keep going.

Also, I didn't trust it. The divorce wouldn't be final for another four and a half months. If her new sentiment was real, it would hold up a while longer. With the world at my feet, life on my back, the choice was simple.

Go, yes—but where?

China and the cheap beaches of the Philippines seemed the two most likely choices. At Okubo House I'd heard several well-tanned travelers rave about a small Philippine island named Boracay. Walter: "Oh, man, it's beautiful. Killer sunsets every night. Bungalows on the beach for a buck, beers for a quarter, big bowls of mango and papaya and pineapple for nothin'. And you'll get a tan that'll melt any woman's heart—maybe even your wife's."

The Philippines offered another attraction: brewing public discontent. Instead of hearing about all of them secondhand, I thought it would be interesting to see a revolution up close (rock-throwing mobs, tanks in the streets, all-night curfew), and the newspapers were predicting one any day now in Manila.

If I went directly to the Philippines, I guessed that I would return to Hong Kong in a few months, then go on to China. On the other hand, an immediate move toward China was a move toward "home." Like a ravenous animal, China would swallow me whole, digest me quickly, secrete me backward toward Russia and Europe. Within a matter of weeks, at most a few months, I would be back in the States.

On the plane I had decided to take a bed in a room on the mainland side of Hong Kong Harbor, in a block-long monstrosity named Chungking Mansions. Although lacking the elegance implied by the word *mansions,* Chungking is highly regarded by the sort of budget traveler who is unworried by pawnshops and girlie shows and men on nearby corners and in doorways, hissing, "Hash! Coke! Smack!"

The complex's ragged corridors form a poorly lit labyrinth of offices, apartments, restaurants, tailors, and gem dealers; tucked between these enterprises are some two dozen "guest houses"—cramped series of rooms and toilets where travelers passing through town find beds for as little as a dollar. A few are true bargains, but most are nothing more than grubby slums with pretentious names: Sheraton, Crown and Astor, the Carlton.

But it is not comfort or a false reputation for cleanliness that attracts Chunking's tenants: the building is a switchboard of up-to-date travel information. The Traveler's Hostel and Travel Agency on the sixteenth floor is a wanderer's bazaar where China visas are expedited, advice is given freely, and huge discounts are offered on airline tickets to everywhere: Beijing,

Manila, Amsterdam, Rio ... All day and most of the night there is a parade of travelers arranging for tickets or visas, posting or picking up messages at the bulletin board, seeking a travel partner, selling a backpack, promoting one scam or another.

Only two years had elapsed since my last visit, so I was sure I'd recognize Chungking. But that first night back, as my bus in from the airport neared downtown, memory failed me. The glare of blinking, dripping neon gave the street scenes out the window the appearance of nighttime in an amusement park; markets were still open, and crowds of dejected-looking shoppers puttered mechanically from one small store to the next, collecting booty in string bags. The blocks began to look identical—clusters of disintegrating boxes crammed together, labeled with splashes of Chinese script, and patrolled by these grumpy elves. Nothing looked familiar. Who would help me?

25
AMY

Such a plot must have a woman in it.

—SAMUEL RICHARDSON
Sir Charles Grandison

SEATED DIRECTLY AHEAD OF ME was a young lady with fingers of dark hair groping down the back of her neck. I leaned forward to see her profile—was she Asian? No, from the side she looked like an American teenager—seventeen years old, I guessed, living in Hong Kong with expatriate parents.

"Excuse me. Will you recognize the stop for Chungking Mansions when we come to it?"

My intrusion interrupted some distant reverie, and at first she appeared not to hear. I was about to speak again, when her trance broke and she turned a friendly face toward me. "Sure," she said, with the hard American accent. "I'm going there myself."

"Are you staying there?"

"No, but I have to check something there."

"Oh. Were you just on the flight from Tokyo?"

"No, I just spent two hours waiting for a plane from Bombay. A friend of mine was supposed to be on it, but I didn't see him anywhere. I paged him, but no response, and the airline has no record of him."

"He's coming from Bombay?"

"Yes."

"Is he Indian?"

"No. His name's Dylan. He's British. We met in Katmandu and fell in love"— she smiled as she said this—"and decided to do China and the Trans-Siberian together. But first he had to go back to India for a bit, and I wanted to stay in Nepal, so we agreed to meet here in Hong Kong. But it's been three weeks since we split up, and it was four days ago that he was supposed to meet me here. I'm starting to wonder what's up."

"That's too bad."

"Yeah, it is too bad." Then she laughed, as though this was the first time it had occurred to her that it was, in fact, too bad. "But it'll work out. What's your name?"

"Brad. What's yours?"

"Amy."

"Nice to meet you, Amy. How'd you like Nepal?"

She sighed and smiled, skin radiating, hazel eyes aglow. "I spent three months there, the best three months of my life. Nepal's so pretty, so different. I learned a lot there. Have you ever been there?"

A few minutes later the bus pulled to a stop at the Star Ferry Terminal, end of the line. Absorbed in our conversation, we'd missed Chungking Mansions. No matter—it was only a few blocks back. "We can walk," Amy said, the "we" lingering nicely in my ear.

In 1842, after the first Opium War, the officer who negotiated the peace treaty was recalled to England in disgrace for accepting what the foreign secretary called "a barren island with hardly a house on it." Now, as we stepped down from the bus, the night glow of Hong Kong Island's skyscrapers shimmered on the harbor's ripples, and hulking ships trimmed with strands of orange light floated noiselessly on the blackness. Amy and I began walking along the harbor's edge. Traffic and hotels swirled and jutted on our left, waves slapped at the sea wall on our right. The night was warm and steamy, and somehow, walking here, talking with my new friend, felt like exactly the right thing to be doing.

She was short, Asian-sized, her walking pace easy. She wore a white peasant blouse, loose blue pants (made in Katmandu, no doubt), and rubber flip-flops—an outfit that lent her the aura of a strolling Gypsy. Her steps were slow, unmeasured; if we came to an opening in the crowd, she wouldn't speed through, but would let things adjust around her. Suddenly I felt very American. What *was* my hurry? Consciously I slowed.

"What did you do in the States?"

"I was a teacher."

"But you hardly look old enough to be a student."

"Most people think I'm about eighteen," she said, unbothered.

"But I'm twenty-six, and I really was a teacher. For two years. And I looked even younger then." She laughed. "It sounds funny to hear myself say that— 'I was a teacher.' I feel like I'm talking about someone else's life. I'm not even that person anymore. I don't see how I can ever go back. There were days in Katmandu when I'd look up at the mountains or the people in the streets and I'd just start laughing: 'I'm in Katmandu! Kat-man-*du*! How did this happen?' "

Amy had a fresh-washed look about her. When she found something particularly amusing, her face would melt into an endearing assortment of scrunched cheeks, flashing eyes, shiny teeth. She was cute, and something about her said: Life is good.

"That's where I'm staying," she said, pointing. I followed her finger to the massive Peninsula Hotel, the British five-star.

"The Peninsula!"

"No," she laughed. "Not there. *There!*"

I looked again. Past the Peninsula was the YMCA.

"I've got a bed in the women's dorm. It's the world's best deal. Next door you pay two hundred a night, but for three dollars I get a bed, air-conditioning, pool privileges, and I can use the café on the roof. You should see the view. I'd tell you to try the men's dorm, but I know it's full. I checked there earlier—for Dylan."

On the street in front of Chungking Mansions we were accosted by a gang of touts attracted by my backpack. They circled like feeding sharks, each taking his nip:

"You want room? Good room!"

"You come *me!* Many hee-pee come *my* room."

I picked the least frantic of these men and asked what he had to offer. He claimed to be the owner of a newly opened ninth-floor guest house. "Air-cah-dih-shun. New betts. Veddy chip—only twenny Honk Honk dollah [$2.50]."

"Amy," I called, interrupting the two touts already enamored of her, "I'm going to look at this guy's room. After that, want to get a bite to eat or something?"

"Uh, sure. But first I've got to go up to the sixteenth floor. There's a message board, and maybe Dylan's somehow left me a note."

26

DYLAN

A man may be a fool and not know it, but not if he is married.

—H. L. MENCKEN
A Mencken Chrestomathy

N HOUR AFTER WE MET, Amy and I were riding the Star Ferry across the harbor to Hong Kong Island. Surprisingly I had found the room offered by the Chinese man to be perfectly decent—exactly as described. There had been no note from Dylan.

Keeping a polite-yet-familiar distance, Amy and I leaned on the railing, watched the ferry's angling sudsy wake, and traded histories.

"I started traveling a year and a half ago. Everything in my life was okay except for this relationship I was in. It wouldn't blossom, but it wouldn't die. Carl and I made love 'one last time' for six months.

"Finally I decided to go away for a while—really give him some space. I'd always wanted to bicycle in Europe, so I saved money, invited a girlfriend, and gave notice at my job. My boss tried to talk me out of it. I was director of a program for juvenile delinquents, the youngest director they'd ever had, and he thought I was throwing away too good a thing."

Now I was glad we didn't have one-page résumés; listening allowed an opportunity for looking at this fresh, smooth face twelve inches from my own. Light, darting eyes, watching mine; thin lips sliding back and forth, words slipping out.

"But I left just after New Year's last year—eighteen months now. We bicycled Britain and then the Continent, camping out. Later we ferried across the Mediterranean and spent a month in Israel bicycling the Sinai. We split up after six months: I went to Switzerland and worked the summer in a hotel and did a lot of rock climbing on my afternoons off. In the fall I biked more of Europe—by myself this time.

"Right before Christmas I went back home. What a shock! I thought people would be as excited when I came back as they were when I left—surprise parties, the whole thing. But they really didn't know what to do with me. I

101

was the first one in my circle of friends to go traveling, and some of them—especially the guys—felt left behind. I got real careful about saying things like 'the Sinai,' or 'When I was in Amsterdam . . .' When people ask 'How was your trip?' they want you to say 'Oooooh! It was neat!,' and then they want to tell you about 'the new guy Linda's been seeing.' It made me sad. That's not me anymore, and it never will be.

"After Christmas I flew to Bombay. I didn't like India—I'm not sure I was ready—but my first night I met this Australian guy who'd been there a year, and I started traveling with him."

"How fortunate."

"Well, it turned into a bad thing. He wanted me to be his girlfriend, but it wasn't mutual. And when I started getting the hang of India, he began to fall apart. He was always crying. He asked me to marry him and move to Australia. After a month I went to Nepal. I was really glad to get out of India and away from him. Katmandu was heaven. I rented a room by the month and had a regular schedule. Every day I went to Buddhist meditation and body-awareness classes. There was a pool at one of the Western hotels, and for five dollars a week you could swim all you wanted. Paradise. I stayed three months; someday I'm gonna go back and live for a year."

Amy stopped and looked at me. "God, this is great." The ferry breeze was blowing the hair straight back from her face. "A couple of hours ago, I was really depressed about Dylan not showing up. Now, I feel a lot better. I haven't unloaded on anyone like this for days. What about you? What are you doing here?"

I told her about my trip and the choice facing me: China or the Philippines? Earlier, I had mentioned my tenuous marriage, and now Amy asked several questions: Did I think my wife and I would get back together? Did I want to? Did she? Why had we split up? Was she seeing other men? Did I see other women? Suddenly I understood the Australian's dilemma. My stomach was winding like a ratchet and my arm was fighting an impulse to slip around her waist and pull gently.

"I'm glad there was no message from Dylan," I told her.

She smiled. "I was just thinking the same thing." We looked at each other, then away, gazing self-consciously at the distant lights.

"Tell me about him." I leaned back from the railing, thinking: In a moment just like this one, smoking was invented. "How'd you meet?"

"Through friends in Katmandu. He looks a lot like you, only he's skinnier and doesn't have a beard. He's twenty-four, and already a real experienced traveler. He's been in Asia for a couple of years. He's funny, well read—he's named after Dylan Thomas—and he likes to play chess. Do you play?"

"Not in years."

"That's one reason Dylan and I want to take the Trans-Siberian together—we're good chess partners. Now if he'd just get here!"

Dylan was my rival. Already I envisioned Amy and me tramping the hazy valleys and hills of China, to Beijing. We would share a Trans-Siberian compartment, and as the train thicka-thacked across the steppes, I would relearn chess. As we pulled into Moscow, I would lean back from the jiggling board and say, "Checkmate." Amy would surrender; we would laugh and cuddle. . . .

"When did he say he'd be here?"

"Last Saturday, four days ago. Now he's missed two planes, and the next one's not until this Saturday. I'm getting antsy. I want to see China. Hong Kong's okay, but I want to get moving."

"What do you think's happened?"

"I don't know. He had to get money from some people in New Delhi and then in Bombay. They owed it to him. He's been living in India for a couple of years, and he made some business deals."

"Drugs?"

"No. I think it was a couple of VCR's he 'imported.' He was supposed to get a thousand dollars each. He had so many deals going it was hard to keep track. He knows just about everyone in Katmandu and Delhi."

"Do you think anything weird could have happened?"

"Nah. Everything was all worked out. But you know India."

She paused. Underneath us, the boat was throbbing; seated on the nearby benches were rows of silent Chinese, stern eyeglass-wearing Buddhas. I supposed the reason for their sullen demeanors was the wall sign: DO NOT SPIT.

"There was just one thing," Amy said.

"What?"

"This may sound funny. I trusted Dylan, but lots of people told me I was dumb to hang around him. He was a junkie."

I tried to sound indifferent. "Heroin, you mean?"

"Yeah, but he kicked it. He didn't want to go back to Europe all strung out. That's why he was in Katmandu—to get away from his friends in Delhi for a few weeks and kick. The night I met him, he said he was going cold turkey and wouldn't be around for about a week.

"But a couple days later I was eating dinner with some women friends and Dylan came into the restaurant looking for me. He looked terrible, all wasted and shaking. He asked if I'd come and see him later. When he left, everyone at the table really came down on me. They said he was just using me—I should stay away from him. I didn't like that—I thought someone should help him. I went over to his room and put cold towels on his face and tried to comfort him. He was shaking and retching, and most of the time he was delirious. Have you ever seen anyone go through withdrawal?"

I hadn't.

"Neither had I. It's really something—they're not human. I went by to see him every few hours for a couple of days, and when he didn't get any better, I got real scared. I thought he might die. The American Embassy gave me the address of a free drug clinic, and I wrestled him into a taxi and took him there. They gave him methadone, and he stopped shaking. He got a lot better. Within a couple of weeks, he stopped using even that.

"He said that when he went back to Delhi, he wasn't going near the stuff. I believed him—I still do. I think he'll show up. Underneath the junkie, he's really a sweet guy. Nepal was definitely the highlight of my trip, maybe of my life, and Dylan was a big part of it. I'm glad I didn't listen to my friends. Later some of them told me the same thing."

I thought: That's right—Dylan's a human being, not a rival. If he'd found love and tenderness with Amy, I should be glad.

"Good for you," I said, and touched her shoulder. "That's a neat story."

27

PLAYING PAST BEDTIME

Whether women are better than men I cannot say—but I can say they are certainly no worse.

—Golda Meir

W E WANDERED THE STREETS on the island side of the harbor until we came to the Poor Man's Nightclub, a collection of food vendors and merchant stalls that materializes nightly on a dockside parking lot. We found an empty table under a restaurant awning and, by pointing at the various tubs of food, ordered roast duck with hoisin sauce, rice-chicken, a side dish of eel, and washed it all down with water (her), San Miguel beer (me), and more stories.

We talked about the people back home—parents, siblings, friends. Amy commended herself for having had the gumption to leave the States and drift over to Europe. I clued her in on The Man 100 Miles Up. She told about rock climbing in Wyoming; I told about building a log cabin in Idaho. She talked about her old boyfriend; I talked about hoping to get back together with my wife someday. We talked about sex—how old we'd been the first time, who with, where. After her trip Amy was going to get married, have kids. I was going to make my living writing.

A warm rainstorm blew in, tugging and pounding at the canvas awning over our heads, trapping us at our table long after the meal was done. Through a curtain of small waterfalls, our waiter appeared, shirtless and barefoot, carrying a second beer.

It was early morning by the time the rain stopped. "They lock the YMCA at midnight," Amy said. "Every night I have to talk the guard into letting me back in. He's getting to know me. Last night he just smiled and opened the door."

"Probably the highlight of his night now."

We paid the bill—splitting it—and walked the steaming, now quiet, streets back toward the Star Ferry. At one point we found ourselves walking beside a concrete railing; on its far side was a twenty-foot fall to the water, on the near side a four-foot drop to the sidewalk. Amy hopped up, tightroped the railing for thirty paces, then jumped down. She grinned mischief at me. I thought: Two kids playing past bedtime, half a world from home.

My perception of her was kaleidoscopic: teenager, strolling Gypsy, reformer of delinquents, sexual being. With the flash of an eye or the scrunch of a cheek, she could change from mystic seeker or helpless younger sister into mother-to-be or acrobat balancing atop a ledge.

"I'm really glad we met," I told her.

"Yeah. It's been great. Usually I'm not this open with people—certainly not with guys. There are women I can talk with this way, but never guys."

"Maybe we feel comfortable because I'm married and you've got Dylan."

She laughed. "I know what you mean. I keep wondering how we'd feel if you were single. It feels safer this way."

"It does. We both have a way out if we get the least bit uncomfortable."

"Yeah," she said, "but I'm not the least bit uncomfortable."

The harbor's fish-and-saltwater stench highlighted the silence that followed, as we pondered our meeting—her groping eastward, me fleeing west, until our head-on collision. Coincidence? Destiny? Would we carom off each other, or somehow stick?

"I don't know where I'm going after Honk Honk," I said, "and I don't know how I'll think in the morning, but right now I have the feeling I'd like to spend more time with you."

"I was thinking about that, too. If you do decide on China, maybe you and Dylan and I can make it a threesome."

"Well . . . That wasn't exactly what I had in mind. If Dylan shows up, you guys go ahead with your plans. But if he doesn't, and if I do decide to go to China, I'd be open to doing it just with you."

"Why do you say 'if' he shows up?"

"I don't know. Maybe it's just wishful thinking, but I have my doubts. I knew junkies in India, and I know you can't count on them the way you count on other people. Besides, I don't know Dylan—I'm not even sure he exists."

She snorted. We fell quiet again. This time Amy broke the silence.

"I don't know why I'm telling you this. Maybe it's because I feel safe with you. But here goes." She looked at me, then down at the cracks in the sidewalk.

"The day he left Katmandu I gave Dylan my Visa card and my passport, and then I reported them stolen and got everything replaced. He's going to sell them on the black market in India and that'll be our money for China and the Trans-Siberian. Right now I'm down to my last few hundred dollars."

My mental image of her began blinking on and off like a Las Vegas marquee. "Reformer of delinquents?" Who had reformed whom? I was speechless.

"Do you think that's terrible?" she asked, voice tightening.

"No," I said, weighing it out. "Not really. I'm just surprised. That sort of thing is a little far from my reality these days. There *was* a time I might have done something like that ..." My tone of voice finished the sentence: *"but I'm beyond that now."*

"It's not like I hurt somebody," she said. "I didn't steal anything. There's no one to feel sorry for."

Cinderella had revealed a tender spot and Prince Charming had shish-kebabed her on the lance of judgment. A canyon opened in the still air between us. I scanned the wreckage of my own past, looking for something to even things up. It's always a short search.

"Five years ago," I said, gulping, "when I was two months into a journalism career, I made a big mistake. A basketball player passing through my town said he didn't have time for the interview I'd been counting on. I knew he'd never be back, and I figured I could write his story without him, so I did. It seemed like such a small thing, but it really affected me. My self-image changed. I began not to trust myself. A year and a half later—I was working for another newspaper by this time—I wrote a letter to the editor of the old paper, explaining and apologizing. I didn't anticipate the reaction. I'd hoped for forgiveness or something, but the editor, who'd been a friend of mine, blasted me in the paper, said that anyone who does that sort of thing"— more gulping—" *'forfeits the right to sit behind a typewriter.'* I guess I took it to heart. Within a couple of weeks, I became a waiter. Six months later, I went to India."

We walked without speaking for a few moments, silenced by the arrow of guilt's 180-degree swing. I heard mental whirrings coming from Amy's part of the sidewalk, and then: "Can you forgive yourself?"

"It's been a struggle. I used to believe I was a writer, but the only writing I've done since then has been in my notebook. Sometimes I hear people say, 'If I had the chance to do it all over again, I'd do everything exactly the same.' Not me. I've never felt quite right since then."

Amy was quiet a while, comparing our indiscretions. "Well, I did feel a little funny at first, but I'm not going to spend the rest of my life regretting it. I'm going to chalk it up to experience. Everyone in Katmandu was doing it. 'You're stupid not to. It's so easy.' I really want to see China—who knows when I'll be here again?—and I didn't think I could do it without the extra money. I'm pretending it's a gift."

"What if Dylan doesn't come?"

"Oh, I've got enough money—three hundred dollars in travelers checks and a couple thousand at home in the bank. I can write a check, but I've been counting on that to go back to. I just wish Dylan would get here." She sighed.

"How much are you expecting to get?"

"Dylan had friends who'd sold things before, and they figured about fifteen hundred. That should make for a pretty nice time in China and Russia."

Yeah, I thought, as we continued on toward the ferry and toward our respective beds, but Dylan's never gonna show. He was in Katmandu or Bombay or Paris right this minute—arm roped, veins popping—with the door locked in a suite of rooms charged to Amy's Visa card. Everyone knew about junkies. I'd been around long enough to see through a scam like that, but Amy hadn't. She was actually the helpless teenager I'd first seen, and to make it through China she would need someone like me.

28
A TIME
TO AMY

*As to marriage or celibacy, let a man take which
course he will, he will be sure to regret it.*

—DIOGENES LAERTIUS
Socrates

THAT FIRST NIGHT altered the context of my visit to Hong Kong. No longer was my only concern: China or the Philippines? Now there was another question: What about Amy? From the first moment, we were embedded in each other's consciousness. During waking hours we were inseparable: movies, long walks, meals together. After I showed up at the YMCA for breakfast three mornings in a row, the staff started greeting me, "Ah, Mr. Amy." At the rooftop café we became a familiar afternoon sight, drinking iced tea at a shaded table and watching the monsoon weather breakdance over the harbor. Sometimes we played chess, but it was no contest—merely an excuse to hang out together.

We developed a routine: each morning after breakfast we walked back to Chungking Mansions to hear travelers' stories, ask questions about China and the Philippines, and check the bulletin board for messages from Dylan. Later we would take the Star Ferry over to Hong Kong Island and check at the American Express for mail or a telex from Dylan. Amy was still certain he was coming: "I got to know him too well. He wouldn't just forget this without at least letting me know."

But as the days went by, her doubts mounted. She made preparations to apply for a China visa, and said that if Dylan wasn't on Saturday's flight from Bombay, and if he didn't write or telex, she would have to make a move.

I, too, was coming toward a decision. At the YMCA and Chungking Mansions, I grilled the darkest travelers for beach recommendations. Most had just come from the Philippines, but warned that the season was finished.

"It's too humid now—the monsoons are about to break."

"The insects are fearless, and they're getting bigger."

"The sky's always hazy. Don't go now. You'll regret it."

At home I had fantasized monsoon season as an "experience," but the reality, seen up close, had pimples. Every day was warm and muggy, or poured rain; a pool of breastbone moisture was now a permanent feature of my anatomy. Gradually I began to sour on the idea of spending significant time in any place with weather like Hong Kong's.

Still, the days there were happy ones. *There's a time to work, a time to play, and now,* I told my notebook, *it's time to Amy.* One morning we boarded a ferry and spent the entire day visiting Hong Kong's less-populated outlying islands. We strolled the quiet villages of Cheng Chau, forty minutes from Hong Kong, but at least forty years and forty decibels behind. On Lantau we hiked high-meadowed hills, gawking down at three-sixty ocean views until we overheated, then caught the boat to Peng Chau.

"You know, I think my wife and I made this same ride." We were sitting next to each other under an awning at the back where the breeze was strongest.

"Did she like Asia?"

"A lot. She's a great traveler. She rode a bicycle from Virginia to Oregon one summer all by herself."

"Seems like you'd be perfect together. Why's she want a divorce?"

"I don't know for sure. When I think about it, I can come up with lots of explanations, but no Ultimate Reason. My most recent one is that it has a lot to do with her being three years older. She's starting to think about security, and worries that I might want to wander around forever. She'd probably say I'm the perfect kind of guy to meet traveling—say, on a bus in Hong Kong—but you might be smart not to marry him."

"Do you still love her?"

"I do."

"I bet she misses you."

"She does. She said so on the phone."

"Why don't you go back?"

"Not yet. I'm having too much fun. *Hey,* what're you?—I've already got a mother!"

"Some people need more than one." She was laughing. "I'm gonna take you to the airport and send you back." She tugged the hair curling at my neck. "But first we're gonna find you a barber."

"Great. We'll put it on your Visa card."

"*Hey,* yourself!" She poked a finger into my right biceps. "Now I know why you're traveling alone. You drove your wife crazy, didn't you?"

Instead of a barber on Peng Chau, we found a cool harborside café. We drank iced tea, played chess, watched the locals watch us, and we talked incessantly—as though every little detail about each other were vitally important.

The return ride featured a spectacular light show, the sun lowering down out of a broken sky and coming to rest on the hills of mainland China, setting them ablaze. Needles of orange light slanted across the harbor and became stuck in skyscraper windows. Above the city the green slopes of Victoria Peak contrasted with a frothing stew of gray-white clouds. Shoulder to shoulder at the boat's railing, Amy and I drank in this passing wonder and gulped an occasional "Wow!"

That night at dinner she asked: "What if you weren't married? How would you feel about me?"

"Let's get a hotel room!"

We chuckled over that for a couple of moments before I repackaged the idea: "Do you think we could share a room and not sleep together?"

"Knowing me," she said, "probably not."

Saturday night came—the flight from Bombay. Instead of going out to the airport, Amy called the airlines and asked if Dylan's name was on the manifest. It wasn't. On a hunch, she spent ten precious dollars on a garbled phone call to a certain hotel in New Delhi. Dylan had just stepped out, she was told, but yes, he was definitely registered there. Then the line went dead.

"He's still in Delhi!" she moaned, slamming down the receiver. "He hasn't even made it to Bombay yet! He won't be here for at least another week!"

We walked back to Chungking Mansions to check the bulletin board a final time: maybe Dylan had called in a message. Nothing. Amy grew silent. No, she didn't want to go out for a bite. "I want to go home and go to bed."

A few days is all it takes to enslave a man to a woman's moods. In silence I walked her back. A block from the YMCA we came to a quiet area not lit by street lights. I steered her off the sidewalk and stopped her. I stood behind her, kneading her shoulders, then her scalp—scratching gently at the roots of her hair with my fingertips. She leaned back against my chest, closed her eyes, and relaxed. For several moments I massaged her head, worked the little hollow where spine meets skull, and softly stroked her cheeks. She sighed, transported. I felt the tension leaving her body and entering my own. From my taller vantage point I looked down past the contented childlike face to the slow rise and fall of grown-up breasts. My rigid position on extramarital affairs came up for reexamination. Maybe they could *strengthen* a marriage. How should *I* know?

If it hadn't been occurring in my own life, I would have recognized this ridiculous situation for the soap-opera plot that it was: on the other side of the Pacific, a wife, half-committed to divorce; on this side, the body of a lovely young felon responding eagerly to my fingers; in New Delhi, her drug-addict boyfriend; in my head, China and the Philippines competing for attention. *This* was exactly the right place? Right thoughts? Right actions?

I gave Amy's shoulders a final squeeze. "Go home," I whispered in her ear. "Sleep tight."

She turned around with a dreamy smile, eyes barely open. "You're so sweet," she cooed. "And so married."

We hugged. She came up to about my chest. We kissed once on the lips, smiled, squeezed hands. She turned and walked away. I stood in the darkness with my erection, watching her disappear down the street and thinking: A blind man could see where this is headed.

29
HORMONAL FOG

He travels best that knows When to return.

—THOMAS MIDDLETON
The Old Law

TOO KEYED UP FOR SLEEP, I stepped into a small, crowded café.

"One iced coffee," I told the waiter, an old, whiskery Chinese who looked none too happy.

"Um bih." *One beer.*

"No. One iced coffee."

"Um bih."

"One iced coffee."

He grumbled and scribbled on his pad. A few minutes later he walked by my table and banged an iced coffee down on the far edge, out of reach. He glowered at me and left. I thought, I hope the Communists come next week.

At other tables Chinese in pairs and in groups drank bih, coffee, tea, and ate pastries from the adjoining bakery. They laughed and swore at each other. The floor was littered with wrappers and scraps of food. A group of four Chinese came in. There were no empty tables. They eyed mine. The iced coffee was finished. I left.

Outside, European couples in tuxedos and glittery evening gowns walked the greasy streets, skipping in and out of the honky-tonks that will disappear the instant the British leave. In front of the Topless Playboy Bar the barkers screamed at me, "Only sixty Honk Honk dollah! Two drinks free!"

Suzie Wong, wearing a low-cut gown and six pounds of makeup, was standing outside the next club. "You look lonely. Come in—I buy you drink."

I bolted for the Star Ferry and paid my eight cents to board. I sat on a bench at the front of the boat, salt breeze licking my face, watched tugboats nudging ocean liners, and read the lights of the harbor-split colony: ROLEX, SANYO, WINSTON, CANON.

It occurred to me that the thoughts I had brought from home were rubbish.

113

A trip around the world was not, after all, a magic elixir. It solved nothing, healed nothing. Traveling thousands of miles had changed only my position on the globe. I still had the same bag of emotions and confusions to deal with, was still uncertain about my marital status, about sex, about how to make a living.

A mental voice chided me for being indecisive, for letting my decisions be based on the actions of others, specifically women. "You'd have already left Hong Kong if you hadn't met Amy. You're weak and unsure of yourself. How low you've fallen—trying to steal a junkie's girlfriend!"

I fought back. In my notebook I wrote ten times: *I am in exactly the right place, thinking, doing, and feeling exactly—oh, but exactly—the right things.*

That cleared my thoughts some. As the ferry sliced across the harbor, as the damp air blotted up my hormonal fog, I jotted this: *Sleeping with Amy will be my signature on the divorce papers. Am I ready for that? Ten years from now, looking back, what do I want to see?*

When the boat reached the far side, I didn't get off. Without disembarking, I rode back and forth across the harbor four times, relaxing, soaking up every bit of energy the water would yield.

ow'd you sleep?" I asked at breakfast.

"Fine, once I sorted my thoughts out."

"All squared away?"

"I think so," she said. "How about you?"

"Yeah, I think so."

"Is it China or the Philippines?"

"I've been kidding myself. I'm too preoccupied to appreciate a beach right now. And *my* revolution is gonna have better weather. I'm going to China."

"When?"

"Real soon. How about you?"

"I've waited long enough. Ten days. I'll leave Dylan a list of places he can meet me. As soon as they give me a visa, I'm leaving. It's Sunday. I can't apply until tomorrow."

"What'll you do for money?"

"Write a check on my savings. Hate to do it, but ..."

"How long will you stay in China?"

"I'm thinking three weeks. How about you?"

"Five seemed about right in Japan. If I stay five in China, I can make it back to San Francisco pretty easy in another four. My wedding anniversary's nine weeks from today."

Neither of us said anything for a moment. Amy spread red jam on her toast. I coaxed a drop of orange juice from my empty glass.

"Could we stand each other?" I asked her.

She bit her toast, not looking at me, and chewed it. "Maybe if you got a haircut."

"Hey, I bet my wife wishes she'd said that just one time less."

We both laughed.

"We could stand each other," she said.

"I know."

We were quiet a moment. Finally Amy said, "There's one thing, though."

"What?"

"I slept with a married man once. It's a bad idea."

"I was wondering how to say that same thing. For all my kidding, I really am married—that's something I got clear on last night. I wrote in my notebook that the line of monogamy is drawn right below the shoulder blades."

"You give a wonderful head massage," she said.

"I was sorting your thoughts out."

She laughed. She stretched her hand across the table.

"Buddies?"

"Buddies," I agreed, and we shook on it.

Monday's sky was packed with gloom clouds and brooding mystery. Chalked onto a blackboard at the ferry terminal was a message: TAI-FUN WARNING—3.

"Three means a tai-fun is heading our way," explained a lady at the tourist-information booth. "Eight means direct hit."

Amy and I applied for visas. "Ready Wednesday morning," we were told. Around noon the Star Ferry shut down, the harbor emptied of boats. High winds howled in off the sea, and a stinging rain began to rip at the city. Businesses packed it in for the day. Shutters were drawn. The YMCA staff closed the rooftop café, folded the tables and chairs, and took them inside. I told Amy I'd see her later and waded back toward my room. Walls of rain blew sideways through the air. Umbrella carcasses littered the streets. Suzie Wong had disappeared. Cars were few, buses empty. At Chungking Mansions only two people were in line for the elevator.

"They say it's a five now," one of them said.

The other: "And it's supposed to get worse."

In my room I slid out of wet clothes and curled up under my sleeping bag. I read *Dragon Seed,* a novel set in rural China, until it fell from my hands.

The next morning the rain had stopped. TAI-FUN HITS EIGHT! screamed the oversized headline of the *South China Post.* At breakfast Amy asked me, "Could you believe the noise last night?" But I hadn't heard a thing. I'd slept right through my first tai-fun.

The sky cleared, the streets dried. By midafternoon there was a feisty crowd on the roof of the YMCA. Double-decker tour boats were once again scooting mobs of upscale tourists around the peaceful harbor. At our favorite table Amy and I spread a map and began looking at China.

PART
THREE

30
AS A MAN SHOULD BE

Any change in China would be for the worse, which is a pity, because it seemed so bad when I sailed through it. Would it always be these people in cheap cotton clothes, walking through the streets, carting the steel rods that are used for these awful buildings, saying nothing? ... It worried me that China might never be better than it is now, and that the water might always be scarce, clothes always rationed, food never plentiful, houses always tiny and the hard work never done.

—PAUL THEROUX
Sailing Through China

THIRTY MINUTES BY TRAIN from downtown Hong Kong, the West drops away and the green world reasserts itself, scrub valleys and forested hills surrounding the tracks in an ominous manner. Communist China, Red China, Mainland China—a billion people, one out of every five in the world—looms like a tidal wave. Until this moment China, to me, had been a gimmick, an ethnic joke. China was where you wound up if you dug too deep. China was surrounded by a Great Wall. It had flocks of peeking ducks and was full of laundry men and barking women who made violent revolutions. Now it was coming at us head on. I hoped the Man 100 Miles Up was watching. Maybe he'd select Amy and me as a team. That's the way my wife saw us.

"Oh, have sex!" she had huffed when I had told her earlier that morning, for some now-unfathomable reason, about the latest developments in my plans. "You're free and I'm free," she said, and hung up. Now, on the train, I tried to fit this curse into the developing scenario, but it just hung there, unanswerable.

The tracks ended at an apparently random spot that marked the limits of Hong Kong. Several warehouse-style buildings had been erected in a clearing hacked from the surrounding forest, and around them a generic frontier town had taken root.

A hitchhiker's sign (cardboard, handpainted; C-H-I-N-A, with a blue arrow) pointed the way to Immigration. Amy and I, the only foreigners on the train that morning, drifted along in a stream of silent Chinese returning from visits to Hong Kong. They appeared overly somber, trying to convey the impression that being away from China had caused them great sorrow. Duty had called them to Hong Kong for the performance of some joyless yet necessary task, at which they'd lingered not a moment, and now they trudged soberly, but unconvincingly, homeward.

The formalities of exiting Hong Kong went quickly, but at Chinese customs a uniformed young girl—straight black hair, white blouse, all business— separated Amy and me from the crowd and led us to a desk where English was spoken. Unsmiling guards with red stars on the crowns of their pea-green caps inspected our packs and took our passports. The girl showed us to a large waiting room and told us to relax while our papers were processed.

"You must be tired," she said. It was eleven o'clock in the morning.

"There is water." A pitcher and row of glasses were spread on a table.

"Sit down and be comfortable." There were fifty chairs in the room; Amy and I were the only occupants.

Immigration Control, the state bank, and the railroad station for trains to Canton were all under the same sprawling roof. After we cleared customs and changed money, we followed the foot traffic to a row of ticket windows. My eye roved in search of an English sign—TOURIST INFORMATION, maybe— but it found nothing. All lettering was the Chinese stuff. The building was busy with people, none of them white. Amy and I were on our own. We discussed strategy and decided she would stay with our packs while I got tickets. When I joined the line, the seven men ahead of me looked back over their shoulders, staring. They had just returned from Hong Kong, I guessed; maybe one of them could speak English.

"Canton?" I asked the man ahead of me.

He stared, frozen.

I tried the Chinese name for Canton: "Guangzhou?"

His head bobbed up and down. "Guangzhou!" he said.

I pulled some money from my pocket. "Guangzhou—how much?"

He seemed to understand. He opened his fist and showed me three and a half yuan in worn bills.

"Shay shay." Thank you, according to the new guidebook.

His face broke into an embarrassed grin. By now the entire queue was smiling and nodding, but it was temporary; the smiles soon faded, unblinking gazes returned. These men just stood there looking at me; the only thing that diverted their attention was the slow shuffling of the line, and the eventual arrival of their turn at the ticket window.

When my turn finally came, I shoved seven yuan across the counter and held up two fingers. "Guangzhou. *Yee.*" *Two.*

The girl in the cage held up fifteen yuan for me to see, about seven dollars. *What?* The man ahead of me had clearly said tickets to Canton were three and a half yuan. Had he been mistaken? Had I misunderstood? Was she trying to cheat me because I was white?

"Guangzhou?" I asked. "Canton?"

The girl nodded twice and shook her money for emphasis. "Canton."

Confused, probably scowling, I slid more money across the counter. She slid back two orange tickets with Chinese characters. But the people ahead of me had gotten brown ones—I had seen them.

"Canton?" I held up the tickets.

"Canton!"

I looked dumbly at the tickets; they could have been just about anything. "Guangzhou?" I asked yet again.

"Guangzhou!"

Behind me was a long line of staring people. I took the tickets and walked back to Amy. "I got something, but I'm not sure what."

o the five hundred people in the station we were objects of great curiosity. They sat on pews across from us and let their jaws dangle. Staring back at them had no impact; they neither smiled nor frowned, nor in any way hinted an acknowledgment of our mutual humanity. Occasionally one would grunt to his neighbor and the two of them would share a laugh. My notebook: *Staring is a sport here.* And: *I am a mechanical robot, a stranger from another time. I am not short with a dark crew cut, as a man should be.*

At a stand inside the crowded station Amy bought a small cardboard box that held a sandwich and fried chicken leg, and sat down to eat. I said I was going exploring, would be back shortly, and fell in with the people heading toward the station's exit. I wondered: Will I be allowed to leave?

But I emerged unchallenged into the bright pages of *National Geographic* magazine. The day was clear now, and the harsh sun gave me permission to hide behind dark glasses. Milling people in sandals, straw hats, baggy blue shirts, and baggy blue pants stopped as one and gaped. A policeman halted bicycle and foot traffic so I could cross an intersection. Wherever I walked, crowds parted and drew back.

Three battered taxis were parked in a row alongside the dusty, unpaved square next to the station. A bemused driver opened his door and beckoned.

I slid past. A food stall—a tattered awning hoisted over a crude wooden counter—offered tea and doughy pastries; tacked to the edge of the counter was a faded round sign, red and black and white: COCA-COLA. Beside the stall, a man with long white chin wisps sat on the ground next to a mound of peanuts, curled hand resting on a rusty scale. The bed of an ancient black dump truck was piled high with striped melons; tomatoes and red peppers were spilled onto a canvas.

But business was slow: vendors and customers alike had chosen this moment for a long, silent staring break.

31
SHANGHAIED

. . . survey results show that most Americans would rather travel than almost anything else . . . One question posed was, assuming they had the money, what would the respondents spend it on. 'A vacation trip of one week or more' was the alternative chosen by 74 percent.

—RICHARD PAOLI
The San Francisco Examiner, November 6, 1983

THE TORPID CROWD STIRRED TO LIFE when our train, seventeen cars long, came hooting into view. The throng, heaving packs and crates and sacks up onto shoulders, stumbled forward in a great surge that drained the station. Third World etiquette prevailed: people jamming bundles through open windows, jousting for space. The train had arrived empty, but within moments it appeared overwhelmed and overloaded; Amy and I began wondering if we'd get seats. We tried boarding each car, but each time we got the same response—a frown from the car's attendant and a wave toward the rear, back toward Hong Kong. And then, after sixteen cars and sixteen brush-offs, with mutual distaste Amy and I spied our destiny: a group of white people were knotted around the doorway of the last car, our car. A panel on its side said LOTUS TOURS.

We'd been shanghaied!

Amy said, "I'm embarrassed."

Like it or not, we travelers were about to enter China in air-conditioned sterility with thirty-two tourists on the fourth day of a two-week Orient tour. The sixteen forward cars were "hard seat"—old cars with rough benches and open windows, bundles of belongings stashed underfoot, and people stuffed in by the dozen. *Chinese* people. Even if we hadn't known our place, the ticket lady had known. The tickets she'd forced on me at twice the people's price condemned us to the last two seats in the luxury car; a conductor standing outside glanced at them and motioned us aboard. So much for walking into China and falling in with the masses.

Inside we found curtains draped across closed windows. Padded seats

123

draped with white linen headcloths clicked back into reclining positions. We were in the last row. Amy sat by the window, I took the aisle. Two young Chinese, a man and a woman, sat across from us.

"Are you part of the tour?" I asked the man, already knowing he wasn't.

"We are guides."

"Where are these people from?"

"America. New York." His English was good. "Where are you from?"

"San Francisco."

"You are American, then?"

I wanted badly to draw some distinctions, but it was useless. We were all the same. "Yes. American."

In front of us the tourists were settling in for the three-hour ride. They were a church group of mixed ages. Half were teenagers, the rest retired couples or single women in their fifties, but there was no one between twenty and forty. The entire mob was prattling about different things—purchases they'd made in Honk Honk, money they'd spent, accommodations.

"What's tonight's hotel like, Laura?" screamed a girl in the seat ahead of me. She directed her question several rows ahead, to a woman with a name-tag: LAURA, LOTUS TOURS. "I hope it's better than last night!"

"You'll like it," Laura said. "They just built it last year. It's the best one till Singapore."

"Does it have *real* toilets?"

"Yeah," echoed the girl's seat mate. "Not like last night."

"It has real toilets."

"It better!"

Amy and I stared at each other. In search of an ethnic experience, we'd found this.

"Sorry," I told her. The tickets were my doing.

"It's not your fault. I couldn't have done any better. But don't worry—it's just until Canton."

The train started without delay. A hostess wheeled a cart down the aisle, passing out cold Coca-Colas. When she came to Amy and me, she held out two bottles, but hesitated; she glanced across the aisle at the Chinese guide.

"Would you like Coke?" he asked me.

"Are they free?"

"Only for the tour." He yammered in Chinese to the hostess. "Two yuan," he told me. Ninety cents apiece.

"No thanks. Could we get some tea?"

When the girl had gone, the guide leaned over to me. "China is a poor country. We have to import Coca-Cola from Hong Kong, so it is very expensive."

32
THOSE THINGS!

At Hot Springs the story is told of a Virginia lady who became extremely irritated with the mass of tourists visiting her state; she was promptly reminded of the fact that those tourists brought more than one hundred million dollars a year to the state of Virginia. "But why," she protested, "couldn't they just send *the money?"*

—CLEVELAND AMORY
The Last Resorts

HE TRACKS CUT A SWATH BACK THROUGH TIME, slashing holes in the centuries. The unrelenting, timeless squalor of the Third World paraded past: mud houses with crumbling walls, dirt roads, water buffaloes, streams of a muddy-brown gruel, and miles of hand-tended fields separated by walls of piled stone.

Peasants pushed carts loaded with rocks and loose earth and scratched the ground with sticks. Most homes had thatched roofs; behind each was an outhouse. Now and then, as if by mistake, a modern building appeared—looking forlorn and misunderstood. The midday sun dumped its searing glare; in the shade of a tree a boy lay on his back, a straw hat over his face. Through the miles these scenes repeated themselves over and over.

The air-conditioner was blowing a cold draft through the car. I pulled on my sweater, sipped tea, and watched, alternating my attention between the two realities. Outside, the ruin of a red brick building sped past. I tried to guess its résumé: Ten years old? A thousand? Decayed naturally, or knocked down during the Cultural Revolution? Inside, two rows ahead of me a slender high-school girl was reading a magazine article: "How to Have a Flat Stomach!"

An hour from the border, and for no apparent reason, the train came to a halt in the countryside. Neat fields of young cornstalks groping for light and gasping for water lined both sides of the tracks. Through Amy's window I saw an old peasant woman walking barefoot along a dirt path next to a row of palms. The path curved away from the railroad tracks, wandered through the corn fields, and led to a village on the crest of a distant hill. Balanced across the woman's meatless shoulders was a yoke with a bucket dangling from either end; the weight of this barbell forced her forward until her torso nearly paralleled the ground. Jaw outthrust, teeth bared, she had the look of an angry, lumbering camel. I wondered: How many times has she plodded up that hill? How many times did her mother? And her mother's mother's great-great grandmother? Did any of them ever taste cold Coca-Cola ... ?

Suddenly a riot broke out in the car. A moment earlier, everyone had been seated, looking out the window or reading. Or sleeping. Or chatting quietly with a neighbor. But when the train stopped and the peasant woman appeared—framed perfectly by two palm trees—the car exploded with people fumbling for cameras.

"Agnes, where is it!" A man in the center of the car sprang to his feet, knocking aside a young girl unsheathing an Instamatic. He yanked down a suitcase with either fist. A vein was throbbing on the side of his neck. "Which one's it in, Agnes?"

A young man wearing a Duke University T-shirt squeezed off the first shot. His Nikon had been strapped to his chest—not stowed away—and while the others scrambled around him, he stood and fired at the old woman. Before she dropped, he fired again. Immediately he spun 180 degrees and blasted at the opposite window. Leaves and tree limbs and several rows of corn were frozen in immortality. Within two seconds, he had ripped off three shots.

Spinning back toward the first window, he bumped into a dark-haired acquaintance wearing braces, thick glasses, Walkman, and a camera with telephoto lens. "Look out, Wilson. I'm trying to get that old lady."

Wilson showed his braces and raised his own weapon. "You already got her twice, McMasters!"

At the front, six of the older ladies stood in the aisle squinting through viewfinders—a row of proper British redcoats firing a volley. Toward the middle of the car a knot of high schoolers pressed against the window, leaning over seat backs and over each other, firing wildly. The zipping shutters were the sound of a presidential press conference.

"Remember the Alamo," Amy said.

A squeaky female voice—a chalkboard being mutilated—was heard: "Oh, look at the rooster!" The press corps flip-flopped to the other side of the car. A squawking complaint died even as it was born, and a plume of red and brown feathers rose in the air.

Excited by their easy kills, the group sought fresh targets. Some lobbed shells at the far horizons; others pumped lead into the corpse of the peasant woman. "This was on a commune near Canton," the slide-show narration would go. "That lady was a Communist. Miserable life."

Soon the mob turned inward, spraying careless fire around the car. The Chinese guides were the first victims; slaughtered in their seats, they went without whimper. Laura of Lotus Tours was next; she took a dozen shots to the head and shoulders and dropped into her reclining chair. Now the high schoolers opened up on each other; girls were gunned down trying to look flat-stomached, the boys died leering. "Hey, McMasters, get one a' me 'n Robbie!" was Wilson's swan song.

The excitement was too much for the twelve-year-old girl directly in front of me—the one who had screamed, "What's tonight's hotel like, Laura?" She walked back to the tour guide and demanded, "Do you have a bathroom?"

"In there." His index finger flicked toward a door behind my seat. I heard it click open.

"*Those* things!!" shrieked the girl. "I can't use *those* things!" She stomped back to her seat and threw her pouting body down. "How long," she asked her seat mate, "*is* this fucking ride?"

33

ASSURED
OF NOTHING

For miles out in the China Sea you see mud
from the Yangtze River, then suddenly you are on
China, and you gasp at the flat fields stretching as
far as you can see. . . . There is something
magnificent about it. A feeling of grandeur and
age. . . .

—ANNE MORROW LINDBERGH
Hour of Gold, Hour of Lead

NE OF THE STRONGEST FORCES ON THIS PLANET is that which makes a person wonder what the guy next door is up to. It makes a human being uncomfortable to not know—or to not at least *think* he knows—what goes on in his neighbor's house. Or town. Or country.

If you don't think this is true, why not test it? Put a sign on your door saying THE DOOR'S UNLOCKED AND I'M RECEIVING VISITORS, and just see if a bunch of people, most of them with backpacks, don't show up!

That is more or less what has happened in China since 1972, the year of Richard Nixon's precedent-breaking knock on China's door. The Chinese were pleasantly surprised with the results of his visit—friendly attention from the international media and a spell as the darlings of the world community. Having visitors could be fun.

But it wasn't until 1978 that the country was officially opened, and even then the Chinese didn't exactly throw down the walls. After the recent decades of isolation—piled, as they were, atop historic millenniums of isolation—the powers-that-be decided to go slowly. As an experiment, tourism would be tried on a limited basis. Foreigners with the money to match their curiosity were invited to pay about a hundred dollars per day for the privilege of joining tour groups that stayed in specially selected hotels, ate in specially selected restaurants, and went on orchestrated visits to specially selected communes.

The people who joined these tours complained about the accommodations, the food, the restrictions, but came back with wonderful tales about "the people." Nearly everywhere they went, these tourists were the first white visitors in decades. To be the first to see an "unspoiled" place is every traveler's fantasy, and even at a hundred dollars a day the people who joined these groups said they'd gotten their money's worth.

The only unhappy faction was the independent faction, the seat-of-the-pants travelers, the backpackers—the ones who couldn't afford a tour group and wouldn't be caught dead with one even if they could. These people groused about being denied first crack at China and worried that it would be "ruined" before they got to see it. But there was nothing to do except wait, and to occasionally drop by the Chinese consulate in Hong Kong and ask for a visa—a request that was continually denied until late 1981, when the Chinese, in the wake of the success of the tour-group experiment, quietly decided to loosen up even more. In Hong Kong travelers who had for years been applying for individual visas suddenly found them being issued matter-of-factly in three working days. Anyone with ten bucks and a valid passport was invited in!

But there was a catch: the new policy would be another experiment, only six weeks long and very, very low key. Its purpose would be dual—to see how the masses reacted to Westerners wandering in their midst, and to avoid the expense of building first-class hotels in every city. The Chinese had chosen the pragmatic approach, the capitalist approach: "Let the independents in, let them wander the country, let them find the good spots, the popular attractions, and let the market respond." The fanfare and the big preparations made for the free-spending tour groups would not be made for the tight-fisted backpackers. They would be allowed to travel certain routes between certain cities in certain areas, but they would not be pampered. No special arrangements, no bold announcements. The experiment would be a simple one. If the independents wanted to come, fine, but they would have to figure out on their own where to stay, where to eat, how to make travel arrangements. If they were crazy enough to come to China, they could do it Chinese-style.

"Fair enough." By word of mouth, the news ripped through the backpacking circuit. Idlers on the beaches of Thailand and the Philippines heard the word, grabbed their packs, headed for Hong Kong. Within days they found themselves in China, bushwhacking through a culture thoroughly unprepared for them. Logistics were a nightmare. A whole day could be consumed trying to get enough to eat or a place to sleep. Hotel keepers—unaware of the government's unannounced experiment and fearing trouble from the police—often refused to admit the white devils stumbling to their doors. Instead, they would refer them to the big tourist hotels, often in distant cities, where prices started at fifty dollars a day—a traumatic suggestion for someone on a backpacker's budget. In the early stages of the experiment, travelers frequently had to spend hours pleading in sign language (tears were useful) just to get a bed for the night.

Restaurants were slightly easier to master than hotels, but the trains were worse. There were three widely divergent classes of travel to choose from— "soft sleeper," "hard sleeper," and the loathsome "hard seat"—and one could never be sure which class he or she was being given. Schedules and prices were nearly impossible to figure out, and even for a Chinese person, getting a reservation was a desperate exercise. Trains were booked full a week in advance, and all business was transacted in Chinese—English being not merely avoided, but absolutely unheard of.

Survivors of the new experiment say that six weeks spent in China was the equal of six years of the infamous frustration of India: diarrhea was a given, bad food and strange bugs a constant hazard, health care a mystery. Colds and sore throats that wouldn't go away inspired the witticism *They come with the visa.* Some travelers made it as far as Canton or one of the other towns close to the border, and then turned back. Others flew into Beijing, stayed a week, and flew out again. But the hardy ones toughed it out, visiting every city that was "open" in the sprawling country. Backpackers began trickling into Lhasa, the fabled Tibetan city that lies on the Chinese slope of the Himalayas and adds luster to any wanderer's résumé. Some ventured north to the Gobi Desert and to the great grasslands of the west, taking their chances, going on faith, assured of nothing. Every meal eaten, every reservation made, every ticket bought, every bed procured in every funky hotel or dormitory or peasant hut, was considered not only a major victory, but a vital piece of intelligence.

Since days often passed before one backpacker ran into another, it became common practice when seeing another white face to immediately huddle and exchange information: Where have you been? Where did you eat? sleep? How did you find your way? How much was the train? When does it leave? Can you get a discount with a student card? Isn't it strange speaking English again?

The notes taken and the maps sketched during these conversations became each traveler's most valued possession. With a fat sigh (and the sincere warning, "Never, ever go hard seat!"), people leaving the country bequeathed their hand-scrawled notebooks to those just entering. Independent travel in China was grueling work, but it was getting easier.

Individual Chinese, sensing the possibility of extra income, began to work around the system. The manager of a dormitory near the train station might see how he could set aside a few beds each night, and then direct the white-faced takers to his brother's impromptu restaurant down the street. An English menu would be scrawled on a piece of cardboard; a few delicacies (apple pie, chocolate cake, peanut-butter-and-jelly sandwiches) would be added, and business would mushroom. Soon a network took shape, connecting every approved city. The Chinese became accustomed to bewildered backpackers walking their streets, and began steering them toward sanctuary. After the initial strangeness, the leaders smiled, pronounced the new experiment a success, and declared it would continue indefinitely. A black market sprang into being, dealing at first in watches and cameras and tape decks, and then, later, when the government began promoting its "friendship stores," made the short leap to money itself. The ins and outs of dealing with China filtered to Hong Kong, and became accessible to anyone with an hour to spend on the sixteenth floor of Chungking Mansions.

The number of visas being issued expanded geometrically, from none to twenty that first week, then twenty a day, fifty a day, a hundred a day... Each succeeding wave found the country more manageable. Crude guidebooks were printed; word went out that China was "a good place." If you went before it got "ruined," you would have a true adventure, and it would cost almost nothing—five to fifteen dollars a day. And now that a faint path had been beaten, you would, if you were like most travelers, spend a good deal of time outwardly cursing and envying, but silently *thanking* and envying, those first curious pioneers who, as always, have gone before.

34
WHAT HAVE
WE HERE?

... and [Delilah] called for a man, and she caused him to shave off the seven locks of [Samson's] head; and ... his strength went from him.

—JUDGES 16:19

"MAY WE ZEET WEES YOU?"

A young European woman wearing a skirt, a crisp white blouse, and too much blue eye makeup was standing at our table. The young man with her wore sandals and the loose cotton clothes Westerners buy in India. They sat and introduced themselves: Heidi and Richard from Zurich.

"Let me guess," Amy said. "You're staying at the Government Service Workers Hostel?"

At Chungking Mansions everyone gets the same instructions for Canton: "Across from the train station catch a number-five public bus. In twenty minutes it'll start going along a canal. At the third bridge over the canal, get off. Walk across it—look lost, it won't be hard—and someone'll point you to the hostel."

"Deed zey make you beg for beds?" Heidi asked.

"No," Amy said. "They were nice."

"When do you arrive?" Richard's accent was not so thick.

"About an hour ago."

Heidi: "We arrive at noon, but zey are mean to us. Zey say zey have no room."

Richard: "In Hong Kong someone tell us that if this happen we lie down—like maybe we sleep in lobby. So we do it. In two minutes they have beds."

"I seenk I am nut going to like zees country."

For dinner the hostel manager had directed Amy and me to a small open-air barge-restaurant moored on the banks of the great Pearl River and decorated with paper lanterns and a string of Christmas-tree lights. An earlier traveler had written out a bilingual menu, and now we had plates of sweet-sour pork and rice-chicken and bottles of warm Tsingtao beer in front of us. On the nearby streets endless thousands of Chinese in sandals and loose pajamas were walking or pushing bikes toward the huge ferries shuttling back and forth across the water. On the river's far side the setting sun was doing something orange and red and wonderful to the air pollution.

"The place seems okay to me," Amy told Heidi.

"Last week I come from Zudeek to Hong Kong to meet Ree-shard. He writes me letter from Eendya, says we should go to Shina for a munts. I have never been to Sird World. Een Zudeek I seenk zees ees great idea, but when we get off train I see ees mistake. Millions of poor people going everywhere, and nussing is in Eengleesh. Zank Guhd zee bus has a real 'five.' If eet has only a Chinese five, I seenk we will be still at zee train station."

Richard: "And we don't do so well with the black market. In Hong Kong everyone says, 'You get one-forty, *no problem . . .*'"

I'd heard the same thing. Chinese would approach us on the street, eager to trade 140 yuan in their people's money for 100 yuan in the foreign-exchange coupons (FEC) the state bank issues tourists. Canton was the best place to do it—farther inland the offers were lower.

". . . but we get only one-twenty."

"Where?" I asked. No one had yet approached us.

"At the bridge. When we get off bus, a man is there. He speaks English better than we do. We say we want one-forty. He says one-ten. 'The rate has gone down. Too many tourists now.' Finally he says one-twenty, so we say okay."

"Ree-shard, luuk! Zey have Peking duck. Can we get zum?"

fter dinner Amy and I went walking. First stop was the bridge over the canal, but it was dark now and no one approached us. We wandered dusty back streets unlit by street lamps; crowds were still out, but in the darkness people paid us no mind. Bullock-powered vegetable carts rumbled by, and every pedestrian seemed to be carrying something—a squawking chicken, a string of fish, a huge squash—home for dinner.

"I seenk," said Amy, "I am going to luv zees country."

A line stretched down the block from a building with a spaghetti of Chinese characters on the marquee; a poster showed a scowling man with a dagger clenched in his teeth, a woman with a bedsheet clutched to her bosom looking over his shoulder. In a nearby park several hundred people were seated on benches, watching an opera troupe perform on an outdoor stage. The heroine wore whiteface and a glittery long-sleeved gown that covered her ankles-to-chin; we watched her shriek at the audience for twenty completely foreign minutes.

"I'm ready for bed," Amy said.

We got lost on the way back. The dark streets all looked the same, and although we seemed headed in the right direction, we never arrived. We stopped several people, but their answers to our questions were as confusing as the opera.

A bright yellow glow shone from a street level window up ahead. "Let's ask in there," I told Amy. A moment later, through the window, we saw a barber finishing up a crew cut for a young boy. Amy started laughing. "Well, what have we here?"

"Don't start."

The man took two steps back when I ducked through his door.

I smiled and pointed at my hair.

He shook his head, terrified. *What did I ever do to you?* Three women seated on chairs along the wall began howling with laughter.

Amy stepped in out of the night. On the train she'd been studying the glossary in the guidebook. *"Ching." Please.*

I held my fingers up, close together. *Just an inch.*

The man shook his head, pointed at his wristwatch.

The women pushed him forward. The crowd that had gathered at the door began yelling at him. He screamed insults at everyone but Amy and me, then brushed the barber's chair clean. The people had spoken—there was no choice. He patted the chair and smiled at me. The women stood and insisted that Amy have all three of their seats. The man tied a bib around my neck. "Don't worry," Queen Amy called from her thrones, "I'll make sure he doesn't scalp you in back."

Before the first snip, two of the women came over to run hands through my hair. Raucous guffawing came from the street. I turned my head; none would come inside, but there were now eight people crowded into the doorway. And what had just been a front window—four feet high, six feet wide— was now an aquarium full of heads, a laughing Chinese face pressed to every inch of glass.

"You never have a camera when you need one," Amy said.

As my hair fell to the floor, a young boy scooped every scrap into a tiny silver box. When it was all over and I'd paid my twenty-five cents—no tip— he took Amy and me by our hands and led us the three blocks to the Government Service Workers' Hostel.

35
WANT TO CHANGE MONEY?

Even if he has lost his religion in childhood and now thinks himself a man, secure in a wise skepticism, there are no atheists by the dawn's early light over a foreign toilet.

—HERBERT GOLD
A Girl of Forty

MY'S BED WAS EMPTY WHEN I AWOKE, and soft murmurs were coming from outside the window. The fear that I was missing something prodded me out of bed and across the room. It was just dawn, but already the masses were gathered on the wide, tree-shaded sidewalks along the river. For several moments I watched while they waltzed, twisted, glided, and preened through the free-form tai-chi exercises that accompany every new day in the People's Republic.

It was a pleasant morning, cool and calm, but even at seven o'clock the air already held a sticky promise of heat. *What was that itch in my throat? "They come with the visa." No. Not this time. I refuse.* There was a hand mirror lying on Amy's bed; my hair was suffering postcut trauma, but my face looked okay and my throat was its usual color. No use taking chances. I dug a fistful of vitamins from my pack, and swallowed them with the room's supply of boiled water and an unscheduled malaria pill. I lay on my bed and wrote affirmations—*I am perfectly healthy. I am in exactly the right place . . .*—until the door slowly opened.

"You're awake! How you doing?" There was reassuring eagerness in Amy's voice.

"Fine. Did you go for a walk?"

"I've been out front watching these people. This is so great! And I found out we can get tickets at the dock." After lingering in Hong Kong, we were

135

ready to rack up some miles. We would leave at noon for China's interior—eighteen hours on an overnight boat, then another ten on a bus. Amy had running shorts on, and now she pulled on running shoes. "I'm going for a run first. Want to come?"

"No thanks. I'm going to find the black market." Amy, passport & Visa card. Brad, foreign exchange coupons. Same-Same. "Want me to change any of your money?"

She finished lacing up her Nikes and dug in her money belt. "Here's four hundred FEC." Two hundred dollars. "But only do it if you can get one-forty."

he masses were still twisting their pajama-clad bodies. The sidewalk along the river was jammed with these people, and the street next to the sidewalk was jammed with buses jammed with more people. There were no private cars, only a few jammed taxis surrounded by hordes of bicyclists, all of whose handlebar bells appeared to be jammed. Near the river it was a jam factory.

I found a clear spot on the sidewalk and scouted up and down the Pearl. Large ferries overflowing with people and bicycles were plowing through the water in both directions, and in the distance I could see a succession of bridges. A century ago Canton was China's Western trade window, and it still has European markings. Massive brick structures—customs buildings and warehouses—lined the water's edge. A square tower with a clockface at the top of each of its four sides stood watch over the commercial jumble of the dock area. Most things had an old and tattered look; nothing was new.

I turned away from the river and walked through a quiet section of garden paths and red brick buildings—a university campus, green and shaded and pleasant to walk in. Through open windows I saw bustling people arriving at their offices—professors in coats and ties, secretaries in light dresses. Groups of book-clutching students were ambling toward classes. As they passed me, they would stop talking. When I called a greeting, only one responded: "Goo mooreen," he said, and hurried onward.

I came to a void where a building had recently stood. Now, the ground was littered with slabs of broken concrete lanced through by twisted iron rods. On the edge of this ruin were a pile of sand, a crate of sacks labeled PORTLAND CEMENT, and a drum for hand-mixing mortar. A dark-suited man picked through the rubble as though trying to find something he'd lost. He looked up with an embarrassed expression, and then went on as before. He did not ask to change money.

I came to the canal bridge Heidi and Richard had mentioned. Here were more tai-chi crowds, stretching, bending, each person looking so much like the next. In midsidewalk four smirking men squatted around an upturned fruit crate, rocking back and forth in happy laughter, enjoying an early morning card game. Would they soon be going off to work in a commune? My guess: No.

Another man was wading hip deep in the mud-orange canal, tossing out a net and drawing it slowly back in. I stood on the bridge for several minutes with one eye on this fisherman and one eye on the stream of people walking by. The fisherman didn't catch any fish. No one asked me to change money.

I walked along the canal for half a mile, watching the eyes of passersby. Most avoided my gaze altogether. Clusters of office workers standing at regularly spaced intervals peered down the jammed street, looking for overdue buses, each absorbed in his or her own world—worried, I supposed, about the job, the boss, the family, the in-laws, the Party. None were worried about changing money.

The tree-lined avenue was old and worn and unkept. Everywhere were small scraps of litter and chips of rock; two inches of a greasy gray sludge ran in a gutter next to the sidewalk. An old man was emptying a boxful of trash straight into the canal, a futile gesture: no amount of cleaning would make the place sparkle.

Across from the canal a vein of commerce ran along the ground floor of the old and worn buildings that faced the old and worn street. A shirtless young man sold roasted chestnuts from a smoking barrel, the smell mingling exotically with the sweet aromas of several bakeries. I passed food stalls, tea stalls, clothes stores, pharmacies with bunches of herbs and leaves stashed in ancient red bottles, and plucked dead chickens hanging from a wire stretched in front of a butcher shop.

Rising above the ground-floor shops were scores of three- and four-story apartment buildings that made me think of Chicago. Laundry was draped in open windows, and small green plants crowded the outer ledges. The buildings were faded and chipped and crumbling and dusty. I thought: Take away the buses, it's 1910.

Spanning both the canal and the Pearl River was a major bridge—the kind that arcs in the middle like a low rainbow, so that anyone crossing it has to first climb a moderate grade, then descend one. The middle lanes were for buses, but the wide outer lanes, fully half the bridge, were reserved for bicycles. Coming from across the river was an endless tide of bicycle commuters, each pedaling a basic-black government-issue one-speed. They rode eight or nine abreast, packed in so tightly that they seemed to keep each other upright.

I worked my way to a vantage point alongside the railing; thousands upon thousands of riders crested the arc and coasted down toward me. For several moments I stood there enchanted, close enough to tap the nearest rider and topple all of them. The sound of their simple machines, a harmonious flowing and clicking, refreshed me like a mountain stream. The rancor and life-threatening smell of the Western rush hour were still decades away. Instead, this atmosphere was transcendental—several million spokes and wheels and gears, quietly ticking.

There was something else about this scene, something I could not at first put my finger on, and I stood there watching until it hit me: I could see these peoples' eyes! That's what it was! They were naked, these millions, there for any foreigner to come and watch and read into their faces whatever he might. They were not hidden behind windshields and tinted glass, but were out in the open and passing slowly enough so that as they went by I could look right at them. Suddenly I felt uncomfortable, as though I'd been given too intimate a gift. I'd been allowed to stand and peer into the millions of eyes— yet the single face—of China going to work.

Many of the riders glanced over, but only fleetingly; they could not stray for long from their delicate commute. Thousands of black irises flicked at me and then away, and still no one called out to ask if I wanted to change money.

I glanced at my watch. It was only eight-thirty, but already the day was heating up. Keeping to the shade, I strolled back in the direction from which I'd come, past the impatient bus riders, past the pharmacies, the bakeries, the butcher shop. As I again neared the bridge, I noticed a circle of some forty people gathered in the street. Excited voices chopped the sluggish morning air. I stood at the back of the crowd and peered over the tops of people's heads. At the center were two females, one old, short, ugly, and very, very angry, the other young and tall and pretty, with long black braids hanging to her bosom and fat tears rolling down her cheeks.

The old one had a handgrip on the younger's bicep and was berating her. The younger stood with back straight and eyes half-closed, biting her lip, convulsing with sobs. The older was addressing the growing crowd, telling them her grievance, telling them what an awful thing this young one had done. Only once did the younger one resist; at a particular remark she opened her eyes and shook her head: *No, that's not true.*

Members of the crowd called out support for the younger one, but the old woman cut them off with a new burst—seniority being invoked. A majority of the crowd seemed to back her up, calling out the Chinese for "Hear, hear!"

I looked around at the crowd, a mixed bunch—men and women, young and old and in-between. Each was completely involved, cautiously assessing the merits of the case and occasionally yelling out advice. I felt sorry for the girl. Whatever she had done could not have been so bad as to deserve this— to be dragged into people's court at nine in the morning and raked over the coals by an angry old woman. I pictured myself pushing through the crowd and shoving the dumpy one aside. I would offer passage to America, a lifetime of wedded bliss, bubbly offspring. . . . I would . . .

I would do nothing at all. It was not my place. Besides, there was Amy, and my marriage, and . . .

It was time to vote now. The elder still commanded center stage. With minimal enthusiasm she called a short sentence out to the crowd, and a handful of people yelled responses, voting—I thought—in the girl's favor.

Now the old woman shook the girl's bicep, rattling her body. She called to the crowd to voice its disgust, and the crowd responded, yelling out loud cries of condemnation, nearly unanimous. I say *nearly* unanimous because there was at least one person who did not vote. He was standing at my side, unnoticed until this moment. But as the crowd was reaching its peak, I felt an elbow in my ribs and distinctly heard these words: "Want to change money?"

36
BUT AMERICANS, THEY ALWAYS KNOW!

*In the Chinese family system, there is superficial
quiet and calmness and quarreling is frowned upon,
but in reality all is in conflict.*

—TING LING
Quoted in *Women in Modern China* by
Helen Foster Snow (1967)

H
E WAS CHINESE, ABOUT FORTY YEARS OLD, with a knowing look in his
eye. We glanced at each other for the briefest moment, then back
at the women.

"Maybe," I said sideways.

"Come with me."

He turned and walked away down the canal; the noises of the
crowd faded, and were quickly forgotten. For a while the man stayed half a
step ahead of me, not looking back, pretending that our walking this close
to each other was mere coincidence. The people on the sidewalks, still
swaying, paid us no attention.

I checked him out from behind: knit polo shirt, Western slacks, Nike running shoes; and hanging from his shoulder, a brown leather bag. His hair
was twice as long as the popular burr cut, and fashionably shaped. His body
was taller and thicker than the standard Chinese model. He looked, I thought,
like an athlete.

I wondered about his upbeat appearance. An undercover agent? Someone
from the Thought Police? Or was his dapper presentation merely the black
marketeer's badge? I checked my gut. *He is safe.*

We walked briskly in silence for a hundred paces, then turned left around
a corner and started down a wide, less busy street, away from the canal.

"We will walk together," he said, dropping back alongside me. He squeezed a quick smile at me and then looked down at the street. "How much you want to change?"

"One hundred FEC."

"How much you want back?"

"Two-fifty."

"Ooooh!" He glanced up at me. "You're an American?"

"Yes."

"You Americans!" His command of English and the playful tone of his voice put me at ease. "I am a poor man. Why do you want so much money? I can give only one-twenty."

"You can do better than that."

"I can give you one-thirty, maybe. That is all."

"I bet you could give me two hundred."

"No. I cannot. Really. I cannot. Nobody in all of China will give you a pfennig more than one-thirty-five."

"But my friends will laugh at me if I take a pfennig less than one-seventy-five."

"You are a smart man. You know that one-seventy-five is impossible. Absolutely impossible."

"One-thirty-five is also impossible. Unless you can do better than that, sir, I'm afraid we can't do business. The lowest I could possibly go is one-fifty."

"I am sorry, my friend. I wish I could help you."

We walked silently for ten paces.

"But because I like you very much, and because you are today's first customer, and because it is unlucky to lose one's first customer, I will give you a very special price. One-forty."

"One-forty?"

"Yes. One-forty."

"Deal."

"Good," he said. "I will give one-forty. But you must tell me one thing. How do Americans always know where to go, how much to pay? You come so far from your home and you know just what to do. You find the cheap hotel, you find tickets for the train, the boat, you know how much money to take from a poor man like me. You are too smart! I thought maybe you were Swiss. Or Australian. Or German. I can sometimes trade with those people for one-twenty. But Americans, they always know."

It sounded sincere, but maybe it was his standard line. Maybe the top rate had gone up in the last few days and he was trying to sucker me. Either way, I liked him. He was the kind of man one would not mind being cheated by, just a little.

"Tell *me* something," I said. "Why do you speak such good English?"

"Do you think I am Chinese?"

I looked him over again: polo shirt, slacks, Nikes, stylish haircut, strong physique, the spark of literacy in his eyes. Indeed, he did not look like one of the masses, but I sensed a trick.

"Yes. I think you are Chinese."

"Aaahh!" he laughed. "You Americans! Too smart! You are right, I am Chinese—but I was brought up in foreign places. I have seen your good life, and now I cannot be a good Communist. I like Western systems. The Chinese system is no good. You see our streets—they are filthy. Most people here do not know they are filthy. But I have seen your streets—I know the difference."

"Do you have to stay here?"

"My family is here. I have six brothers. I came back to be with them."

"Are you married?"

"Yes, I am a man like all the others. And you? You are not married," he guessed.

"I am married."

"Where is your wife?"

"San Francisco."

"Ah, you Americans. You are too smart! Leave the wife at home. How very clever you are. What is your name?"

I told him.

"My name is Thomas," he said. "Brother Thomas. I am a Christian. I have a Bible with me. Do you like to study the Bible?"

"Well ..."

"Of course you like the Bible. I can always tell a good Christian. You have been baptized. Am I right?"

I stammered.

"It does not matter," he said. "I can tell you are a good Christian. We will study my Bible now. In a minute I will give it to you. Do not open it right away. Take it and hold it for a moment. When you look inside, you will find one hundred and forty yuan. Count them and put them in your pocket. All the time keep talking like we are talking now. Do you understand?"

"I understand."

"Good. After another moment take out your FEC and put them in the Bible. Hold it a while and then give it back to me. Do you understand?"

"I understand."

"Good. We will turn left at this corner."

We made our second left, turning onto a street that ran parallel to the canal and two blocks away. We were the only people here. Brother Thomas began to sing:

"Onward, Christian soldiers, marching as to war ..." His voice was loud and happy. An ox yoked to a wooden cart at the side of the street looked up from the trash pile it was browsing.

Brother Thomas, fidgeting with his shoulder bag, sang a couple more verses—"With the cross of Jeeeeee-sus, going on before ..."—and then, out the side of his mouth, "Americans don't like to sing?"

And suddenly I was singing with this jolly man. "Crowns and thrones may perish, kingdoms rise and wane ..."

A back street in Canton, a sunny Thursday morning in June, trading black-market money with a Chinese Christian—this was all a man could ask for! I might switch places with this Brother Thomas. Let him have my America and my credit cards and television and the freeways full of smoking cars. I would walk back to the canal and find that tall young girl with the braided hair and wipe away her tears and together we would take over Canton's black market.

"... but the church of Jeeee-sus ... constant will remain ..."

Brother Thomas passed me his "Bible"—a thin green pamphlet about forty pages long. The title: "Twenty-one Christian Hymns." Inside was a wad of bills. I palmed them.

"Onward then, ye people, join our happy throng ..."

There were fourteen 10-yuan bills: 140 yuan, people's money. I slipped the foreign-exchange coupons out of my pocket, tucked them into the "Bible," and a moment later passed it back. Brother Thomas took it, held it—blessing it, no doubt—sang one more refrain, "... with the cross of Jeeeee-sus ..." and then, without counting it, put the money into his shoulder bag.

"Praise the Lord," he said.

"Ha-du-du-du!"

"Yes, Hallelujah! I am a good Christian." His voice was full of mirth. "I'm the best damn money changer in all of Guangzhou, or Canton, as you say. God is with me. He protects me."

"Is this dangerous?"

"Not with God watching. But without Him it is very dangerous. The police stop me sometimes, but I won't speak Chinese to them. I pretend I am a tourist. I call a taxi. 'Taxi!' I say. 'Take me to the airport.' The police cannot understand me. They think I am a Japanese tourist with lots of money, and they leave me alone."

"What would they do if they really caught you?"

He drew a finger across his throat.

"Really?"

"Yes. Really."

"What would they do to me?"

"Send you home."

We walked in silence for a moment, and then Brother Thomas began to spout the Lord's Prayer. "Our father, which art in heaven—"

I interrupted. "What do you do with the money?"

"When I leave you, I will meet my brother at the next corner and give him the money. He will go to another corner and give it to another brother, who will take it home. Then, if the police stop me, they will find nothing. Even if I have ten thousand yuan in people's money, it is okay. But if I have FEC, they will make trouble."

"But what do you *do* with it?"

"I buy Western things at the friendship store and sell them to Chinese people for more money. When I get enough, I will buy a motorcycle. A Yamaha Seven-fifty. You know it? It will be the first one in Guangzhou. Vroom, vrooooom!" He laughed, and gripped imaginary handlebars. "Now we turn left again. Soon we will be back where I met you."

"Those two ladies? What were they arguing about?"

"The old lady was the girl's grandmother. She says the girl is selfish."

"That was all?"

"That was all."

At the corner we made our third left turn (The Man 100 Miles Up would see us tracing a square), and suddenly we were in a narrow alley, a dirt marketplace crowded with squealing piglets and live chickens. Fruit and vegetable stands overflowed with cherry tomatoes, green bananas, crimson chile peppers, mounds of melons, bushels of peanuts. Slabs of fly-covered pork hung from hooks. Peasant farmers crowded the cramped alleyway, haggling and recoiling in shock at the sight of me. Vintage Third World.

Brother Thomas led the way through the throng. "Do you have any friends who would like to study Bible with me?" he called over his shoulder.

"Is it okay to speak English here?"

He snorted. "Nobody understands one word we say. They understand only chickens and pigs."

"I have more money to change, but it's back in my room."

"How much?"

"Eight hundred in FEC. Can you do that?"

"Of course. Why did you not bring it?"

"This was my first time. I didn't know if I would meet a thief or a good Christian like you."

"Aaaah, you Americans!" he screamed. "Too smart. Too smart."

37

IN CHINA, ON A SLOW BOAT.

*I'd love to get you
On a slow boat to China,
All to myself,
Alone.*

*Out on the briny,
With a moon
Big and shiny,
Melting your heart of stone.*

—FRANK LOESSER
"Slow Boat to China"

A DOZEN WESTERNERS WERE SPRINKLED among the hundreds of Chinese crowding the dock in Canton, waiting to board the boat up the Gui River. Our ultimate destination was Yangshuo, a small town of renowned scenery only two hundred air miles northwest of Canton. Getting there, however, was a proposition that involved a combination of boat and bus travel that would last nearly thirty hours but cost less than ten dollars.

The boat—it looked like a small troop ship salvaged from the first World War—would drift south down the Pearl River (briefly heading back toward Hong Kong), make a right turn onto the Gui, and take us upriver, west and north, to the small town of Wuzhou. Amy continuously mispronounced it— "Wa-zoo"—but she'd tolerated my "Honk Honk" for so long that after a while I quit correcting her. At Wuzhou the Gui would become a river of untamed rapids, narrow canyons, hidden boulders, and twisting currents, and we would become bus riders.

It was truly a people's boat—four hundred passengers, one class of travel. The middle of each deck (there were two) had a small common area with folding chairs and a snack stand. Huge wooden platforms—giant two-tiered bunk beds—ran the length of the ship, and were divided by removable wooden slats into individual "sleeping spaces" two feet wide and long enough, just barely, for me to lie down flat. At the head of each sleeping space was a window. "A ventilated morgue," Amy said.

Even though all of us had purchased tickets at different times, we Westerners found ourselves bunched; the Chinese policy was becoming clear—Us and Them. On one side of me were two women from Calgary, Canada; on the other was Amy, and beyond her was a mixture of young Europeans. We settled in, arranging packs, nodding hellos, making "apartheid" jokes, and sharing the ripple of excitement that accompanies the start of any adventure.

It was noon. We were due to arrive in Wuzhou at six the next morning. Eighteen hours of fun. Four of the Europeans—two braless women in tank tops and two shirtless men—immediately removed the slats separating them and broke out a pack of cards. Biscuits and fifty-cent beers were bought from the snack stand, and a rowdy game of hearts was dealt out. A loudspeaker spat out several announcements in Chinese and then played hours of loud wailing music—People's Republic Top 40. The Chinese across the way, nearly all of them men, sat trancelike in a row on the top bunk, legs dangling, faces set, eyes fixed on the card game. Whenever one of the Westerners—especially one of the braless women—got up to walk around, scores of eyes followed. The men appeared to be country folk heading back upriver after coming to Canton for supplies. Who could blame them for gawking? It might be months or years before they again saw bleached people, and they wanted to remember each confusing detail.

For a while I talked with the Canadian women—a banker and a nurse, midthirties, on a six-month tour, traveling mainly by bicycle and eager for information on the Japanese Alps. We swapped travel stories and bits of intelligence about the route ahead.

A midafternoon torpor spread over the boat. Amy thumped me in a game of chess. The card game faded away. The Westerners took to napping or reading or writing in journals. The Chinese practiced staring.

But the main event was outside. Baking in steamy heat, real, live China was drifting past our windows. The Gui was not a river but a rusty-brown soup afloat with junks, sampans, houseboats, coal barges. Near Canton towns and factories had dominated the shore, but now the agricultural world had taken over. Rows of banana trees, fields of grain and corn and vegetables, tumbled down the levees right to water's edge—"fencerow to fencerow."

Naked boys swam in the river, splashing at a rubber tire, then climbing onto a raft to stand at nude, innocent attention as we slid past. I waved. They didn't. On shore more boys, clothed and not so innocent, threw rocks that splashed fifty yards short of our boat. Pastoral scenes dotted the levees: a bicyclist bumping along a rutted path; a woman beating laundry on a rock; a boy with a stick swatting a reluctant bullock; a peasant staggering in the sun beneath the familiar barbell of buckets. In the water a crude canoe with sail hoisted at the bow was fighting the current. In the stern a ragged sailor with straw hat pulled at twin oars. Even with sail raised, he was barely breaking even.

There was tapping on my shoulder. I pulled my head back inside.

"This is amazing," Amy said.

Across the aisle the Chinese were staring.

In the late afternoon a man from the small kitchen below deck came to collect half a yuan (twenty-five cents) from anyone wanting a cooked dinner. An hour later he returned with huge bowls of rice and beans and pork scraps. I saw bowl after bowl of it being tossed out the window, and not only by the Westerners. "*Chinese* food is not like *Chinese food*," Amy said. I unwrapped the chopsticks she had given me, gift wrapped, as we left Hong Kong, and picked timidly at my food. The itch was gone from my throat, but who was the last person to use my bowl? How had it been washed? Finally I emptied it out the window and joined the line at the snack counter, but before I reached the front all the beer and biscuits were sold out.

I crawled back into my sleeping space and stuck my head out the window, escaping the kitchen smells and the sour odors of four hundred people packed together. A breeze had cooled the air. The dying sun splashed a purple tint on sagging cloud bottoms. The wide plains of the afternoon had disappeared; tall mountain ridges crowded in. As the river narrowed, we got a look at homes on the banks, primitive buildings with tiled roofs and bricks of mud. White pagodas—Buddhist shrines, I presumed—appeared along the shore at frequent intervals. *Red China?* I had anticipated a godless country-side divvied into busy work units and ordered production cells, but the reality was different. All was tranquil, unhurried, haphazard.

Where are the communes? I asked my notebook. *Where are the Communists?* A Japanese expert ten days ago, I was once again a cultural illiterate.

The boat pulsed onward. The sun sinking behind the mountains ahead of us threw horizontal rays of light that highlighted silent waterfall wisps on the steep green hills. On upper slopes, faint foot trails, like veins, joined together a network of planted fields.

Ellie, the Canadian next door, stuck her head outside. "Want some company?" A fingernail clipping of new moon had appeared. Stars were popping out. Twenty feet below, the river rushed by, fading into blackness as Ellie told about life in Calgary, about the job she quit, the marriage that had fell apart. Traveling had renewed her, she said. The strength she had acquired while battling through Asia was her most valuable asset. "I'm going to do something like this every other year or so for the rest of my life. If you don't get out with the masses, go places where you can't speak the language or drink the water, you lose all perspective on yourself. You begin to think the life you live at home is the life everyone lives."

It was night. At intervals the boat's captain blasted a warning signal and swept a blinding searchlight across the inky river. The loudspeaker, which had been turned off around dinnertime, came back on with an announce-ment, followed by soft Chinese lullabies and then the English song "Rivers of Babylon." The Chinese began unrolling mats and bedrolls; the Westerners took the hint. There were the sounds of teeth being brushed and noisy spitting out the windows. The inside lights dimmed.

During our chess game Amy and I had removed the board separating us and had never replaced it. Now we lay next to each other, bodies brushing, talking in gentle voices about how glad we were that things had worked out the way they had. Dylan had run off with my wife, and no one was going to go looking for them. Reality was a bowl of rice and beans and pork scraps, and a slow ride up the Gui River. We were far from home, free of our pasts, free of everything and everybody. Life is wonderful, no?

And then we were quiet. I lay on my back and looked at the stars being drawn past my window by invisible strings. The noise of the engine and the rasp of nearby snorers were the only sounds. I thought about Amy. Our infatuation had cooled, hardening into friendship. Ten days earlier, we were strangers; now, we counted on and looked out for one another, shared wins and losses, kept track of each other's moods. She was an easy traveling partner—independent, flexible, good with others, and had a sense of humor similiar to my own. We *had* become "buddies." Who could tell? Maybe if I did wind up divorced ... Yeah, who could tell?

I reached out a hand and began massaging her neck and head. She had almost been asleep, but now she began purring. I purred back and kept massaging.

She murmured something I couldn't hear. I opened one eye to look at her. A Chinese man was standing in the dim light of the open area, watching us. I ignored him.

"What'd you say?" I asked Amy.

Her eyes were closed over an easy smile. In a soft and distant voice: "That feels wonderful ..." A moment later: "Is it okay if I fall asleep?"

"Sure."

Later, when my hand wore out, I left my arm resting on her back, my fingers twisted in the hair at the base of her neck. She didn't stir. I lay there a while, listening to the boat throb, inventorying life. Now and then I popped open an eye just to check on the Chinese man. He was still there, hypnotized.

Drifting toward sleep, I pulled my arm back and shifted away from Amy.

She stirred and moaned. We looked at each other, smiling weakly. In China. On a slow boat.

"Do you want a kiss?"

"Mmmnnnn," she said.

We did a little peck on the lips, and then I rolled away from her. She turned on her side and drew near from behind. She laid an arm across my back.

"Is that okay?" she asked.

"That's great ..."

I fell asleep with her arm lying over me. For a while I was aware that her fingers were stirring softly, stroking the skin over my ribs ...

girl who had sold us our tickets was standing at the door smiling. "Up," she said, and waved at our backpacks. I climbed the ladder at the rear, lashed our gear to the rusted luggage rack, and tied a tarp over it. Before climbing down, I looked at the view. It was one of the few times on my trip that I wished for a camera. In the streets below were hundreds of Chinese. Vendors were selling pastries and drinks, but most of the people were just watching. At the far end of the pier was our small boat, rocking gently, now looking exhausted, shrunken, absolutely incapable of carrying four hundred passengers anywhere. A chain of shoeless coolies were unloading burlap bundles. Beyond was the river, flowing wide and brown from the distant heart of China. Spikes of gentle light poked through low gray clouds. In the air the smell of rain fought the smell of garlic. Another morning in the Third World ...

The horn blew loudly, and the bus vibrated beneath me. I climbed down. Amy had grabbed double seats for each of us in the first row behind the driver. As I was settling in, he was blowing the horn again. *Buuu-ahh! Buuu-ahh!* At first I thought he was impatient to start, but later I realized he was just excited. Here was a man who loved his job: it had granted him parole from a life sentence in Wuzhou, freed him from a career on the docks, and now he was celebrating, using the horn to gloat over and terrorize those he'd left behind. He spent the next ten minutes shattering the peaceful morning calm—*Buuu-ahh! Buuu-ahh!*—and occasionally turning around to grin at Amy and me or deliver a Chinese monologue. Six A.M.

The "Deluxe Luxury" bus departed ten minutes ahead of us, fully loaded. Our bus left two-thirds full—six Westerners, sixteen Chinese—rattling like a rolling hardware store through Wuzhou's rutted streets. Three kids floating toy boats in one of the larger potholes refused to scatter until the driver blasted them aside. *Buuu-ahh! Buuu-ahh!* If the bus was his savior, the horn was his prayer wheel, and during the day he proved to be a dedicated worshiper. In town, during one 60-second span, he squeezed off forty-seven distinct and separate salvos. During another sixty seconds in the countryside I counted seventeen blasts. My notebook: *If that horn breaks, I know he'll refuse to drive.*

Lounging in a homemade cot opposite the driver was another person— an apprentice driver? a Horn Repair Academy graduate? He wore a faded white tank top, loose pants that were once possibly blue, and hair that was buzzed into a short flattop. His bare feet were propped on the dash. In a country where per-capita income is less than thirty dollars a month, he wore an impressive silver wristwatch.

Buuu-ahh! Buuu-ahh! The driver blew a mother and daughter off the road and glanced proudly over at Wristwatch. They guffawed and then resumed their animated discussion of, I presumed, the works of Confucius and Lao-tzu sprinkled with the aphorisms of Chairman Mao.

I couldn't take my attention off this pair, particularly Wristwatch. He had the workman's cocky confidence and sense of clear purpose, and seemed perfectly content with his role—as though there was nowhere else he'd rather be, as though he actually *was* in exactly the right place, thinking, doing, and feeling exactly the right things. I became lost in thought about his life. What was the source of his carefree, happy-go-lucky manner? Was he married? religious? a Communist? Was he *really* content? He seemed full of life, full of himself. He was almost always grinning, and nearly every comment he made to the driver elicited a chuckle. They were the prototype Third World bus-driving team, and in a simple way I envied them.

39

AN IMAGINATIVE MENU

China was proud now—of herself and of her potential. She had pulled herself to dignity and unity and that spirit literally pervaded the communes, the backbone of China. The Chinese countryside was where the revolution was won and the countryside was the secret of China's future.

—SHIRLEY MACLAINE
You Can Get There from Here

THE ROAD TO YANGSHOU CURLED AND TWISTED through a series of low mountain ranges whose names I didn't try to learn. It was enough to know that we'd left the coastal plains and were now in the mountains of southern China, heading for somewhere I'd never been.

On the downhills the driver switched off the power, saving gas by coasting. He tried to straighten each curve with his horn. *Buuu-ahh! Buuu-ahh!* He sent animals and bicyclists and people on foot leaping from our path, as though they had no right at all to be there. *Buuu-ahh! Buuu-ahh!* After every confrontation he would glance sideways at Wristwatch and snicker.

Emerald fields, tall with grain, bordered the narrow, unmarked highway. A deep stream the green color of army fatigues snaked alongside the roadbed. Light rain started to fall; beads of water formed on the windshields. I wondered, Do the wipers work? Does Wristwatch fix wipers? or just horns?

Outside, countless peasants were sliding into clear plastic ponchos and chin-strapping their straw hats. In the valleys these peasants were everywhere: stacking bricks, herding flocks of tottering ducks, flogging bullocks, toting barbells, washing in the stream, riding bicycles along the highway—*buuu-ahh! buuu-ahh!*—or squatting in idle roadside gangs.

The road looked as if it had been shelled during some recent war and never fixed. *How does the work get assigned?* I asked my notebook. *Where are the Red Guards?* There were no visible signs of authority or regimentation or coercion, just a vast countryside of war-damaged villages and thriving fields worked by peasants for whom the words *Industrial Revolution* had no meaning. All looked sleepy, uncaring, oblivious.

At around ten o'clock we stopped at the Third World prototype bus station. The driver came bursting—*buuu-ahh! buuu-ahh!*—into a small village of overhanging trees and two hundred mud-brick homes. He tipped sharply into a circular drive and squealed to rest beneath a giant banyan tree, blew the horn several times—*buuu-ahh-buuu-ahh! buuu-ahh-buuu-ahh!*—turned around with a big smile, and held up all his fingers. Ten minutes.

A wooden refreshment stand offered unlabeled bottles of carbonated sugar water. Amy treated me to a red one and chose a green one for herself: eleven cents each. The woman at the stall offered us small red fruits, like apples, but we weren't buying. The guidebooks had warned us.

"Those are fertilized with human waste," Amy said, joking with the woman. "We know."

The woman grinned. We grinned. The instant crowd around us grinned. The whole town grinned. The world grinned.

There was not much to grin about at the Third World prototype toilet. Bombed during the war, ignored by the Cultural Revolution, it was in a state of crumbled disrepair. I thought: *Those* things!

The last person to use the place had left a dark turd on the rim of the drain hole. I tried to piss it down into oblivion. The first jet raised a swarm of previously invisible flies which buzzed annoyedly, levitated briefly, and then resettled nearby to watch and await the outcome. After token resistance the turd gave up and slid down the drain, half an inch at a time, as though crawling.

In the distance, a horn was blowing. . . .

he rain had stopped. Through my streaked window I watched the world pass: fields yellowing with ripeness; a muzzled water buffalo; wiry men with rocklike biceps, wearing red tank tops dark with sweat. An open meeting hall with squiggle-character notices posted on the walls outside. A naked three-year-old boy waving at the bus. A lone sunflower, nine feet tall, winking at me from behind a stone wall. On bicycles, straining men and women dwarfed by their loads—mountainous stacks of rushes and bundles of sticks. Wristwatch was driving now. *Buuu-ahh! Buuu-ahh!* No improvement.

The first driver was chain-smoking hand-rolled cigarettes, which he kept in a black plastic coin purse on the dash. When he leaned forward to reach for one, he would sneak a look back at Amy, sleeping on the seat across the aisle from me, head bouncing against the window.

The air-conditioned tour bus was about half an hour ahead of us now. When we stopped for lunch, we saw its distant glint and breathed the cloud of dust raised by its departure. (Later we learned that the air-conditioner quit fifteen minutes out of Wuzhou.) Wristwatch pulled the bus into a mud-walled courtyard, and grinned. *Welcome to the Third World prototype diner.* Inside the courtyard was a mud-brick hut with tin roof, wobbly tables, a barefoot waitress, Afghani health standards, and an imaginative menu. The "very pork and tomatoes," was a very disappointment. I stripped the one piece of flesh from the pork bone, fished a few tomato slices from the oil slick, and ordered the "very egg fried beef."

Wristwatch and the first driver held court at the next table, entertaining the locals with stories of how they'd captured the strange foreigners. An Australian couple who had been sitting in the back of the bus joined Amy and me. As we laughed about the food—"*Chinese* food is not like *Chinese food!*"—and traded résumés, it became apparent that the Australians had briefly crossed paths with Amy in Switzerland a year earlier, when they spent a night in the hotel where she worked. And now in China we ate what we could, drank hot tea, and marveled at the miniature thing the world has become.

40
THE EMERGING CHINA

Travelers are vital to this planet the way blood is vital to your body. When a body is ill—diseased or parched or withered—the job of doctor, masseuse, or therapist is to improve the circulation of blood to the afflicted area. I say that a healthy flow of Travelers (travelers—not tourists; tourists never visit diseased places) will work better than anything else to heal the sick, impoverished, illiterate, malnourished parts of our world.

—LANCE FREE
The Art of Tripping

HE SKY HAD CLEARED SO COMPLETELY that the morning's rain now seemed like a mistake. The first driver was back in the saddle, and both the horn and the afternoon were heating up. Wristwatch offered me a cigarette, rolled his pant legs up over his knees, rigged a curtain across his window, glanced back at dozing Amy, winked at me, turned around, and went to sleep.

Most of the passengers were napping. In the back the Australians were catching flies; all of the Chinese were unconscious. Only two people were talking. In the row behind me a fortyish man from New Jersey, dressed as if he had wandered away from an optometrists' convention (clean knit sport shirt, gray tweed slacks, black tie shoes), was explaining to an English punk rocker (nose ring, and red hair so short it was a coat of rust) that he had spent eleven months in the Philippines, then six in Taiwan learning Mandarin, and would now spend three more in China. I made a mental note to investigate.

The scenery was getting dramatic. Shrub-covered rock formations—pillarlike, several hundred feet tall—were poking through the surrounding fields. All askew, no two alike, they gave the region the look of a graveyard after an earthquake.

The road surface was marked now with fat, evenly spaced dung bombs, and lined with eucalyptus trees, rice paddies, and fields of cornstalks five and six feet high. At the top of every pass was a squatting tea seller. *Buuu-ahh! Buuu-ahh!* We passed a platoon of marching school kids—boys and girls with hoes and shovels and plenty of work to do.

Amy awoke from her nap, looked out the window a while, leaned across the aisle, touched my forearm. "Why are we on this bus, and not out there in a field scratching out a living?"

"You got me."

"Hey, are you sweating?"

"I am a little warm."

"A fever?"

"No, no—it's just hot out here. Aren't you hot?"

"Not like you, but I bet those guys are."

Outside we were coming onto a road-construction project—one hundred men with picks and shovels and sledgehammers. Huge white boulders, delivered by dump truck, were being smashed apart by hand. Men with wheelbarrows transported smaller rocks to the new roadbed; an antique steam roller crushed them flat. The driver was not impressed. *Buuu-ahh-buuu-ahh! Buuu-ahh-buuu-ahh!*

A peasant riding a bicycle three hundred yards ahead heard our bus coming, pulled to the shoulder, and dismounted. As we drew near, I saw he had the vacant look of the dimwit. The driver swung right toward him. *Buuu-ahh-buuu-ahh! Buuu-ahh-buuu-ahh!*

Dimwit's eyes widened in terror. At the last minute the driver swung back. Driver looks at Wristwatch. Hearty laughter.

The emerging China?

I asked the optometrist what he was doing with his life.

"Oh, I've had lots of different jobs."

Like what?

"Oh, I worked in a hospital, I worked landscaping, I was a gardener, I've been a teacher."

What was he doing in Taiwan for three months and the Philippines for eleven?

"Teaching."

English?

"Yes. And the Bible."

The Bible as history or the Bible as religion?

"Religion."

Did the religion have a label?

His eyes rolled. He took a deep breath. He hadn't told this tale for at least a couple of days:

"When I was a young boy, God appeared to me and told me to teach the Bible. But he didn't tell me who to teach it to. So wherever I am, I teach it to whoever is around. In the Philippines it was mostly Catholics. In Fiji it was Methodists. In Taiwan it was Episcopalians. In the Solomon Islands it was Anglicans."

What about the vision? How did it go?

"I've had it several times in my life. The sky opens up and I see Jesus sitting on the throne in heaven."

Is it in color?

He smiled. *These laymen* . . . "No, it's not like that. I don't see Him the way I see you. I feel His presence around me. Sometimes when my eyes are closed, He touches my hands with His." He held up his palms as though to play patty-cake. "He tells me He loves me and that He's always nearby to support me. Several times I have been able to transmit His power to others—to have It come through me and hit them directly." Behind his glasses his watery blue eyes widened and bored into mine. "Sometimes when the Lord works through me, people have visions. By myself I can do nothing, but with Him sometimes things happen. I have been fasting and teaching for many years now, and I'm hoping to do some big miracles soon."

Had there been any miracles so far?

"Only small ones. Now I want to do some big ones." His voice was solemn, his expression joyless. "I'd really like to see the dead rise." He paused to let this sink in. "I think maybe here in China it can happen. The time is right."

I thought: How about starting lower, down around zapping a fever, or bringing a marriage back from the grave? But I held my tongue.

Did he travel a lot?

His eyes went into his forehead again. He forced a dim smile. "It's been almost three years this time."

Was it as it appeared? Did he want to go home?

"Yes. I've been away so long. I'm nothing but skin and bones now." He shrugged. "After China I may spend a month in Israel, but then I'm going home."

Once uncorked, he did not close back up easily. "We don't have much time left, anyway. We're sitting on twenty-five different time bombs—Iran, Iraq, South Africa, Afghanistan, all of Asia, the debt situation. I really think there's not much time left. The end is near." He paused, then said it again: "The end is near."

He waited for me to ask another question, but when I didn't, he plowed ahead. "I've known all of this for a long time now. I was a conscientious objector when I was a young man. I was out at Stanford during Vietnam and got drafted. Have you heard of David Harris? He married Joan Baez, and then she divorced him. That was sad. He and I were at Stanford at the same time."

What happened when he was drafted?

"They told us all to step forward, over the line. I refused. The FBI was there. They came over to me and said, 'We really don't want to send you to prison. Let's not make this a big thing.' Some of the other guys there, like David Harris, made it a big thing. They went to jail for five years. I didn't want to put my family through that. I spent two years doing alternative service, working in a hospital." He hesitated. "Sometimes I wonder if all of this is doing any good. It seems like I've been doing the Lord's work for an awfully long time." He sighed heavily and looked out the window.

Outside the sun had burned off all the clouds; a hot breeze blew in through the windows. The bus slowed as we entered a generic small, dusty town. *Buuu-ahh! Buuu-ahh!* In the center of town was another mammoth banyan tree, a mob of Chinese lounging in its shade. We stopped. The driver held up one finger.

I went to the tea stall. The owner pointed to his cups. I shook my head. He pointed to a short stack of flat bread, black with crawling flies. Without disturbing the flies, he lifted the top two pieces, pulled out the third, and extended it to me. When I declined that, he had nothing else to offer.

A peasant boarded the bus as we were pulling out. He held a short conversation with Wristwatch and sat down next to me. He had a string bag filled with long green beans and a slab of fresh meat, fat mostly, sitting at the bottom. The beans kept falling through the bag's holes, and Amy kept picking them off the floor and handing them back to him. At the next stop she received a reward; the peasant bought two popsicles from a boy who shoved them through the open window, and gave one to Amy. I wondered briefly about the water from which it had been made, but when Amy held it to my lips I took a big bite. It was cold and fruity, and felt great sliding down my throat.

The peasant now began to lecture us on the countryside. He pointed at a woman leading an ox, and spoke in a burst of Chinese. Wristwatch laughed at him, but our new guide wasn't swayed; he pointed at a field and cupped his hands. "Melons," I said, and made a slurping noise. His face wrinkled like an accordion. He jabbered and bobbed his head from side to side.

I tried to imagine myself in this man's body, my consciousness centered between his temples, behind his eyeballs. Did he read or write? Had he ever seen a real city? Did he know of Nixon's visit? of Reagan's? Did he understand "American tourist"? Did he think Amy and I were "rich capitalists?" Were we?

In a few minutes he began gathering up his things. Amy retrieved three stray beans and returned them. The man pointed at a mountain several hundred yards from the road, then to himself. "That's where he lives," Amy said. The man grinned. The bus was slowing. He stood outside for a moment, waving his hand at us. As we pulled away, I watched him for as long as possible, sloshing through a rice paddy, bag full of beans and meat fat slung over his shoulder, on the way home to tell his wife about the foreigners he met on the bus.

41
STUCK
WITH
A PIG DAGGER

*. . . On fine days they bathe in the sunlight;
in the rainy season they are in the misty rain; in
the morning the glory casts upon them; at dusk
the mountain haze enwraps them—all in all, they
are colorful and in different postures, and make
you feel intoxicant.*

—A Chinese brochure describing the towering
limestone formations around Yangshuo

THERE WERE NO FIRST-CLASS HOTELS IN YANGSHUO. There were no second- or third-class hotels either, but a couple of places did take backpackers. Amy and I stayed at a remodeled villa that formerly belonged to one of the rich people Yangshuo has seen come and go during the thousand years of its history. Our $2.75 room had an overhead fan, thin mosquito netting, fat mosquitoes, weak light bulbs, and a giant green canister that the staff kept full of scalding tea water. Down the hall were toilets that backed up with stinky excrement two days out of three, and outside was a shower that, when working, trickled cold water.

Richard Nixon came to see Yangshuo's wondrous scenery in 1972, but for lack of a good hotel the Chinese took him to Guilin, sixty-five kilometers away, to spend the night. Even now, the only foreigners staying in Yangshuo were backpackers, and a small service network had sprung up to cater to them. The tiny Yellow Lotus Café had an English menu and a steady Western clientele; the owners of motor launches offered cheap boat rides along the bluffs and steeples of the winding Li River; and bicycles could be rented for one yuan per day.

Each morning, huge tour groups arrived by boat or bus from Guilin. The tourists snapped pictures of each other with the cliffs towering in the background, and raided Yangshuo's riverside shops for "genuine scroll paintings," "antique" knickknacks, and T-shirts that said "I Love Yangshuo." But for all this, the town seemed authentic. When afternoon came and the boats and tourists headed back to Guilin, Yangshuo resumed its timeless pace. A day there was a series of bucolic images: an exploded watermelon lying in the gritty street, seeds and juice and pink meat staining the dust; a bullock pulling a cartload of cabbages; two laughing boys chasing a frantic chicken.

Still, I sensed something unsettling about Yangshuo. At first I mistook it for grinding poverty, but it wasn't that; the people were all well fed and healthy looking, yet seemed to lack fundamental human curiosity. They were either unnaturally polite or overly distant. I guessed that those who worked with foreigners had been coached on how to act, the rest warned to keep their distance. People walking past the Yellow Lotus Café glanced inside as though expecting to glimpse a murder in progress, and then scurried onward, faces bent to the ground.

I felt there was a secret I was not being let in on, that a battle was waiting to break out if only we white witnesses would leave. I wanted to talk this over with someone, but contacts with English-speaking Chinese were very limited. The waitress at the Yellow Lotus Café communicated by giggling and pointing at the menu. The lady at the hotel desk knew six or seven lines, which she repeated over and over:

"Bicycles are one yuan per day."

"Shower is being repaired—maybe try later."

"No people's money! You must pay FEC."

I considered myself fortunate to meet Yang Di, a launch owner who approached Amy and me at the café and spoke English. After we settled on the time and price of a boat ride, our conversation drifted to the Cultural Revolution, the landmark event in the lives of the few Chinese I did talk to.

"I was eight years old in 1968," Yang Di said. "I remember those times. Mao said the old leaders should not have power anymore. The students should have power. The Red Guard made the old leaders go into the fields and work like peasants. Then there was fighting. In the next town hundreds were killed." He stood and pointed out "Yangmeiping" on the wall map. "I did not see that, but I know it happened. Here in Yangshuo many people were led in processions through the streets. They were made to wear a hat. The hat meant they were bad people. After the processions they were killed. Sometimes they were shot with guns. Yes, against a wall. Other times they were stuck with a pig dagger." Yang Di jammed an imaginary blade into his heart and died. "I was eight years old. I saw this many times."

"Where are the Red Guard today?" I asked.

"They are no more. They have no more organization."

"But where are the *people* who were in the Red Guard?"

Yang Di's eyes darted up to the ceiling, down to the floor.

"Is it okay to talk about this?" I asked.

"Yes, yes. It is okay. The Red—"

Just then another launch owner tapped Yang Di on the shoulder.

"I must go," he said. "Something about my boat. I will come back."

But he didn't.

The next day Amy and I went for a bike ride. The plan was to cycle downriver through the fields and limestone towers, to the small village of Fu-Li, where Yang Di's "steersman" would be waiting to give us a lift back.

In the midst of the countryside's storybook scenery it was not 1910, but 1019: heating and cooking were done with wood; rocks to build roads and homes were hauled in baskets; bicycles and bullocks were the transportation system, watermelon and tea stalls the fast-food outlets; still groups of people—adults, children, whimpering babies—squatted under trees, waiting ...

The village of Fu-Li was half a pace this side of the Stone Age: crooked cobblestone alleys meandered between homes of mud and sticks; mute peasants—"Cave people," Amy whispered—squinted out at us from smoky interiors; a hybrid cart—wooden deck, rubber tires—rumbled by with a load of firewood; a mangy gray dog woofed at us and slunk away; a naked baby boy crawled through a brackish puddle; the entire village was foul with a urine stench. Beneath the stone towers lining the Li river, silent women thrashed wet pajamas on the rocks. The Li, brown and confident, eased its way among the looming ramparts. Bamboo trees thirty and forty feet tall sprouted along the banks like giant lime-colored ostrich feathers, bowing gently in the midday agitation of heat and air. The overgrown ruins of an ancient village lurked in the jungle, awaiting the arrival of modern China. In the nearby water naked children splashed at a buffalo. Beached on a spit of sand was Yang Di's boat; the steersman sat with his feet up, patiently waiting.

We were silent on the ride back. On the launch with us were our bicycles and eight Chinese. The steersman's little girl sat across from me, skirt raised and legs spread, showing me her wrinkled four-year-old thing. A screaming boy ran around the boat, beating his fists on his mother and grandmother. A man tied his canoe to our little boat, and later, when our engine burped and died, he poled us to shore. The embarrassed steersman cursed and dismantled the engine. His hands were soon black with grease, his expression pained. This was his livelihood; if he couldn't fix the engine, Yang Di might find another steersman. He pounded on the disassembled engine with a cooking pot, then put it back together. It sputtered and caught. For the next hour we held our breaths. The engine chattered and whined and beat itself toward death, but made it back to Yangshuo.

42
I'M ACTING STUPID

I have finally kum to the konklusion, that a good reliable sett ov bowels iz wurth more tu a man, than enny quantity ov brains.

—JOSH BILLINGS
His Sayings, 1865

"ARE YOU MAD AT ME, BRAD?"

We were back in our room on our respective beds, underneath our respective mosquito nettings, ceiling fan thumping the dead air.

"Mad at you? No. Why?"

"You've gotten awfully distant."

"Sorry. I'm not feeling so great. Didn't know it showed."

"Your throat still?"

"Yeah, and walking back from the boat I was dizzy. I hallucinated I was twenty feet above us, looking down."

"Oh. You were so quiet I thought I'd done something wrong."

"Well ..."

"What?"

"Nothing you've done. But I am jealous."

"Dylan?"

"No, no, no. Whenever I travel I watch what I eat and drink, but it never seems to matter. Ten years ago I lost thirty-five pounds in Morocco. Dysentery. As soon as I got over that, I went to Afghanistan and nearly died from hepatitis. In India I got worms that didn't go away till months after I got back."

"Are you kidding?"

"I wish I were. My wife says I get sick if someone whispers 'Third World'

166

within half a mile of me. And now I get to China and don't even last twenty-four hours. So when I see people like you and her eat whatever they want and stay perfectly healthy, it pisses me off. Why can't I do that? Yes, I'm angry—but it's not at you."

"Why didn't you tell me all that before?"

"Didn't want to be a crybaby."

"Well, how bad is it?"

"My throat hurts all the time now, and you've seen me blowing my nose. Probably just a cold, but something's going on."

Amy worked out of her netting and went to the door. "Hang on. I'll be right back. Anything I can get you?"

"Air-conditioning, a hard bed, clean sheets. And a big bowl of chicken-noodle soup."

She shut the door. *Going to get a damp washcloth.* During two awful days of Delhi belly, my wife had paid constant attention to my forehead. *Thank God for women.*

Amy came back emptyhanded. "I asked at the desk if they have a doctor ... "

"Let me guess: 'Shower is being repaired—maybe try later.' "

"They have an acupuncture guy who doesn't speak English."

"I don't do needles. All I need is a little rest."

"We don't have to leave tomorrow. We can stay a couple days and let you ride it out."

"Nah. We're done here. We should get moving. Dylan's going to meet you where—Guilin?"

"Beijing, probably. But that's not as important as your health."

"I'll be okay. Maybe you should just go on ahead. I could stay a few days. Meet you in Beijing or something."

" 'Leave me here to die'—right?" She was disgusted. *"You* wouldn't leave *me* here."

There is no resentment so profound, so twisted, as the sick person's envy of the well. "You're right. I'm acting stupid. Look, I'll take a nap. When it cools off later, I'll go for a long bike ride and sweat whatever it is out. Tomorrow I'll be fine. We'll go to Guilin and catch that night train. By the time we hit Beijing, I'll be myself again. Promise."

43
IN
A FIELD
BY THE RIVER

You might as well expect the rivers to run backwards as that any man who was born free should be contented penned up and denied liberty to go where he pleases . . .

Let me be a free man—free to travel, free to stop, free to work, free to trade where I choose, free to choose my own teachers, free to follow the religion of my fathers, free to think and talk and act for myself—and I will obey every law or submit to the penalty.

—CHIEF JOSEPH, an American Indian,
addressing a group of Cabinet members
and congressmen in 1879

SUNSET WAS FORTY-FIVE MINUTES AWAY, and the street was busy with people heading home from work. I nosed my bike into the traffic in front of the hotel, and fell in alongside a young Chinese man who was riding in my same direction at exactly my speed. From the corner of my eye I saw him look at me two or three times; I expected him to gawk a while, then disappear, but he stayed right with me. In a moment I sensed his presence attach to mine.

Our misshapen shadows stretched out ahead, long and thin on the dusty pavement. A dump truck was stopped in the middle of the road, hood up, and together we veered around it. We came to a fork, the last turnoff in town; ahead was the bridge over the Li River, beyond that was the countryside. He did not turn off.

In the middle of the bridge, clearly and gently, he said, "Hello."

I supposed he was one of those tourist-area residents who has accidentally learned two or three English buzzwords, but he surprised me. When I said hello, he said: "How are you?"

I glanced over at him. "I'm fine. How are you?"

"I am fine."

This was a major exchange. I waited to see if he would take it any further.

"Where are you going?" he asked, slowly and deliberately. I sensed he was fighting shyness.

"I'm just out for a ride. Where are you going?" I said it quickly, to test his English.

"I am riding, too."

"Where did you learn English?"

"In my factory." He spoke in an expressionless monotone, weighing out each word.

"They teach English at your factory?"

"Every day there are English lessons."

"You mean lots of people here speak English?"

"No. Most people do not learn."

"How many people work in your factory?"

"More than one hundred."

"How many of them know English?"

"Not many."

"Ten?" I guessed.

He gasped. "No, not ten."

"Well, how many?"

He was particularly slow with this answer. I turned my head toward him. From earlier glances I had concluded he was clean-shaven, but now I saw wisps of black hair—some an inch long—sprouting randomly on his cheeks and chin. He wore glasses and his face was a stiff mask, but I detected excitement tugging at its edges. "I think I am the only one."

His name was Shi. He was twenty years old and worked in Yangshuo's "small engine factory," where once a day an English lesson was broadcast over the television. Most people ignored the lessons—"They do not listen"—but Shi had decided to learn. Every word of his more than competent English had been gleaned from a television! Without trouble, I understood his pronunciations, and in order to be understood I had only to avoid running my words together. I remarked that he was very clever and guessed that he had lots of fun talking with tourists. His face clouded. He looked over. "No. This is the first time."

Was I the first tourist he'd ever spoken to?

"Yes. It is very difficult to meet a tourist. I am lucky that you are riding tonight. I have been hoping."

I suggested he get a job working with tourists.

"No, I cannot. I must work in the factory."

For how long?

He hesitated. "Forever, I think."

I protested. He was only twenty years old. Surely he would not spend his whole life in the factory?

"Yes. That is my job. It is hopeless."

I asked what sort of work his father did.

"My father is dead. When I was six years old, the Red Guard arrested him. They did not say why. I think he had some enemy. They kept him for two months. Then they killed him."

How did Shi find this out?

"Some people told my mother."

Didn't anyone say why?

"They said he was enemy of the people. They put him against a wall and they shot him."

How did Shi feel about this?

"I am bitter," he said, without emotion. "I am angry." He might have been describing the road: *It is flat. It is long.*

What became of the Red Guard?

"They are no more."

But what became of the people in the Red Guard—the ones who killed his father?

"They are still in Yangshuo. They are the Communist party."

The same people who killed his father?

"Yes."

Did Shi ever see them?

"I see them every week."

The very same people?

"Yes. I know exactly who did it. They know me."

Was there nothing he could do?

"No. There is nothing. They are the politicians in Yangshuo. After the Cultural Revolution I received a letter from the government. They say a mistake was made with my father. They are sorry. That is all. They invited me to join the Communist party."

Was Shi thinking of joining?

"They are murderers," he muttered. "I will never join." It was the largest show of emotion I would get from him.

How many other people were killed?

"In Yangshuo County there are fifty-thousand people. Six hundred were killed."

Were things better now?

"Maybe. There are not so many executions."

But there were still *some* executions?

A hint of a smirk came to his lips. "Yes."

Executions? In quiet Yangshuo?

"In a field by the river they shoot people."

On a bike ride just a day earlier Amy and I had started down a dirt road next to the river, but were forced to turn back when it dead-ended into an empty clearing. I described the road and the clearing.

"That is the field," Shi said.

How often are people shot?

"Not so often now. Before, they shot people every week."

When did that stop?

"When the tourists came."

Just two or three years ago?

"Yes."

Was anyone going to be shot the next morning?

"I do not think so. This year in Yangshuo only five people have been shot. One hundred are in prison."

Where is the prison?

"No one knows. But everyone knows there is one."

Why would someone be shot?

"Maybe for anything. Stealing. Cheating. Begging. Sex. Things like that."

Sex?

"If a man has sex with a woman and they are not married, the man is shot."

Shot?

"Yes. Shot."

And the woman?

"She is not shot."

What if you have more than one baby? Is that a reason for being shot?

"No. But maybe that and something else is a reason."

What did people think about the "one baby" law?

"It is a good law. There are too many people."

Were the rumors true? Do Chinese parents kill baby girls?

"I cannot say."

Did Shi have brothers and sisters?

"One brother. He is fifteen. He was one year old when our father was killed. My mother had two little boys but no husband."

Did Shi still live with his mother?

"No. She lives in a village in the mountains twenty kilometers from Yangshuo. Because she has no husband, no one will speak to her. People are afraid, because my father was killed by the Red Guard. My mother cannot have a job. She is very lonely. I go to visit her on Sundays. She has very little money. I give her ten yuan every month."

Each month Shi earned fifty yuan, about $22. He paid two yuan for a room in a housing complex, gave ten to his mother, spent some on food, which he cooked in his room, and tried to save the rest. Was he happy?

"Not me."

Were most people in China happy?

"Maybe some are, but I think most are not."

We were riding through low hills now, past fields punctured by the strange limestone columns. Not one car or truck had passed us. We felt the eyes of hushed peasants watching us from clusters of homes set back from the road. But for the scream of an occasional rooster and the clicking of our bikes, all was quiet. This green and rustic countryside looked like paradise. Surely, I suggested, the people living here were happy?

"I cannot say."

We rode ten kilometers through a maze of jagged walls streaked with soft pastel colors by long shafts of twilight. Clouds of gnats and mosquitoes—invading our eyes and nostrils, clamping onto our necks—kept us moving.

Shi was as eager to know about my life as I was to know about his. He asked about women: I was married, I must be an expert. He wanted to get married, but he was "embarrassed" around girls. He was lucky he was a tall man; if he were short, no woman would have him. He wished having a girlfriend were as easy for Chinese as it is for Americans: he saw happy boys and girls from America walking together in Yangshuo, but he could not do that with a girlfriend. He could not even talk with a girl. If he wanted to marry a girl, he would have to first mention this to her friends; if she was interested, she would send back a message. They would marry. Then they could talk. It was a "difficult situation." But for Americans it was "easy." For Americans everything was easy. Americans were always taking "vacations." Money was "free" in America. The only bad thing about America was that it was full of "criminals" carrying guns.

Where did Shi learn that?

"Our newspapers tell us. It is very dangerous to walk on the streets of America."

Was there no crime in China?

"Small things. A boy stole ten yuan from my pocket last month. I know who did it, but I cannot prove it."

Ten yuan! Almost a week's pay.

"But there is nothing I can do."

He asked how much my bike cost. It was a shiny new one with fresh paint and deep tire tread. I said the daily rent was one yuan. Shi sucked in his breath. He was riding next to me on a beaten, rusted clunker that groaned and squeaked. He had bought it for fifty yuan—one month's pay. "I borrowed money from the bank."

Did the bank charge interest?

"One percent."

If he had some extra money—say, five hundred yuan—what would he do with it?

He had a ready answer: "Buy things. A tape player, new clothes, books, some furniture, a new bicycle, shoes ..."

We came to a hill. "Ride as fast as you can," Shi said. I let him get a lead, but felt stupid holding back. I blew past him to the top of the hill. My nap had done wonders. When he caught up, in his soft manner he said, "That is a good bike."

From the top of the hill we had a spectacular view. Spread between the limestone spires was a valley of yellowing fields, shimmering irrigation ditches, and neat rows of palm trees. Peasants were giving their fields a final pat, or leading beasts home for the evening. The air smelled of fresh-cut hay, the sky was a brilliant orange. We stood on the hill for a few moments catching our breaths, feeling very comfortable with each other. I thought, So *THIS* is China!

As darkness filled in the landscape, we rode back to town. Shi told about being sent to school in Canton ("Guangzhou," he called it) for six months to learn about engines; he didn't much care about engines, but he'd loved Canton. The big city was intoxicating: the wide river, the uncountable people, the huge boats from other countries, and shops full of manufactured things. "I bought this shirt there," he said proudly. It was a simple white shirt: collar, short sleeves, a row of plastic buttons up the front.

What was it like to fly in an airplane? Shi asked. What was Hong Kong like? Were there many Chinese people there? What was America like? Why was America so rich? Did Americans really go to the moon?

Yes, I told him, some Americans really did go to the moon. Americans think that anything is possible. Shi had learned English; if he could do that, I said, he could do anything. If he really wanted to leave Yangshuo and go to Hong Kong, or even to America, well, it was possible. I told him that he was young, only twenty years old: if you told a twenty-year-old American that he would have to work in the Yangshuo engine factory his whole life, he would prove you wrong.

"It is hopeless," Shi said sadly.

He asked if I had any extra books. I said I had one written by an Englishman imprisoned in China during the Cultural Revolution that he could have, and invited him to my hotel room. I told him about Amy; if Shi would be my guest, we could all go to dinner. He said he would like that very much, but he had never been to the foreigners' hotel. He hoped it was okay.

Would he, I asked, get in trouble if he came inside?

"I cannot say."

44
WE DON'T HAVE THAT HERE

I consider myself a Hindu, Christian, Moslem, Jew, Buddhist and Confucian.

—MOHANDAS GANDHI

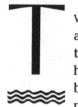

WO HOURS HAD PASSED since I'd left the hotel. Stars were out now, and crickets were singing in the garden. We parked our bikes in the darkness, and I whisked Shi past the front desk and down the hall. Amy was sitting on her bed reading. Feeling like a hunter bringing home a live Bigfoot, I introduced them, summarized the miracle of Shi's television English, and mentioned what had happened to his father. I mixed sweet tea from Hong Kong, and we each drank a cup. Shi sat on the edge of my bed, speaking ever-so-gently with Amy. She was fascinated. So was he. They asked each other lots of questions.

Later we went to dinner. I suggested the Yellow Lotus Café, thinking I could introduce Shi to the people who worked there, or to Yang Di, the boatman. If someone saw that he spoke English, that foreigners were comfortable around him, maybe they could find him work outside the factory. "I should not go there," Shi said.

"Oh, it's fine." I thought he was just being shy. "You can meet some more foreigners."

"My leader lives near there. If he sees me with you, there will be trouble for me. I cannot go."

"Who is your 'leader'?" Amy asked.

"He is from my factory. He is a Communist."

"Is that unusual?"

"In China we have one billion people, but only forty million are party members. They make big trouble."

He led us to a restaurant—three tables, one overhead light bulb—run by friends of his. Yang Di, the boatman, was leaving as we arrived. His eyes widened when he saw the three of us.

"Hello," I said.

"Hello." He looked uncertainly at Shi.

"Do you know Shi?" I asked him.

They nodded at each other and spoke cordially in Chinese. I sensed it was awkward. Later I asked Shi, "He wasn't one of the men who killed your father, was he?"

"No. He is a good man. I do not know him well, but we have seen each other. He is surprised to see me with tourists. Only a few people know that I speak English."

Our presence made Shi a celebrity. He introduced Amy and me to his friends, translated our questions and jokes, but was reluctant to order for us. "I always eat in my room. It is very unusual for me to come here."

I reminded him that he was my guest, and asked if he liked to drink beer. "Sometimes," he said. We sent the waiter, a barefoot ten-year-old, in search of beer. Shi took us back to the dark, garlic-reeking kitchen. I asked what was simmering in the pot on the fire; Shi pointed at a chicken strutting at the backdoor.

When our food arrived, I found that Shi had ordered only one plate (chicken and rice and vegetables) for the three of us to share. I ordered two more platefuls, and we ate every bite. Even with beer, the bill came to only six yuan. When it was time to pay, I gave a ten-yuan note—less than five dollars—to the waiter. He flinched, took my money, and ran out the door.

"Where's he going?"

"He has to find change. That is very big money."

When Shi was distracted, Amy whispered to me, "I'd like to give him some money."

"I was thinking the same thing."

"How about ten yuan? The same that was stolen from him."

"Great. And that's what he gives his mother each month. I'll split it with you."

"Okay," she said. "But he won't accept it."

"I can slip it in the book I'm giving him, and he won't find it until later. When we go back to the hotel, you keep him out front. I'll go in, get the book, and put the money inside with a note."

"Perfect."

Later, when I came out of the hotel with the book, Shi and Amy were in the driveway, talking.

"I don't understand," Shi was saying.

Amy turned to me. "He just asked what 'God' is," she sighed. "You tell him."

"Oh, wow. God ... Let's see ..."

We laughed. Shi stood there waiting. Finally Amy found an answer: "God is what makes the trees grow ... what makes the grass green." She took a deep breath. "God makes the air. God is what makes Yangshuo's mountains so beautiful."

"That's good," I said. "Yeah, that's good. What do you call that, Shi? What's your word for that?"

Shi looked confused. His eyes flicked back and forth. "We don't have that here."

"Don't the Chinese have a reason for why the trees grow? How did your mountains get so pretty?"

He thought for a minute. "They just are that way."

"Have you ever heard of Jesus?" Amy asked him. "Or Muhammad? or Buddha?"

The confused look came back to his face. He scanned his inner skull, looking for clues that weren't in there.

Two college friends of mine had a recurring religious argument. One proclaimed Christianity "the Way." The other argued, "Jesus Christ! A billion Chinese have never heard of the guy!" Here, fifteen years later, was proof.

"Wait, Shi. Let me get this straight. Have you ever heard of Jesus Christ?"

"Or Christ Jesus?" Amy added.

Shi paused and pondered again. "No. What is that?"

I told him about the healings, the feeding of the multitudes, the resurrection, but I could see he was starting to wonder about me, so I dropped it.

I gave Shi the book. There were bows and handshakes all around. Amy and I said how very glad we were to have met him. He thanked us for the book and the dinner. We promised to write.

45

EVERYONE IS IN THE MAFIA

You can get anything you want, At Alice's Restaurant . . .

Exceptin' Alice.

—ARLO GUTHRIE
"Alice's Restaurant"

HEN WE REACHED GUILIN and began looking for train tickets to Beijing, Amy and I found that we had two choices: we could wait—the train station had available space on a train three days away; or we could go to the LaLa Café. According to the grapevine and the guidebooks, a traveler in need could obtain just about anything by dropping into the LaLa and asking for either "John" or "Mister Ma." Between them, these two men had a finger in all of the essential backpacking pies: John owned the LaLa, Mister Ma ran the adjacent hotel; both dabbled in the black market.

"Sit down," John greeted us. "Have a soda, a bite to eat. Chocolate cake?"

"You have FEC, yes?" Mister Ma inquired. "Very good. What can we do for you?"

Amy and I sat down, ordered dinner, and mentioned our need. John and Mister Ma spoke of a "brother" in the train-station ticket office willing to do periodic favors for "friends." To join this select circle, one needed only to give Mister Ma enough foreign-exchange coupons to cover the ticket price. Mister Ma would sell the FEC on the black market and buy the tickets with his own people's money. Nothing drastic, just a little grease for the wheels of commerce.

It was late afternoon, and Amy and I wanted tickets for the 2:00 A.M. train to Beijing, a thirty-four-hour trip that cost about thirty-five dollars. "I will try," said Mister Ma. "But it is late—I cannot promise." He stood to profit fifty-five yuan, China's average monthly salary, on the deal: we knew he would try. We handed over our FEC; Mister Ma left for the station.

When he was gone, John let us pick at his résumé.

"I am twenty-nine years old. I was fifteen when the Cultural Revolution started. If I am twenty-nine when it starts ... I die. I have been very lucky. I studied English for four years at university. In China, maybe one out of every fifty people goes to university. It is very difficult to get in."

What if there is another Cultural Revolution?

"I will see it coming. Just before next Cultural Revolution, Mister Ma and I will disappear."

Will there be another?

"It is our history. There has always been another."

Where will you go?

"Someplace very good." His eyes said, *I already have a plan, and I won't tell it to you.*

Earlier we had joked about John and Mister Ma being mentioned in all the guidebooks. Now I guessed they would go to Hollywood to be with all the other celebrities.

"Yes, very good." John laughed uproariously. "Maybe we go to Hollywood."

Are you a happy man?

"No." He paused. "People see me. They see I have restaurant, I have been to university, I am always smiling, always laughing. They think I am happy man. But I am not happy. Happy on outside only. Inside I am thinking too much. Always thinking. Sometimes I just want to be alone. When I am alone, I never laugh, never smile. Always thinking. My girlfriend tells me it is dangerous to think too much, but I cannot stop."

Girlfriend? Can one have a girlfriend in China?

"Yes. For five years she has been my girlfriend. If we borrow marriage paper from friends, we can travel together, like you. We can get room in hotel. We sleep together, but we will not marry. She is too independent. So am I."

Isn't that dangerous, sleeping together without being married?

"Very dangerous! Very exciting, too."

What was his girlfriend's job?

"Civil engineer. She builds dams. She went to university in France."

What did John do before he opened a restaurant?

"I was English teacher. Now my English is very rusty. Once it was very good."

Was it easy to quit teaching and open a restaurant?

"Easy to quit. Not easy to open restaurant. I borrow much money."

How much?

"Twenty-five-hundred yuan." Eleven hundred dollars.

Did he borrow from the bank?

"No." His laugh said it was a silly question. "I borrow from everyone I know." He pointed at imaginary people surrounding our table. "One hundred from you. One hundred from you. From you, and from you ... Now I owe money to everyone. But I have no choice. I think too much. I know that if I am teacher, in my entire life I make twenty thousand yuan. If I have restaurant, I make twenty thousand yuan in ten years. So I must quit being teacher. I will work in restaurant for twenty years and save my money. After that I can write books, travel, enjoy my money."

"Ah, you are a good capitalist!" Amy told him.

"Yes. But I spend too much money."

"Then you are a *very* good capitalist!"

"Maybe. I go to Christian church sometimes. There is one church in Guilin. It is very small, very quiet. Many Chinese who have been to university go to church. We know about your world a little bit. Many people listen to 'Voice of America.' All day long it comes in Chinese, very weak. But at night it comes in English, very strong."

"Is it true that people kill baby girls in China?" I asked.

John was thoughtful for a moment. "If people talk about something a lot, then it is probably unusual. If people talk only a little, then it probably happens a lot."

"Which is it?"

"People talk a lot, I think."

A my went to the telegraph office, searching for a message from Dylan; I went to a park and lay down under a tree. Before dozing off, I saw Heidi and Richard climb into a taxi on the far side of the park. After five days, I wondered what Heidi'd say now about zee Sird World. But they were too far away and I was too wiped out. I lay there and recalled the day we'd met them, the first day in China, when I thought "hard seat" would be preferable to riding with Lotus Tours. Only the foolhardy travel lower than they can afford for any length of time.

In the evening Amy and I rendezvoused back at the Lala. We were recounting our adventures—no messages—when Mister Ma returned from the train station, smiling.

"Good luck." He sat down and slid us our tickets. "Last two. You are only foreigners on train." He began recounting all the problems he'd run into. As he was talking, a fight erupted without warning on the sidewalk in front of the restaurant; there was scuffling, a woman cried out, and ten feet from our table two young men were swinging at each other. I recognized one of them, a stocky Chinese who had been sitting quietly at a table next to ours all evening. Now he was landing sharp blows to the head and shoulders of a gangly teenager. A crowd was forming. The fight was a mismatch—not the graceful kung-fu contest one would hope for in the Orient, but the sloppy grappling of a junior-high hall fight. The teenager was hardly fighting back, retreating instead with an astonished look. *Why is this man hitting me?* Suddenly he was knocked backward over a bicycle and fell to the ground.

John, who hadn't risen from his chair, barked a warning. The stocky man who had been throwing all the punches glanced back at John. He said something loudly to the flattened teenager and waved his hand toward the distance. *Get out of here and don't come back!*

"What's going on?" I asked John.

He flicked his hand at Amy and me. *Soon I will tell you.*

Calm had returned to the sidewalk. Now the teenager was on his feet. A man was standing between the two antagonists, speaking sharply. The fight was over.

"He is police." John nodded to the newcomer, a man dressed no differently than the millions of other men we'd seen in China: sandals, faded green work pants, faded green work shirt. "He has gun." John patted his hip. "This side. You see?"

Underneath the policeman's shirt I saw the bulge; when he turned, his long shirt swung away from his body, allowing a brief glimpse of a black, holstered pistol. "How did you know he was police?"

"I know every police near here. I must. That is why I can trade money with you. If I don't know police ..." With an index finger, John blew his brains out.

Are the police that bad?

"No. Police are good. If policeman doesn't come to this fight, then someone will have a knife. Someone will die. And later no one will remember anything. Everyone here will be a blind person. Last week at the stoplight"—John pointed down the street—"one man was killed. Two men fight with knives. One man dies. The other man rides away on a bicycle. This was evening time. Thousands of people are nearby. Nobody sees anything. Nobody hears anything."

Why is that?

"Mafia. Everybody is afraid the men are from Mafia. Guilin is big city. There is North Guilin and Central Guilin, and this is South Guilin. Every area has Mafia. This boy"—John pointed at the beaten teenager—"is from North Guilin. He was smiling at our girls."

For the first time I noticed the two cook-waitresses standing at the back of the restaurant, enjoying the attention, lips pursed to suppress smiles. "A boy from North Guilin should not be here bothering our girls," John said. "But our man is too aggressive. He uses fists too quickly. He is always fighting. It is good the police come."

Did they always come this quickly?

"Every block there is policeman. Always. Even if you can not see, there is policeman. Sometimes many policemen."

On the sidewalk the teenager, dark eyes glaring, was yelling at the man who had beaten him. He held up his hand and showed blood: *You hurt me!* The aggressor was unimpressed. He raised a meaty fist: *There's more where that came from!* The policeman was smiling, telling the crowd to break up: *The fun's over, folks! Go on home now.*

"Is that boy in the Mafia?" I asked John.

"Everyone is in the Mafia."

"Are you in the Mafia?"

He answered with a look: *EVERYONE is in the Mafia!*

Before he left, the wounded teenager called out to the girls: *I'll be back, ladies!*

They smiled at him: *Anytime, big boy!*

The stocky attacker was back in the café now, strutting among the tables. He had won a great victory. He gave John a cocky grin and flexed a bicep for Amy and me: *Showed that sucker!*

The policeman drew a chair up to our table. He was smiling: *Boys will be boys, eh, Johnny?*

46
VISION
OF
HELL

There was a young lady of Spain,
Who often got sick on a train,
Not once and again,
But again and again,
And again and again and again.

—Quoted by Osbert Sitwell as a favorite
of John Sargent

S ICKNESS IS THE ULTIMATE MOCKERY, its cruelty multiplied by one's distance from home. In Nepal I'd been four days' walk from telephone, radio, or medical care, but I'd stayed healthy. Now, in Guilin, only a cab ride from an airport or hospital, I felt centuries from assistance.

The LaLa Café closed at eleven, and Amy and I were faced with a three-hour stay in the train-station waiting room. Five hundred Chinese were camped there, waiting to catch a one o'clock train to somewhere. Miraculously we found two empty benches, side by side, and lay down. Amy fell asleep easily, the way she did everything, but I could not.

My notebook: *At midnight the waiting room in the Guilin railroad station is a vision of hell.* Overheated people in tattered clothes were squashed together in endless rows, too stunned to move. Those sleeping were curled up on sheets of dirty cardboard or sprawled on the grimy floor; those awake slumped against stacks of possessions, shaking their heads in bewilderment, fanning themselves in futile attempts to cool down or to dislodge flies, while waiting for a redemption that was never coming.

Lying on the next bench was a man with no hair and no shoes, wearing faded purple pajamas. He would have been equally at home in a barnyard. His twisted facial expression—open mouth, bared gums, blackened teeth— was that of an angry braying donkey. He was breathing loudly, imitating the harsh rooting noises of a pig into the burlap sack that was his pillow.

On the other side of me is Amy, a much prettier sight, but no less disturbing. Who is she, and how did we wind up together? That we so recently considered being lovers now seems ridiculous. When she asks, "How do you feel?" I hear, "What's wrong with you, jerk?" I should have stuck to traveling alone. When you're alone, you can't afford to get sick. Now that I'm sick, I can't afford to be alone.

Temporary redemption eventually arrived in the form of our train. Mister Ma's tickets proved genuine. An amused conductor showed Amy and me to our bunks in a small nook occupied by four sleeping Chinese. Ours were the topmost bunks, across from each other in a triple-tier arrangement. The Chinese below us briefly roused to witness our arrival. They stared blankly— first at us and then at one another—wondering what inauspicious twist of fate had brought foreigners to *their* compartment. I sprawled out on my bunk and fell instantly asleep. A comfortable bunk, a rocking train: by Beijing I would be as good as new. It seemed too good to be true.

I t *was* too good to be true.

I came to life the next morning at the same instant as the loudspeaker, which was closer to my bunk than to any of the thirty-five other bunks in the entire car. While lying flat, I could, without stretching, touch it with my toes. From six o'clock in the morning until well into the next night, it spewed a mixture of announcements, propaganda, and shrill Top 40—the volume up so loud that an ugly tremor of distortion constantly hissed from the box. Occasionally there were comedy segments—shrewish wife, henpecked husband—which the Chinese chuckled at, but I suspected they resented the incessant noise as much as I did.

I came to recognize a Chinese phrase—"*Goo-bah-day kooo*"—which was repeated over and over during announcements. Most of the day I stayed in my bunk, dizzy, oozing sweat, dreaming nightmares punctuated with "*Goo-bah-day kooo . . . Goo-bah-day-kooo*" and scheming ways to silence the loudspeaker. I came up with a plan.

With my pocket knife I would sharpen the handle of my toothbrush into a dagger. In the cloak of noise and blackness provided by one of the periodic tunnels, I would murder the loudspeaker, stabbing as many holes into it as possible before the tunnel ended, and then sleep in peace all the way to Beijing.

But I was chicken; if the tunnel turned out to be only fifty yards long, I would be caught mid-murder, flailing maniacally with my toothbrush-dagger.

And what if I succeeded only in mangling the box, not silencing it? And wouldn't the murder weapon be found in the search? Wouldn't I be the obvious suspect? Who but a Westerner would attack state property during a nonrevolutionary period?

And where would I get another toothbrush?

Toward midday I was stricken with the first attack of diarrhea. I climbed down from my perch, smiled weakly at Amy, sitting by the window with a dreamy look on her face, and spent twenty minutes in the wobbling squat-toilet: *those* things.

Later I sat at the window trying to mentally reverse my wretched condition. I visualized a favorite backcountry meadow in Yellowstone Park. I saw my wife's tiny fists lifting a fat sandwich—ham, Swiss cheese, pickles, sprouts, and avocado, on light rye—to my mouth. I washed it down with a glass of cold milk. I wrote affirmations—*I am in exactly the right place, thinking, doing, and feeling exactly the right things*—and then tried to believe them.

On my map I now see that our train covered twelve hundred miles from the deep south of China to the far north. Along the way it crossed the Yangtze and Yellow Rivers and passed through towns named Henyang, Wuhan, Zhengzhou, and Boading. But at the time, the only route I paid attention to was the six steps to the toilet.

Between visits I drank tea with Amy and the Chinese men from our nook, accepted their offers of peanuts, declined their kumquats and pomelos, and watched central China pass by the window. Yangshuo's rugged scenery was a memory. The area between Guilin and Beijing was comparable in distance and flatness to the land between Houston and Minneapolis. Hills were few, and never closer than the far horizon. The scenery was always the same: peasants and crops, peasants and crops, a cluster of homes, peasants and crops . . .

I was struck by the numbers of people laboring in the fields. Never, it seemed, did we come to an uninhabited area; at any given moment at least a hundred people were visible out the window. Every available piece of ground was planted, every plot tended by straw-hatted workers. Images met my eye, were transmitted down my arm to my fingers, and wound up in my notebook:

> In the thin pencil of shade provided by a utility pole, a man lies on his back reading a book; ten feet away a buffalo is calmly browsing. Thirty peasants, ankle deep in muck, plug seedlings into a flooded rice paddy. Everywhere: ponds, paddies, power poles, and more fields. Occasionally a truck; never a car.

It was 1928 outside. Inside it was 98: 98 degrees at three o'clock in the afternoon. In my bunk at eight o'clock that morning my minithermometer read 86 degrees. Shorts and T-shirts were standard attire. Everyone in the car, with the exception of Amy, looked ready to drop. There were no conversations; other than the racket of the loudspeaker, the only sound was the jarring snarl of people, both men and women, spitting on the floor. About once an hour the car attendant came by with a mop and a bucket of scalding water and wiped away the peanut shells, the fruit peelings, and the drying dollops of phlegm.

Amy and I were the only white people on the train, and I saw none out the window. When the train slowed to pass through towns, I would sit at the window and try to catch the eye of anyone who would look back. People would see me, point excitedly at my receding image, and scream for friends who came rushing from the brick houses with dirt floors that lined the tracks. A small boy leaning against a wall spotted me; I saw his eyes dilate briefly while his brain cells rearranged to accommodate the possibility of hair that is not black.

When seeing a new place, I often think: I am going to come back here later—when I am rich, or when I have more time, or when I have a purpose, or when I am with someone I love—and do this right. But it is self-deception. More often than not, my feet lead me somewhere new rather than somewhere I've already been. And as I sat at that window watching the train bore through the heart of China, I had a different, more probable thought, and I wrote it down: *I better remember what this place looks like. I will never be back.*

47
CONSUL!

. . . somewhere over China
Shanghai or old Peking
On a plane or a boat or an envelope
Real adventure has its ring
Just to put a little distance
Between fact and fantasy
Still six thousand miles away from
  where I really want to be

—JIMMY BUFFETT
"Somewhere over China"

I HAD STARTED MY TRIP with grand and lofty ideas about the magic of travel. "Travel," I told myself and anyone who would listen, "is transformational, the strongest human urge, the thing that keeps us and our world vibrant and alive. It is one's duty to travel, to keep moving, to expose oneself to foreign cultures, foreign landscapes, foreign ideas. Any fool with a thought in his head is out traveling every chance he gets."

Now that I am back, I again half believe all of that, but a perusal of my journal shows that by the time I hit Beijing, I did not believe anything of the sort. My entries for Beijing are not those of a happy man, but moaning laments over my wretched condition and whining complaints about the backward locals. I experienced everything through a haze of dysentery for which I held the entire country accountable. My wife was completely off the hook now, replaced by a billion Chinese.

I could no longer remember my last properly digested meal or decent night's sleep. My notebook: *Beijing is a drab, colorless, hot, flat, bleached, dusty, unremarkable place.*

The thought of four or five weeks in China was quickly abandoned; upon arrival in Beijing my first act was to book a reservation on the next available train to Europe. My Trans-Siberian would leave in eight days.

My second act was to go to a doctor, an Australian recommended by the U.S. embassy. He weighed me (I'd lost fifteen pounds since Hong Kong), shined a light in my eyes, tapped my knee, and ordered me to consume nothing but clear fluids and certain drugs for forty hours. I'd have paid any price, but he asked only seventeen dollars. I holed up in my hotel room and followed his exact instructions.

Two days later, the most dramatic symptoms had passed, and I was able, just barely, to straggle aboard the visas merry-go-round. The Chinese threaten to cancel your Trans-Siberian reservation and give your berth to someone else if you can't show proper transit visas for Mongolia, Russia, and Poland twenty-four hours before your train leaves. Now it gets tricky. The Mongolians won't give you a visa unless you already have a Russian one. You can't get a Russian one unless you already have a Polish one. The Polish one is easy—ten American dollars, five-minute wait—but the Russians are a problem; they make you wait hours for a ridiculous interview— "Why do you come to Russia? You cannot to stay, you know?"—and they hold your passport three "business" days for processing.

My train was due to leave early on a Wednesday. On Monday morning I got my passport back from the Russians. All I needed now was Mongolia. Monday afternoon, during posted business hours, I went to the Mongolian embassy.

"Closed," said a guard in the lobby.

"Closed!"

"Tomorrow," he said. "Afternoon."

I protested. Mine was an emergency. If I didn't get my visa that very day, the Chinese could give my seat away the next morning.

The guard didn't care. "No one here." He shrugged. "Mongolian holiday. Everybody at party."

Instead of leaving, I waited by the front door. Fifteen minutes later, a gray-haired, business-suited man came strolling through the lobby. I stopped him and told my dilemma. "There is nothing I can do," he told me in perfect English. "It is a Mongolian holiday—like your Fourth of July. The entire staff has gone to a party."

I pleaded; without that visa I would have to spend another week, maybe two, in Beijing. If he were I, what would he do?

The gentleman paused and studied the floor. "Come back tonight. Nine o'clock. Maybe ten." He looked me in the eye. "I will help you." And then he walked out the door.

By day the tree-shaded streets of Beijing's diplomatic quarter had been cool and quiet and pleasant to walk in, but at nine o'clock that night the place felt haunted. The half-moon overhead was veiled in shifting clouds, hardly a lamp was lit anywhere, and the entire neighborhood was blanketed with an eerie, gone-to-bed silence that gave the shadows new meaning. Not a sliver of light shone from the massive Mongolian embassy. I stood in the darkness of the street out front, muttering, and trying to ignore the prickling at the back of my neck. One inner voice urged me to forget this, to come back early the next morning, begging; another assured me I was in the right place, getting my visa was the right thing to do, and spooked was the right way to feel.

I entered the gate, crossed the blackened courtyard and climbed the steps. The front door was ajar. I nudged it open and went inside. In a small, dimly lit cubicle off the lobby, a Turkish-looking man in a white T-shirt was reading a newspaper. A radio in the background was playing the Rolling Stones' song, "You Can't Always Get What You Want."

The man looked surprised to see me. Annoyed, too. "I do not speak English," he said right off.

"I need a visa."

"Visa closed. Tomorrow."

"No. Tonight."

"Tomorrow."

"Tonight."

He eyed me warily. "Mo-ment." He picked up a telephone and began speaking excitedly in a language I did not recognize. The song "Uptown Girl" came on the radio. Soon another Turkish-looking man arrived wearing white pajamas patterned with little blue diamonds.

"May I help you?" he said, rubbing his eyes. I thanked him for getting up at this late hour, and told my story. "Who told you nine o'clock?" he demanded.

I described the man: Gray hair, glasses, nice suit, this tall . . .

Both men's eyes enlarged. They spoke rapidly to each other in their own language. I picked out one word: "Consul!"

The mood in the lobby changed instantly. Lights were turned on. I was ushered into a waiting room. A glass of tea was brought. My passport, two photos, and some money were accepted. Fifteen minutes later, the man I'd met that afternoon arrived, wearing slippers, shorts, T-shirt, and a smile. In his arms was a young granddaughter, clutching something.

"I told you I would help." On cue the girl reached out both hands; I had my passport back, stamped with the precious visa. I thanked them profusely and talked with the man for a few minutes. He was the consul, the acting ambassador, Mongolia's head man in Beijing. He wished me well and instructed me to pass his kindness on to someone else. I promised.

Soon I was walking back through the dark night, the moon now completely blotted out. My steps echoed across the courtyard. At the street I stopped and glanced back at the embassy. The lights were already off; the building was once again black and eerie.

I thought, Mongolia will be a very interesting place.

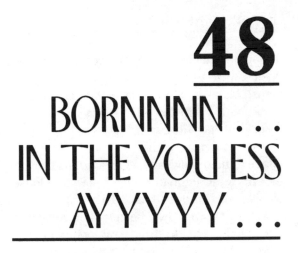

48

BORNNNN . . .
IN THE YOU ESS
AYYYYY . . .

Let a hundred flowers bloom.
Let a hundred schools of thought contend.

—MAO TSE-TUNG
Speech, Beijing, February 27, 1957

BEIJING, IN MY MEMORY, is a series of sleepless nights, endless trips to the toilet, taxi rides from our hotel to various restaurants, several embassies, the doctor's office. Even as I write this, I feel a drippy nose coming on and a fluttering of bowels. But while my body urges me to skip over this part, there are memories begging me to linger, to tarry and ruminate—an ambivalence symbolic of my time in China. One voice said, "Stay, it'll be better." Another: "Move on or die."

But I cannot move on without mentioning a few things. The handbag-sized rat, for instance, that scuttled through a restaurant one day when I was the only patron. The staff shrieked, chased it, beat it to death with brooms, and then apologized to me: Westerners are not supposed to witness executions, even rat executions.

"I disguised myself and went to one execution," said a California man I met, an English teacher two years in Beijing. "Three guys who had stolen slices from a watermelon man. They lined 'em up against a board and put bullets in their heads! Can you beat it? Just last month they had a roundup—grabbed every petty thief, beggar, and political misfit they could get their hands on and executed 'em. They zapped five thousand in Beijing alone." Every foreigner in China had an execution story.

Amy and I spent the Fourth of July at the American embassy, at a party catered by McDonald's of Hong Kong. Betty Hummell, wife of U.S. Ambassador Arthur W. Hummell, Jr., was sitting behind a card table in the embassy driveway. Six weeks earlier she had been busy entertaining the Reagans;

today her official duties included saying "Welcome home" to Amy and me. Inside were three hundred happy Americans, a couple thousand Big Macs, Pepsi, Miller Lite, hot dogs, potato chips, and a stereo blasting Springsteen: "Bornnnn ... in the you ess ayyyyy, bornnnn ... in the you ess ayyyyy." Fourth of July 1984.

On a day trip to the Great Wall Amy and I ran into Heidi and Richard. Since Canton they had had an amazing transformation. Heidi had abandoned her makeup, and had traded her white blouse for a bilingual black tank top sloganned: "I Love China." They'd flown to Guilin, Xi'an, and now Beijing, and everywhere they'd been treated royally. Richard: "In Xi'an I get one-fifty for my FEC." Heidi: "Brad, you look not so good. Do you eat well?"

Months later, Amy sent me a picture: The Wall looks as it always does in pictures, but at fifteen pounds underweight I am the sharpened toothbrush from my loudspeaker plot. I do not remember where I got the energy for the smile.

But if I was drooping, Beijing showed signs of stirring to life. The masses were being encouraged to dress with a little flair. "These bright colors some of the ladies are wearing," said a woman at the embassy party, "two months ago you didn't see any of that. The government's trying to prod China into the twentieth century."

Arguments in support of this thesis were everywhere. Building cranes dotted the low, sprawling skyline like oil derricks in Oklahoma. A story in the *China Daily* spoke enthusiastically of China's participation in the upcoming Olympics—a first. Numerous billboards proclaimed in Chinese: TIME IS MONEY.

"Everything is good today," said a man who worked for China Airlines, and who, I noticed, was missing every tooth on the right side of his head. "Much, much better. We are not so afraid now. In the Cultural Revolution my son cut off my wife's high heels. I had one silver dollar from your country. I could not break it or smash it or hide it. Finally I threw it in the river. I wasn't caught, but I spent three years in the countryside anyway. It was horrible for everyone. My son also learned some horrible lessons. No more Cultural Revolutions. That was our last one."

In the lobby of our hotel a smiling man approached me. "Where are you from?"

I told him, and although he was obviously Chinese, I asked where he was from.

"I am from Beijing," he said, surprised by the question. "It is difficult to tell Chinese from Japanese for you, no?"

"Not anymore, but a Chinese person can turn out to be from Hong Kong, Taiwan, Malaysia—even America."

"Ah, yes. This is true. We do move around. I myself have just returned from Sweden." He smiled.

"Have you been there before?"

"Oh, no!" His smile grew brighter. "I am fifty-five. I am a middle-school physics teacher. This was my first time out of China"—he leaned closer and lowered his voice—"*and my first time on an airplane*. I have been back only three hours." He held up three fingers and smiled some more, the smile of the new groom or first-time father: life was going to get no better than this for a long, long time. He'd been to Sweden. He'd spent many hours with his nose pressed to an airplane window, thirty-five thousand feet above the earth. There had been the mountains and the rivers and the great deserts. He'd seen cities jammed with cars and towering buildings. It made Beijing's skyline, its handful of tall hotels, seem quite primitive. And the colors!

"Everything was so green in Sweden," he marveled. *"Everything*. Things grow so well there. Everywhere I looked, there was more green. How can a place be so green, so pretty, I wonder? It makes Beijing seem drab and dirty and dusty to me now.

"Oh, and the people! So nice, so polite! Never pushing and shoving, always very courteous to each other and to me. And so many fair, blond ones. They were all so tall and healthy. I fell in love many times." He was winking.

It is good to travel, I suggested.

"It is wonderful. I am the luckiest man alive today. And now I want to go everywhere. I want to visit your country. I want to see the Grand Canyon. And Yosemite Park. And ... what part of America are you from? The East or the West?"

I told him.

"Ah, San Francisco! I want to visit the famous Chinatown where there are many Cantonese people, and I want to see the Golden Gate Bridge. It must be very beautiful!"

How did he plan to arrange his next trip?

"Who knows the future? I was able to go to Sweden to attend a physics conference. I consider that a miracle. And if I am ever again allowed to have a trip abroad, that, too, will be a miracle. I think the truth is that I will never again leave China, but I will never forget what I have seen. Never! And as long as I am alive I will hope and pray"—he winked again at the word *pray*— "that I am allowed to visit the West once more before I die. I am a grandfather. I have everything I need or want. Life has been very good to me. But last week for the first time I saw that there is a whole world that I do not know. How can I rest now? Only a fool can be given a glimpse at a new world and then return to his old one without a second thought. Well, I am not a fool. I am a very curious man."

I shared this man's unrest, but not his curiosity.

I already know everything I need to know about China. When I'm ninety, in my mind's eye I'll still be able to picture the landscape, remember the feel of a worn ten-yuan note, see the faces, recall the streets and monuments, smell the garlic, taste the oily foods. I don't need to speak Chinese or be an "expert" to know that China, like every country I've seen, has its hands full trying to figure itself out. I travel with the eternal hope that someday I'll find a country of excitement and enchanting beauty, where people are happy and well taken care of, and where there is not an undercurrent of weirdness. China is not that country. That country does not exist. Countries have problems.

I wanted out of Beijing, out of China, to be on my own again. Amy and I had entered different worlds. She had sightseeing, I had my illness. She was staying a week longer than I, and checked every day for news from Dylan. I was certain she would never hear from him. But in spite of my pessimism, the afternoon before my departure she rushed into our hotel room, smiling, waving a piece of paper.

"Read this." She dropped a telegram from Hong Kong onto my bed. ASSUMING KARMIC POWERS STAY BENIGN, ARRIVE TRAIN THURSDAY. DYLAN. Cosmic timing. He would arrive the day after my train left.

"I was starting to wonder," Amy said, ecstatic.

We celebrated our last night together with a heaping platter of Peking duck in a crowded local restaurant. By now my body was again processing food in the usual manner, my mental state was almost back to normal, and with my departure imminent, Amy and I relaxed and enjoyed being together. She really had been a good traveling partner, better than I, and I wanted to tell her a million different things: that meeting her had given me a badly needed, much appreciated boost; that I hated the turn things had taken; that I loved her spirit, found it so unavoidably attractive that I suspected my sickness was the only device my mind could concoct to keep my body on its marital moorings. Explanations. Apologies. Groveling.

But now we were withdrawn from each other a number of notches—hell, Dylan was coming in two days—and I could see that gushing all over our Peking duck wasn't the thing to do. I had an eight-day train ride ahead; everything would sort out along the way. Amy sat at my right elbow, oblivious to my torments, so happy with life that her smile seemed permanent; so contented that she looked pregnant; so confident, I thought, that her face had *I am in exactly the right place thinking, doing, and feeling exactly the right things* written all over it. I wondered: Why can't *I* feel that? Why did *I* get sick? It was almost too much: I wanted her, and I wanted away from her.

Several stanzas of the male anthem gathered in my throat: If I'd been single, this would have all been different; I like you, gosh, an awful lot, and wish you the very best; you'll find a good man, a better man probably, and you'll make perfect babies; there'll come a day, I know, when I'll look back with the deepest regret. And the anthem's refrain—*I want to sleep with you, sleep with you, sleep with you*—with my own private kicker, *but I'm, somehow, glad we didn't.*

I spilled none of this. We talked instead about what Russia would be like, where we'd go on future trips, what we'd do back in the States. Amy was going to get a job for a while, find a man, have babies.

"Might Dylan be the one?"

She hesitated. "No ... I can't imagine him coming back to Baltimore with me. He's been a good romantic fantasy, but I can't see him as the father of my kids." She asked, "What do you think will happen with your wife?"

"I have a sense we'll get divorced."

The next morning, on her side of the room, Amy propped herself up on an elbow and watched me pack. When I was finished and had checked under my bed half a dozen "one-last-times" she got up and came over, wearing a gauzy white T-shirt that fell to mid-thigh. Through good and bad, sickness and health, we'd been together for three straight weeks. We would remember each other very, very fondly.

"Sorry I fell apart on you. I wasn't myself."

"Ah, you were fine. You're a good person, Brad."

In our sixth floor hotel room we hugged tight. Over her head, out the window, I saw noodles of rain streaking the Beijing sky.

"Last one to London's a rotten egg," I told her, and fled in a taxi.

49
NO MONEY MISSPENT OR TIME FRITTERED AWAY

Money half gone . . .
Not knowing what else to do, I drove west-
ward . . .
The loneliness again. Now I had only the idea
of the journey to keep me going . . . Instead of
insight, maybe all a man gets is strength to
wander for a while.

—WILLIAM LEAST HEAT MOON
Blue Highways

S OMEWHERE IN THE FARTHEST nook of the mind of anyone who travels
is a half-completed picture titled, "How It Will Look the Day I Board
the Trans-Siberian." Although unclear on the details ("Will I be riding
east or west? Where do I get a visa? buy a ticket? How much?"), the
serious traveler never doubts that someday a set of circumstances
will come along requiring or allowing him (or her) to board that train.
And when he does, he already knows, sort of, how it will look: he will be the
only traveler on board; someone important will be on the platform to see
him off; a photographer will record the momentous event—the hearty smile,
the jaunty wave, the traveling bag full of books, postcards, food, and possibly
a nip for the cold nights ahead, slung nonchalantly over one shoulder.

But experience has a cruel way of sluicing fantasy from reality, and my
particular fantasy had to be abandoned on the mid-July Wednesday morning
that I boarded my Trans-Siberian. It was drizzling, the wet season having
finally reached Beijing. The masses had taken refuge beneath thousands of
black umbrella-mushrooms lining the slick streets through which my taxi

197

maneuvered on the way to Beijing Station. In the money belt under my shirt was a second-class ticket to Berlin, with a train change and two-hour layover in Moscow. One hundred and seventy-one measly dollars for eight days of riding; nine thousand miles through six countries and eight time zones.

By the time I reached the station, the small crowd pacing the waiting room contained several other backpackers; eventually nearly two dozen showed up. We stood around telling stories of sickness, executions, and black-market hassles, until I remembered something, and withdrew to the telephone-and-telegraph room.

The unanswered phone call is the last free lunch—no answer, no cost— but from halfway around the world, verifying that I could still make my wife's phone ring, was certainly worth *something.* It was five o'clock on a Tuesday afternoon in San Francisco, and the phone rang and rang and rang. For several moments I just stood there, in a phone booth in Beijing Station, listening to the sound and trying to picture her apartment—the wobbly telephone stand, my stereo on the bookcase, the red Indian rug, the wicker sofa, the "N Judah" trolley rumbling past in the street. But no Her.

By the time I got back to the waiting room, people were already boarding. In my compartment I found one man.

"Brad! You're looking a lot better. Where's your friend?"

It was Russ, a thirty-two-year-old Mennonite farmer from Kansas. He had seen me one day slumped miserably against a wall in the Russian embassy and had offered to pick up my passport and bring it back to the hotel where we both stayed. I'd declined, but we'd spent a few minutes exchanging résumés. Russ had just finished six years on a church mission/farm in Bangladesh.

"Amy's spending another week here."

"Too bad. Wonder who else we'll wind up with? Say, you don't smoke do you? Good. We've got at least a tie then."

The compartment had four well-padded berths, a hot-water canister, drinking mugs, a foldout table with white linen cloth, and a wide-view window. Russ had already staked out one of the lower bunks and was stowing provisions in the locker beneath.

"Did you stock up at the friendship store?" he asked.

In Beijing, like Russ, I had bought ham, cheese, nuts, tea bags, canned fruit, crackers, bread, strawberry jam, and a precious handful of candy bars. No nips for the cold nights ahead.

"Promise not to tell anyone, and I'll share something." Russ showed me a small jar of Skippy peanut butter—chunk-style. "I got it in Hong Kong. It's still half full."

We sat and watched passengers straggle across the platform. Older tourists and a group of Japanese businessmen were climbing into the first-class cars at the front of the train; dour-looking Russians were filling the second-class cars in the middle; but every backpacker who appeared on the platform headed right for our car, Carriage Number Eight, the train's caboose. Once again, we had been segregated.

Suddenly the train shrieked, lurched, and started rolling.

"Hey!" Russ was smiling. "Looks like we get it to ourselves."

The door slid open.

"There's only two of you in here? You lucky fuckers!" It was Bill, a young guy from North Carolina whom Russ and I'd both seen around our hotel. "These stupid Chinese. My friends in Beijing wanted tickets for this train, but the reservation office swore it was full. I just counted twenty-four berths in this car—and five of 'em are empty. You guys have two, and I'm stuck with three German guys."

"Clean living," Russ said, and smiled.

Bill slammed the door.

The moment of freshness at the very beginning of a trip—when *everything* lies ahead—is easily the best. None of the mistakes have yet been made, no money misspent or time frittered away. On that first morning the days stretched ahead like ... well, like Siberia. I would be able to sit back, relax, ponder, watch the countryside, read, write, and along the way solve all the problems in my life.

By Moscow I would know the Russian character firsthand, would know Russia in a way Russia's own majority never would. By Moscow I would have scholarly insight into this business of travel, would know whether it was the Answer or mere motion, and would be able to articulate why. I would have adequately field-tested the travelers-are-the-blood-of-the-earth theory, would have full health restored. I would have Amy completely resolved, would have extracted from our stunted coupling any available lesson and released her back to the world. And I would have devised a strategy, a clear, workable blueprint for dismantling whatever frame of mind my wife had built around her life and body. I would step off the train in Moscow a transformed man.

At the start of a long journey it is easy to believe that one is in exactly the right place, thinking, doing, and feeling exactly the right things, and as my Trans-Siberian pulled out of Beijing, as I unrolled a blanket and spread it over me, as I fluffed up a clean pillow, lay back, and closed my eyes, that's precisely what I was thinking.

50
RHYMES
WITH BIB

I should like to spend the whole of my life in traveling abroad, if I could anywhere borrow another life to spend afterwards at home.

—WILLIAM HAZLITT
Table Talk: On Going on a Journey

HEN I HEAR MYSELF DESCRIBING MY TRAVELS to strangers (usually during interviews for jobs I have decided I don't want) I become almost self-envious. When I hear my own words, and when I see the envy on the faces of my no-longer-hopeful employers, it hits me how fortunate I've been. If I had never been to China or Russia or Japan, I would be insanely jealous of anyone who had. When I hear travelers' tales of the Philippines or South America or Australia or other places I have yet to see, I begrudge them their countries. I want it to be *me,* not someone else, out having wild, exhilarating adventures in the far corners.

But in reading my own notebooks, I am struck by how much travel time is spent in states other than wild exhilaration. Excitement and satisfaction come in spurts that tend to sneak up on one, and by the time I boarded the "Trans-Sib" (rhymes with *bib*), I was not at all confident that I had another spurt left in me. My only conscious desire was to get to Europe and eventually back home, to find some routine job, some easy activity that would allow me to spend the rest of my life in health and comfort. I had had enough ticket hassles, enough restaurant food, and changed beds a few times too many. Once the train was in motion, *divorced* or *married* didn't matter nearly so much as whether or not Russ and I had the compartment to ourselves.

We didn't talk much that first day: it seemed wise to save our stories and leak them bit by bit over the thousands of kilometers ahead. Instead, we spent our time snoozing or peering out the window. My first nap ended a couple of hours from Beijing, when Russ nudged my shoulder. "Brad, maybe you'd rather sleep, but there's the Wall. Do you want a last look?"

My inclination was to sleep, but then I remembered the yearning from months and years before, the warm desire that had seeped through my being whenever I had considered the possibility of actually *seeing* the Great Wall. How had I now become so jaded? I sat up and looked out the window. The Wall, in ruins at this location, ran up the spine of a nearby ridge, its towers notching the hill like arthritic vertebrae. Russ was focusing his telephoto lens.

"Darn! Not enough light."

Over the next several days the occupants of Carriage Number Eight would become accustomed to Russ's three main photographic laments: not enough light, train moving too fast, and too many power poles. Across the plains and through the forests and mountains we were serenaded by the click of his camera and the immediate cry: "Darn!"—never "Damn!"—"Another pole!"

Off and on during the afternoon a drizzle fell; beads of water rubbed across our window at a slant. It was mid-July, but when Russ lowered the window to take pictures, a frigid wind stung my cheeks and arms.

The dozing towns punctuating the endless, shrub-dotted hills north of Beijing were always the same: several dozen houses; muddy streets; idle, rusted machinery; a cinder-block schoolhouse with 150 kids in heavy coats running wild in the yard, and one boy at the fence pointing at our train; a black-and-white-striped bar lowered across the main road to block eight docile bicyclists and three pedestrians; a large pig, the only occupant of a mud basketball court, scrimmaging himself in a midcourt puddle; and outside town on the crest of a hill, a man and browsing horse silhouetted against dark, shifting clouds.

Click. "Darn! Another pole!"

The horse's neck arced downward, and swept back and forth through the grass like a suction hose. The man stood nearby, erect, motionless, watching the train; his clothes, twice as big as needed, flapped in the breeze. He did not return my wave.

These morsels of action were always at least an hour apart. Russ stayed awake for the first couple, then sheathed his camera, lay down, closed his eyes, and practiced very regular breathing. I read the first 150 pages of Hemingway's *Islands in the Stream,* ate one of my three chocolate bars, and sometime during the afternoon made these notes:

I should have brought more books and more chocolate.

And: *Outside I see a peasant man chasing one sheep across a dry riverbed. I can see for miles in every direction, and this peasant, that sheep, and our train are the only moving things.*

51

AS FAR
AS THE EYE
COULD SEE

Détente sounds a fine word. And to the extent that there has really been a relaxation in international tension, it is a fine thing. But the fact remains that throughout this decade of détente, the armed forces of the Soviet Union have increased, are increasing, and show no signs of diminishing.

—MARGARET THATCHER
In a speech, 1978

ONTHS BEFORE MY TRIP, an idyllic magazine photo caught my eye: beneath a sky showing pink slices of sunset, a peasant woman and a horse were sprawled in a carpet of brilliant wildflowers stretching to the horizon. Looking closer, I noticed an extraordinary detail—the woman's head resting on the horse's stomach! *Staged?* In what country do women and horses lie like comfortable lovers in fields of flowers? Below the picture was a one-word caption: "Mongolia."

As it turned out, my day in Mongolia, Day Two on the Trans-Sib, was perhaps the most enjoyable of the entire trip. I awoke early to endless green prairies and intoxicating springlike weather, and made my way to the dining car. In China there had been a Chinese waitress and an English-Chinese menu, but now the waitress was a dazzling Mongol with long black hair, colorful embroidered vest, and a smile hinting at ancient wisdom. I imagined her fresh-bought from a wandering tribe—the woman from the photograph, perhaps, parted from her horse. We shared no language, but by pointing at the English-Mongolian menu I ordered "eggs with tomatoes," bread, butter, jam, and muddy coffee, $2.

Alternately I watched the lovely nomad go about getting my order and looked out the window, where the grayness of monsoon season was a thing of the past. It had been so long since I'd seen a brilliant blue sky that I'd forgotten just how exhilarating one can be. My eyes, it seemed, had been overhauled during the night. Billowing over a spacious, virginal landscape were heaps of bleached clouds—pure white, and thick as drifted snow. Our train, curling through green hills dotted with camels and horses and the white yurts the nomads lived in, seemed as miniscule and insignificant as a worm inching across Russ's Kansas. At the peak of its short summer, Mongolia looked the way America must have looked when the Indians owned it: no painful gouges, no signs of plunder, just miles of thick grass and bright flowers. Everything was pristine, shiny, sparkling, as though created only yesterday.

Throughout the long day, passengers stood in the halls gawking at the marvels out the window. Clumps of red and purple wildflowers and patches of mustard grass laced the green hills with traces of color. One sprawling valley was occupied exclusively by two yurts and a herd of untethered horses.

If a place can be "underpopulated," Mongolia is that place. My pocket atlas showed the country as being larger than California, Nevada, Utah, Arizona, and New Mexico combined, but with the same population—1.5 million—as the city of Phoenix. Wyoming, the least densely populated of the forty-eight mainland states, was credited with six people per square mile; Mongolia, less than three.

Signs of civilization were scant. A two-wheel truck path was worn in the grass by the railroad tracks, but trucks were seldom seen. Once, in the distance, I spotted a bus laboring over a hill on what looked like a paved road. Towns were small, clean, simple, and very, very rare; the houses— sturdy looking, widely spaced—were apparently Russian-built. In fact, all permanent structures had the "Russian look": cinder-block walls, hammer-and-sickle billboards, murals of Lenin.

At an early morning station stop, the train's numerous photographers moved out in force, shooting anything that moved or didn't. A baggy-uniformed security guard—an embarrassed-looking Mongol—came hustling down the platform, waving his arms at Bill from North Carolina, who was zeroing in on a huge poster of Lenin. Immediately all camera-toters rallied to Bill's defense, snapping the same poster. Mocked by the noise of zipping shutters, the guard shrugged, turned and disappeared inside the station.

A round midday, an Australian named Tom burst into our compartment along with Bill from North Carolina.

"Okay mates. Put y' bukes a-why. Time f' some spides."

It was my first card game in countless years, and I made a terrible partner for Tom, but we all were too excited that morning—China behind, Russia ahead—to be bothered with the outcome. The window was down; the air slicing in was just right, crisp and fresh and earth-scented, and the view was an animated impressionist painting—cream-colored clouds lofting over the horizon like great cotton planets.

"This looks a lot like heaven," said Bill from North Carolina.

"This looks a lot like my country," said Tom the Australian.

"This looks a lot like Kansas," said Russ the Mennonite.

For a while the train hugged the side of a high ridge, with the scenery stretching away for miles in series of curvaceous bumps and hills tinted with the mustard grass and purple flowers. Green-and-blue pea fowls flashed by at random intervals, strutting through the lushness. Groundhogs popped in and out of holes in the earth. Beneath a hoop next to a lone block building, two boys and a girl fought over a basketball. A woman carrying a double armful of books, and dressed like a San Francisco office worker (high heels, wool skirt, light blue blouse), stepped from the building and called to the children. The game stopped.

I found myself thinking of my wife, remembering the contented look on her face as the Delhi Mail tugged us through Rajasthan. She'd have loved this train, too. What was she doing today? Where had she been when I called?

I knew where Amy was—entwined with Dylan in what used to be "our" Beijing hotel room, the T-shirt she wore yesterday morning now lying in a crumpled, possibly shredded, mound on the rug beside her. Her persistence had paid off. I wondered: Will mine?

I n midafternoon a buzz of anticipation ran up and down Carriage Number Eight. The schedule posted next to the samovar at the head of the car said we were due a half-hour stop in the Mongolian capital. I stood at the window and watched Ulan Bator, a notch in any traveler's money belt, materialize out of the countryside. At its heart were several modern buildings, eight and nine stories tall, surrounded by a sprawl of squat urban bunkers. The atlas said half a million people lived there, an estimate my notebook challenged: *It doesn't look a whole lot bigger than Gunnison, Colorado—5,000 people.*

Whoever took the Mongolian census must have counted lots of Russians—

in spite of the independent façade, Mongolia is a Soviet colony. In and around the Ulan Bator station, blue-eyed Russians, not at all similar to the happy workers on the shameless billboards, easily outnumbered those with high cheekbones, narrow eyes, and the ruddy Mongolian skin.

A scowling Russian soldier stalked the platform, hands gripped angrily behind, silently daring anyone to look him in the eye. He wore black knee-high boots, a green cap studded with medallions, and had a monstrous pistol lashed to his hip. Other Russians lounged around the station, looking suspicious and bitter, as though Mongolia were the most dreadful exile of all. Alcohol seemed the local pastime; three-fourths of the men—beaten spirits, shabby clothes, several days' beard growth—looked like winos.

People were desperate to board our train. Hopeful travelers paced beside mounds of twine-wrapped luggage on the platform; inside the station every ticket window was besieged by a long line of silent, grimacing Russians. There was no friendly banter, no conversation of any sort, not even whispers. If someday the existence of a horrible death camp is reported in Ulan Bator, I will not be surprised.

Most of the passengers stayed in the train, but I saw this as my one shot ever at Ulan Bator, and went for a look. The square in front of the station was a weed-choked "people's park." At its center was a concrete monolith; I imagined the dedication day headline: THE PEOPLE GET THE SHAFT. On this beautiful summer day I was the park's lone visitor.

On a nearby street I was surprised by three passing Mongols wearing leather slippers, fringed tunics, winter caps with long earflaps, and daggers tucked in their belts.

"Hello."

But I was from the wrong continent, the wrong century. This trio, the largest collection of Mongols I would see in Ulan Bator, eased into wide grins, and once past me, exploded into laughter.

Two blocks from the station I noticed people passing through an unmarked door into a building with no windows. I followed. It was a small grocery with only a few Russians, no Mongolians, shopping. The party elite? Loaves of bread, a few food tins, and some bottles of wine were scattered among mostly barren shelves. People weren't speaking to each other, or to me; I stayed only a moment, bought nothing, and went back to the train.

Most of the occupants of Carriage Number Eight, having found nothing to spend money on, and having been dissuaded, by the black looks of the scowling soldier, from taking pictures, were already back in their compartments. The Russians had never gotten off.

Soon the station and the Ulan Bator skyline were fading behind us. Stacked in an industrial yard near the tracks was a stockpile of cement sewer pipes. Newly minted dump trucks, rusted tankers, and a fleet of dusty municipal buses were parked in rows on a storage lot. On the outskirts of town I saw a cement-mixing plant, several factories, several oil tanks, a shantytown, and one communications dish. And that was it for Ulan Bator, Mongolia.

Within moments we were back in the land of camels and tents and mustard grass and clear-flowing streams, and—as far as the eye could see—nothing more.

52

WE HAVE BORROWED SOME OF THE RUSSIAN ARMY

By the end of the 13th century the Mongol realm stretched from China to Poland, taking in all of Asia except India, Burma, and Cambodia. The whole of the Mongol people itself numbered, apparently, not more than a million; yet at its zenith their empire, based on fewer than 150,000 troops, was sitting firmly on the necks of some 100 million people.

—JOEL CARMICHAEL
A Cultural History of Russia

THE HARSHNESS OF ULAN BATOR had scuffed Mongolia's utopian luster, and for the next couple of hours a subdued atmosphere settled over Carriage Number Eight. Russ drifted into an afternoon nap. I went to the dining car to buy postcards and Mongolian stamps; a single card with postage to the United States cost $1.35! I splurged on six of them, wrote short messages, and turned them over to the Mongolian steward who ran the car. (Somehow all six found their destinations.)

After dinner a "discussion" broke out between several Westerners and the steward. This tough-looking man was a stew of ethnic features—Turkish, Chinese, American Indian. He was well built, wore Western clothes, and looked as though he might once have been in someone's military (intelligence services, probably). The expression on his face said that he had learned something very nasty about every one of us on his train. He was drunk.

"It is Mongolian holiday," he said by way of explanation. His English came to him with painful slowness. He stood in the aisle between tables, weaving unsteadily from drink and the motion of the train, feeling his way through each sentence as though opening a combination safe by touch. When asked a simple question, he would roll his eyes—"You imbecile"—and then launch into a long, broken soliloquy. His intoxication stifled any semblance of "conversation," but since no traveler wants to pass through an entire country without meeting a single native, and since he was the only English-speaking Mongolian any of us were likely to encounter, we primed him with the conversational pellets that fuel a monologue.

Are the Mongolians and Chinese friends?

"Mongolians ... are ... friends ... with everyone. Mongolians ... have ... always ... been friends with ... everyone."

Even the Russians?

"Mongolians ... are ... friends ... with ... everyone." While his answers took shape, he would search the half-dozen faces of his audience, making sure we understood the full import of each word. "Everyone has ... two arms ... two legs ... one head ... one nose ..." He paused for steadiness. "Two ears ... two eyes. ... Right?"

Right.

He nodded.

"The Chinese ... If their leader ... goes to the top of the hill and says ... 'Everybody go to the toilet and make pee-pee! ... then you will see one billion Chinese ... go *rushing* to the toilet! And every single one of them ... will make pee-pee."

Laughter.

"Yes ... this is true! You have seen the Chinese ... for yourself." He swigged from his drink, grimaced, continued: "The Russians ... If their leader goes to the top of the hill and says ... 'Everybody go to the toilet ... and make pee-pee' ... then everybody will go to the toilet.... But they will not make pee-pee! ... They will stand in the toilet ... and look at their watches ... until it is long enough time for to make pee-pee.... Then they all go to Red Square, and clap and cheer...'YEA, LENIN! ... We make lots of pee-pee.' ... Then they drink vodka all night to celebrate making lots of pee-pee ... that they did not make."

More laughter.

"Yes ... I am telling you the truth.... The truth makes people laugh." He stood a little taller and cleared his throat. "Mongolians ..." He waited for the laughing to die. "If our leader goes to the top of the hill ... and says ... 'Everybody go to the toilet and make pee-pee' ... we ..."

Here he snarled and shot his right fist toward the ceiling; when it was head high, he clapped his left hand against his right biceps, stopping his right arm in midflight. Arm and fist hung in the air, forming a right angle— the obscene European gesture: *Up yours, buddy!*

"Maybe ... in one hour we go to the toilet...." he growled. "Maybe! ... And maybe we make pee-pee ... But maybe *not* ... Mongolians are independent! We pee-pee for ourselves!"

Joe, an Australian who earlier had told me he was a "bush pilot," had a question: "What would the Russians say if you independent Mongolians asked them to leave?"

It was the obvious question. All day long we had witnessed the occupation: posters of Lenin, Russian billboards, Russian buildings. At each station there had been Russian policemen, Russian parks, Russian monuments, newspapers, soldiers, women, children. In the countryside there were convoys of Russian army trucks. Near Ulan Bator we had seen jet fighter planes hurtling along a hundred feet off the ground. "Russian MIGs," Bill from North Carolina had proclaimed.

Our dining-car host sighed. He sat down at an empty booth. "Let me explain.... We are very few people here.... How many do you think? ..."

One and a half million.

"Yes ... One and one half million." He was surprised, even disappointed, that we knew this. "And how many people are there in China?"

A billion.

"Yes. And since you never know ... what's going to happen in China ... since you never can tell ... what the Chinese leader is going to yell ... from the top of his hill ... and since there are so few Mongolians ... and so many, many Chinese ... we Mongolians have done a very smart thing. We have bought many, many weapons from the Russians.... And we have done something ... something even smarter. We have *borrowed* ... some of the Russian Army."

Laughter.

"No, no ... Do not laugh!" He glared at us. "We Mongolians have been around ... since before there was America. ... We are very smart people. ... And when we borrow the Russians' army ... this saves us lots of time and money.... The Russians ... they watch the Chinese for us ... and then we are free to do all our favorite things ... riding horses ..."—he leered at the two women in the audience—"making babies ..."—he turned away, raised his hand to order another drink, and then turned back to us, trying to look fierce and independent—"celebrating Mongolian holidays...."

"If we ask the Russians to leave ... the Russians will surely leave.... Are Mongolians not ... the sons and daughters of Genghis Khan? ... Mongolians are peace-loving people, but ... you do not want to make a Mongolian angry. ... People in every country know the strong spirit of the Mongolian warrior. ... Right?"

Rrrrrright!

He scoffed. "You are brainwashed.... Your CIA ... has made so much propaganda that now ... now the world ... all Westerners ... are afraid of the Russians.... But the Russians ..."—he had a politician's grin—"they are nothing to be afraid of.... If they ever need a beating ... myself and a few friends can give it to them.... But they will never need one.... The Russians ..." said the drunken Mongolian dining-car steward, "are incapable of killing."

"What are a hundred thousand of them doing in Afghanistan?" asked Joe the Australian Bush Pilot.

"Last year ... just last year ... I myself went to Afghanistan."

You!

"Yes ..." He puffed up his shoulders. "Me ... And I see things with my own eyes." He patted his face. "In Kabul ... all is peaceful.... The Russians are among friends.... The Afghani people love the Russians.... There was no killing.... To say anything else is a lie! ... A C-I-A lie!"

"Now wait a minute ..." said Joe the Australian Bush Pilot.

I avoided the conversation's rapid and predictable disintegration by slipping out of the dining car and back to my compartment, where I caught Russ, alone, spreading peanut butter on a row of crackers.

53
OFFICIAL POSTURES

Russia is a riddle wrapped in a mystery inside an enigma.

—SIR WINSTON CHURCHILL
In a broadcast, October, 1, 1939

A FLASH OF LIGHT.
Loud foreign grunting.
Someone shaking my shoulder.

I opened an eye. Two uniformed Mongolian men were in our compartment; I saw a green thigh three inches from my face. Having been warned that the Russian border crossing would happen in the middle of the night, Russ and I had slept clothed, documents handy. Russ, still under his covers, was sitting up, holding out his handful of papers. I dug mine from under the pillow. One of the men removed the customs' declaration forms we'd been given only twenty-four hours earlier, and handed the rest back. They left.

"How long were we asleep?" I asked Russ.

"An hour and a half."

We sat there for a few moments. Outside our window it was pitch-dark. I got up and went into the hall. The two men were standing on the ground outside the train, talking and smoking. There were no buildings in sight, no noises coming from the train. I went back into the compartment. Russ had lain back down, eyes closed. I switched off the light, and slipped under my blankets. . . .

A flash of light.

Loud foreign grunting.

Someone shaking my shoulder.

"Puss-purt."

I looked up, blinking at a burly Russian man with a row of silver buttons on his coat. "Puss-purt." Behind him was a slim, beautiful woman with a serious pout. They took our passports and left.

"How long was that, Russ?"

"Forty-five minutes."

I waited two minutes, leaned up, and switched off the light. Ten seconds later two armed soldiers, barking rapid Russian, switched it right back on. They pointed at the compartments beneath our bunks. We got up and showed them our belongings. My copy of *One Day in the Life of Ivan Denisovitch,* with *Solzhenitsyn* in large letters on the cover, was ignored, but Russ's black leather Bible was not. The two guards huddled with it, speaking in loud voices; they flipped from Genesis to Revelations, inspected the handwritten notes inside the cover, said something in Russian to Russ, handed his book back, and left.

Right behind them came a conductor. "Teeck-ets." He took them and left. We straightened our things, shut the door, and climbed back under our covers. I hit the light.

"Wouldn't you love to know what they were saying about my Bible?"

Before I could answer, the door slid open, the light flicked on. The body of a stern woman filled our doorway. "You will now exchange *hud cuhdency* for *Rrrrashun rrubles.* Cash only! No traveler chake!"

She directed us down the dark platform to a building with a makeshift bank. A row of lamps turned the scene into a prisoner-of-war movie. A ring of rifle-toting soldiers had surrounded the train, eliminating the chances of anyone bolting into the night, back toward Mongolia.

"These fuckers." Bill from North Carolina was in line ahead of us. "They're only giving fifteen rubles for twenty dollars. In Moscow you get sixty no sweat on the black market."

"Yeah," said Russ, "but look at the bright side. Once they get our money, you know they'll let us sleep."

"Lake Baikal."

Russ had opened the shade, allowing in a haze of gray light that shattered a vague dream I was having.

"There's Lake Baikal," he said again, trying to coax me to life. Then: "Darn, not enough light."

"Wha'timazit?"

"Six-thirty local time. One-thirty in the morning in Moscow."

In Russia, at a latitude equal to that of Hudson's Bay in Canada, clock time is meaningless. Each day brought more than nineteen hours of light, and the train and all stations operated on Moscow time; before long I would grow accustomed to dawns at 1030, breakfasts at 0330, dinner at high noon, high noon at 0700. En route to Moscow I was never certain what time it was, or which meal to eat next. Russ wore a fancy watch and tried to keep me informed, but after a while the sun became my only guide.

But at Lake Baikal the sun was hidden. The intoxicating Mongolian weather had disappeared. Streaks of rain smeared our window. Beyond the glass was a large body of whitecapped water, its banks lined with groves of poplar and aspen. Offshore, under a dark and sagging sky, small boats battled foaming three-foot waves.

Russ poured two cups of tea and proposed a toast: "Home-lund, cum-rad! Und peace!"

We clinked, and sipped, and grinned at each other.

"Did that really happen last night?" Russ asked.

"The border?"

"Yeah. How many of them were there? It seemed like one of those long bad dreams that just keeps going."

Before the tea was finished, we stopped briefly at a station. Sitting on the track next to us was a train full of Russians. The accommodations we could see through their windows, sixty sleeping berths squeezed triple-decker into one open car, made Carriage Number Eight seem luxurious. A lady peering into our window shrugged off my wave and shook her head. The rain had stopped, and now Russ lowered our window. The lady turned her back, moved away.

When their train started to roll, its occupants began to loosen up, smiling and waving now at those of us in Carriage Number Eight. A couple of compartments down a man leaned from the Russian train and aimed a camera at me. I leaned out and waved for him. He snapped the shutter and saluted a thank you. People in both cars began poking heads out windows. Knowing we would never again see each other, it was okay to be friendly. Men, women, children, young and old, capitalist and Communist, were smiling, waving, laughing, getting in free, unabashed gapes. Someone on our side started clapping, and it spread to the entire car, then to the Russian one. As their train pulled away, each passing window revealed a cargo of grins and at least a few clapping hands. A chuckling babushka stretched an arm across the no-man's-land, and clutched playfully at the hands from our car.

"Yea, Babushka!" someone yelled.

I felt a surge of exhilaration. Every now and then some incredibly human moment pops out of the sea of suspicion and sarcasm in which we swim. This was such a moment.

54
THE LAIN-EEN SPOTTING COMPETITION

So often, back in the big cities of the West, you hear people saying, "If I could only live my life again, I'd travel." The sad part of it is that many of these people are in their twenties and thirties.

—RICK BERG
The Art and Adventure of Traveling Cheaply

I

N TRUE COMMUNIST FASHION the others in Carriage Number Eight regarded Russ's and my half-full compartment as a blessing intended for all. Our room became the Gathering Spot, a place to drink tea, play cards, tell lies. There were Swedish women in the next compartment, and down the hall several Australians, some Germans, a sprinkling of Americans, two French, and a lone Brit.

During one card game, with endless Lake Baikal winding past our window, Bill from North Carolina suggested we play for money, but was quickly outvoted. "Oh, that's right," he said. "I forgot about Tom. You've got what, ten dollars, Tom?"

"Seven now," said Tom the Australian, throwing down a card.

"Really?" I said. "Seven dollars to your name?"

"Yes. Really." Tom's left cheek had a rectangular patch of facial hair, an inch and a half by three-quarters. The rest of his face was clean-shaven, but these few whiskers had been groomed to a length of more than two inches—the coat-of-arms of a young man crazy or daring enough to drop into Europe flat broke.

"What'll you do when we get to Berlin?"

"Have you seen his socks?" Bill asked me. "Show him, Tom."

Tom kicked off a shoe and raised his foot to the seat cushion. He was

wearing green and red knee-high hand-knit socks with an unusual feature—
a toe area divided into two separate niches as though designed for a cloven
hoof.

"I've got forty pairs of these."

"What are they?"

"Two-toed socks. I got 'em in Japan. Japanese fishamun wear 'em. I'm going
to sell 'em on the street in Europe. They'll boy anything there. I figure I can
get ten dollars. Foyve at least!"

"But even if you get ten for all of them, that's only four hundred dollars.
Then what?"

"I don't know. Everybody else seems worried about it, but I'm not." He
was full of blond and blue-eyed twenty-one-year-old energy. He was riding
the Trans-Sib. Nothing mattered. "If I get cold, I'll make my socks into a
sleeping bag."

"I guess that's not so strange," I told him. "When I was twenty-two, I landed
in Boulder, Colorado, with a sleeping bag and exactly nine dollars to my
name."

"Roit. And what happened?"

"I was taken in by the woman who's now my wife."

Bill from North Carolina: "Two years ago I arrived in Athens from the
islands, with *no* money—only a Magic Bus ticket to Paris. I knew a French
family, and if I could get to them I'd be able to think of something. But I had
to wait three days for the bus to leave, and that nearly killed me. I slept on
the street outside the railroad station, scared to death. To eat I had to dine-
and-dash. Going through Europe on the bus was a bitch. Everyone else would
go to the restaurant and eat—I'd go to the backdoor and say I was starving.
I never want to do that again."

In the mid-seventies Russ the Mennonite began a Bangladesh-to-Kansas
odyssey with several thousand dollars, and arrived in New York eight months
later with $102. "Greyhound had a deal going—ninety-nine dollars any-
where—and that left me three dollars. I had a jar of honey, and I ate bread
and honey for a few days. In Illinois an old man befriended me. In Missouri
he bought me a big breakfast, and that got me home."

"Hey, what's that?" Bill from North Carolina was pointing at an odd assortment of white metal pieces strewn across a clearing on the side of a
hill. If they hadn't all been the same color, and if the clearing hadn't been
so obviously tended by a gardener, it might have been a scrap-metal
dump.

"It looks like a plane wreck," said Bill, trying to answer his own question.

"It's Lain-een!" screamed Tom the Australian.

It was obvious as soon as he said it. We were seeing artwork, an item of
sculpture. The metal pieces formed an abstract bust of Lain-een; to see what

the artist had intended, one had to look at what *wasn't* there. The white shapes were his clothes, his eyes, his hat; it was his face that was missing. The grass in the clearing was his flesh.

"That's moin!" screamed Tom the Australian. "That gives me faw."

"Four *what?*" asked Bill.

"Faw in the Lain-een Spotting Competition. The whole car's in on it. Where've you been?"

55

A CASUAL AFTERTHOUGHT

*A Moscow friend told me of a Russian woman
who had lived forty years in Paris and who, after
her first chance to visit Russia, flew back to Paris
with the one gift that all of her emigre friends had
prayed for—a suitcase full of Russian earth.*

—HEDRICK SMITH
The Russians

HE EARLY-MORNING CLOUDS YIELDED to clear skies that spread over a countryside with the same lusty rawness and spacious grandeur as Mongolia. Although considerably more developed, Siberia, too, struck me as underpopulated and underworked. In towns I was surprised at the degree of idleness we were witnessing. Silent, brooding people loitered in the stations. Crews of plump women with picks and shovels dug halfheartedly at the railbeds. The only people who seemed to relish their work were the policemen wagging fingers and hissing *"Nyet!"* at anyone with a camera. I had come to Russia expecting to see full employment, a paradise of untiring workers marching devotedly toward Communist heaven. Instead, I saw plodders, beaten drifters who, if they bothered to go through the motions at all, affected only an unconvincing imitation of labor. I was reminded of the Soviet witticism: "As long as they pretend to pay us, we will pretend to work."

For the first day or two in Russia I felt conned. I had come with a vague hope that my presence and interactions with "the people" would chip away at our mutual misconceptions and contribute to that groundswell of human solidarity which is surely coming. But now I felt like a fool. Whom was I kidding? I was going to pass through Russia without making a dent.

Aside from the chuckling babushka and her briefly smiling comrades, the vast majority of my interactions were with other backpackers. The train's Russian passengers glowered and retreated into their compartments whenever I passed through their cars. I was a clumsy intruder, an unwanted do-

gooder. My greetings, even in Russian, were pointedly ignored. The staff
people in the dining car were gruff and seemed nervous, as though they were
being watched to make sure they didn't derive incidental pleasure from their
work. I imagined their thoughts: "Our lives would be easier without you rich
tourists coming to mock us."

One day our frumpy waitress took the following order from the group at
my table: "One biff stroganoff, one feesh, one shikken, one biffsteak."

"Bet you don't get your shikken," Tom the Australian told me. "They ran
out last night."

"They could have picked some up along the way."

"I'll mike you a why-juh. If you get shikken, I'll give you a pair of socks. If
you don't, you pay for my beefsteak."

We agreed.

During the next half hour Tom and Joe the Australian Bush Pilot swatted
dozens of flies and lined them up one by one on the tablecloth, underscoring
the car's general dishevelment. Each time she passed, the waitress—embarrassed, jabbering—would flick them onto the floor. Finally she brought
four servings of "biffsteak"—a wad of cooked hamburger hidden under a
pile of rice, with a fried egg laid over the whole mess.

Joe the Bush Pilot: "Hey, where's my fish?"

Bill from North Carolina: "And my stroganoff?"

She pretended not to understand.

Tom the happy Australian: "Eat up, jints. Yaw in beefsteak country."

f I had been conned about Russia, I had conned myself—thinking I
was going to change places simply by passing through! One tourist
changes nothing. The nineteen of us in Carriage Number Eight would
make no measurable difference. Travel, as a means of social change,
was a hoax. Insights gained at home have a way of unraveling en route.

I was not the only one with misgivings. I found Bill from North
Carolina sulking in the hall one beautiful afternoon. Outside, miles of forest
and an enormous river were zipping by at ninety kilometers an hour.

"The earth is so pretty," he said. "I can't imagine a more ideal setting for
life! But when I look out the window and see how beautiful everything is, I
can't help but wonder: How'd everything get so fucked up? Who's to blame?"

We stood for hours, assessing guilt and worshiping this large, empty land
cut only occasionally by a dirt road or a solitary strand of power lines.
Idyllic farming lives, remnants of the eighteenth century, were laid before
our eyes: a horse pulling a wagon toward a ramshackle farmhouse; mounds

of drying hay dolloped out in distant fields like scoops of eggnog ice cream; on a smooth black pond, three boys fishing from a rowboat ("Darn! Another pole!"); near the tracks a gang of bent peasants scything grass; in a wide, lawnlike meadow, a man on horseback rounding up cows; nearby, another man standing on the giant tire of a baby-blue tractor, peering perplexedly beneath the raised hood.

"If you sleep or read or even lower your eyes," Bill said, "you might miss something."

Russia seeps deep into one's bones. Carpets of purple flowers, forests of pines and birches, and the endless green hills, all explained the famous Russian reverence for the Motherland. The place *was* compelling. I felt an urge to jump the train, scoop up handfuls of the deep black topsoil, build a cabin, sign on for the next five-year plan. The power lines were already in, the crops grew tall, the sun shone until nearly eleven each night, and during the four hours preceding sunset, soft colors bled together in a psychedelic western sky.

One afternoon, for no apparent reason, a rainbow formed on the southern horizon, stabbing itself into the ground like a huge painted wicket wide enough to drive a buffalo herd through. Indeed, the countryside could have swallowed up millions of the beasts without having to gulp. Is it any wonder that Russian novelists routinely dash off thousand-page novels? Such an enormous land demands enormous books, enormous thinking, enormous dreams, wild, enormous plans. It's only natural that the Russians want to run the entire world—from central Siberia the rest of the world is a casual afterthought.

56

THE THIRD WORLD DIET

*As a member of an escorted tour, you don't even
have to know the Matterhorn isn't a tuba.*

—TEMPLE FIELDING
Fielding's Guide to Europe

ETWEEN NAPS, MEALS, CARD GAMES, and sessions of staring out the
window, Russ and I hosted résumé swaps. On the full moon night of
Friday-the-thirteenth of July a stream of people flowed through our
compartment, telling stories, passing time, waiting for the main event
to come sliding up over the horizon.

Tom the Australian told me he had worked as a registered nurse
in a mental hospital in Sydney.

"Then your problem's solved. Registered nurses can find work anywhere."

Tom made a face. "I quit n'sing."

"Why?"

"Didn't loik it. A man died in my arms, and none of the doctors cared. He
was an alcoholic with diabetes, and he had these big swollen veins in his
throat, and one of 'em popped. He started choking, and I grabbed him and
sat him up. He said, 'One . . . two . . . three . . .' then puked blood all over me
and went unconscious. I tried to get a doctor, but no one would come. There
was one Indian doctor in particular—said he'd be there soon, but he didn't
come for twenty minutes, and by then it was too late. He was just waitin' f'
the guy to die. I quit pretty soon after that, and I won't go back."

"What'll happen when your seven dollars run out?"

Tom leaned closer and lowered his voice: "I've got nine thousand dollars
from an insurance settlement. It's in a bank in Berlin." He held up a slightly
crooked wrist and showed where it had been broken. "Motorcycle exa-dint.
I ran into the utha goy, but he caused the exa-dint."

220

"I'll have to revise my mental image of you."

"You really thought I was a sawk m'chant?"

"I really thought you had balls."

Joe the Bush Pilot was only twenty-five, but already he was set financially. Flying was just a hobby; he made his money farming. "My father left me thirty-five hundred fertile acres in southwestern Australia. I've got wheat, lupin, and some cows."

How can a farmer up and leave thirty-five hundred acres?

"My stepdad suggested that while I was still young I should follow the great Aussie tradition—go have a look around, see what's out there. So he's watching my place for the next eighteen months."

Bill from North Carolina, in spite of his dine-and-dash story, was also bona-fide bourgeois: "My grandmother left me two thousand acres of Arkansas timberland. It's in a trust. When I'm thirty, I get a lump of eighty to a hundred thou. I'll either use it for down payment on a house or set up a permanent income. If I can get ten thousand dollars a year from it, I can travel forever."

"What about you?" he asked me.

"I'm spending my meager life's savings on this trip, and I don't know for sure what's going to happen when I get home. I'm thinking of writing a book."

"About your trip?"

"I'm not sure what it's about anymore. Once I wrote a booklet—*The Art of Tripping,* I called it, by 'Lance Free,' a pen name from a newspaper I once worked for. . . . It was full of thoughts about what a great thing traveling is. Sometimes I've thought this trip—people I've met, things I've seen—would make a good background for all those thoughts, but now I just don't know."

"You're not gonna write it?"

"Just don't know. The trip hasn't turned out the way I hoped. I've been preoccupied a lot with whether or not I'll wind up divorced. And I got sick in China—that's not something I recommend to anyone. Remember yesterday when you asked me, 'How'd everything get so fucked up?' I've spent a lot of time wondering the same thing. All those people in China and Hong Kong and Japan—am I dreaming to think we're gonna work all this out? And what kind of confused book would this make?"

Bee, a British nurse who had wandered into the compartment, had been listening. "You should write it. My trips never make sense till they're over. When you get home, you see things more clearly."

Terry, a ponytailed young man from Madison, Wisconsin, spoke up. "*I've* thought of writing a book about what traveling's really like. I've read lots of books about the Trans-Sib, but they never tell you the real stuff. They're full of who did what on what river, how to tell tundra from taiga—but they never tell you about *us.* They never tell you that no one knows what the fuck they're doing on this train, or that by the third day you'd kill for a decent meal. Or that what you mostly do is sit here playing cards and bullshitting in your own language. There hasn't been a real good book about us since *The Drifters.* And we deserve one. How many of us are there, you think? In Nepal? China? Japan?"

"Don't forget all the Aussies driving around America in Volkswagen buses," said Tom.

"Right," said Terry. "Or people cruising the world on their own boats. There're millions of 'em—out there right this minute—but nobody writes about 'em. If you read all the books and newspapers, you'd think everyone had a job in a corporation and spent their one-week vacation in sunny Spain or charming England. Hell, Europe's nothin' but a yuppie summer camp anymore."

"Thank God everyone's *not* out here," said Bill from North Carolina. "Prices would triple. Can you believe how cheap this is? I did eleven weeks in China for seven hundred bucks!"

"People won't believe that," said Terry the Longhair. "All they know is the Sunday travel ads."

"Yeah," said Bill. " 'Hong Kong and China—Ten Days from Seventeen Hundred Dollars! *Land Cost Only.'* "

"People are scared," said Terry. "I hitched the Africa Road last year. In Zaire, every night I'd arrive in some village in the middle of the jungle. People'd come rushing out like I was Jesus. 'Where'd you come from?' I'd name the last village. *'WHAT?'* they'd scream. *'Are you crazy? Those people are thieves, murderers. They'll slit your throat.'*

"Then we'd party all night; they'd be the nicest, most shirt-off-your-back people you'd ever want to meet. They'd kill a pig or a dog, break out their brews, offer one of their daughters and their best hut. Next morning they'd beg me to stay—offer *two* daughters, they'd make me chief, *three* daughters, anything I wanted. I'd say, 'Thanks, but I gotta go.'

" 'Well, which way are you going?' And I'd name the next village. *'WHAT? Are you crazy? Those people are thieves, murderers! They'll slit your throat.'* Then I'd reach the next place, and they'd come runnin' out: 'Where'd you come from? ... *WHAT? Are you crazy?* ...' This happened every night for weeks.

"And it's the same way with people at home. They'll think you're nuts if you tell 'em you've been here. Those Russians are *thieves! Murderers! They'll slit your throat!*"

People laughed agreement.

Terry went on. "But even if you tell 'em how it really is, people still won't come. Not if they hear about the raunchy places you sleep and the greasy meals and how everyone gets sick. People don't stand in line to get sick. Look at you, you toothpick." He pointed at me. "I bet you've lost thirty pounds."

"Hey, that's *my* book," said Bill from North Carolina. *"The Third World*

Diet. Combine travel with weight loss. I won't have to do anything—just get all the fat people out here, drop 'em off in India with no money, and come back and get 'em a week later. They'll lose fifty pounds. I'll be rich.'"

Joe the Bush Pilot had a spin-off: "Third World Survival Camp. 'Hands-on experiences with highly trained counselors.' "

"Obedience training," said Bee the British Nurse. "Take people's spoiled brats to Calcutta for two weeks, and guarantee they'll never hear another peep out of 'em."

A round of entrepreneurial hilarity swept the car until Terry the Longhair steered the subject back to my book: "Don't tell people about *your* trip. Tell 'em to get out for themselves! Tell 'em they don't have to work, wear a tie— you really *can* spend your whole life this way. There're people like us all over the place—on the Trans-Sib, on the Nile, thousands of 'em hanging out in Tokyo and India, South America, Europe—people who aren't working, never will, and they're laughing at anyone who does. Working sucks. I wouldn't be caught dead at it." Bee laughed. Bill from North Carolina was clapping.

"Hell, there're only two legit industries anyway," said Terry the Longhair. "Tourism and agriculture. And if we can get enough people to boycott that whole 'arms-race-and-new-car-every-year' crockashit, someday we'll all just be traveling around, hangin' out together." He glanced around the car. "Look at us! How long you guys been out?"

"Three years," said Bill from North Carolina.

"Two years," said Tom the Australian.

"Six years," said Russ the Mennonite.

"See! We're already livin' it," said Terry the Longhair from Madison, Wisconsin. "And, hell, if we had more people moving around, we could all live damn well off the American defense budget. We wouldn't need the bombs. If we're everywhere, who'd attack us?"

He paused. No one said anything for a minute; everyone was debating which of his more obvious weak points to pick on.

"But you've got to warn people," he started up again, preventing debate, "it's addicting. You find yourself stretchin' your money forever, hopping checks, always scammin'. Going home gets real scary. You'd rather spend a hundred bad days on the road than ten so-so ones at home."

"Sounds like you're broke," said Tom the Australian.

"Damn close," Terry said.

"Why don't *you* go home and write a book?" Bee the British Nurse asked him.

"Nah," said Terry the Longhair. "Sounds too much like work."

There was a scream from the hall.

"Oh, wow! Get out here you guys! There's the moon!"

57

"BRAAH-DEE, YOU BE GOOD BOY!"

Trips start when the last familiar face recedes from view, and end the instant one reappears.

—LANCE FREE
The Art of Tripping

I T WAS 3:15 THE NEXT MORNING, Moscow time, when I was awakened by the train's gradual halt. A crack in the blinds revealed a weak sun attacking the clouds on the northeastern horizon. I put my shoes on and eased open the door.

"'Za bigstop?" Russ asked, through a fog of sleep.

"Can't tell yet," I said, and slid the door shut behind me. At all other stops the wave of photographers had negated the special feeling one has when alone in a foreign place, and I was determined to see at least one Russian station by myself.

But I wasn't allowed off the train. The car attendant, a Chinese man who'd been aboard since Beijing, resented my prowling in the middle of the night. This was his time to himself, the part of the day when all his problems should be sleeping. Refusing to lower the stairs, he pointed to his watch and said, "Only stop three minute." I knew it was a lie, and he knew I knew, but I was too sleepy to argue. I just smiled and went to the open doorway on the right side of the train, and spent the next fifteen minutes observing the dozen early-rising locals milling on the platform.

Several of them were exact replicas of my Slovakian relatives in western Pennsylvania. During my childhood, whenever we made the drive up from Virginia, my mother and her family spoke in a Russian dialect; but it wasn't until much later, maybe it wasn't until I saw this lonely, rural station, that I fully grasped that my grandparents had come from another continent. I had always considered their language nothing more than a family quirk, and never appreciated that they actually had uprooted from their homeland in hopes of a better life for themselves and people like ... me?

The sporadic letters from family members who had not emigrated to America were often sad ones, and were used by my grandfather to justify his contention that he had done the right thing; life in the coalfields around Pittsburgh, no matter how difficult, was, he said, incomparably better than living in a place where a person's biggest obstacle to happiness was his own government—or worse, the one next door. I hadn't understood Mom's tears in front of the TV when the tanks rolled into Prague in 1968, but when I saw these early-morning idlers on a station platform in the middle of Russia, wondering if and when their tickets out would arrive, everything made a little more sense.

Men stood, nursing cigarettes, in quiet, shifting groups of two or three; women clustered on benches that lined the platform. At some point, every person there looked over at my doorway and made eye contact with me. I supposed that I, too, had I lived here, would have risen at dawn to study those fortunate enough to be heading for places I could but imagine: if I couldn't go myself, I would at least want to inspect the people who could.

The scene had a theatrical quality: the platform setting, the shuffle of characters, my inability to interact with them. But had this cast assembled just for my benefit? If I hadn't gotten up at 0315 Moscow time, for whom would this slow drama have been performed?

My attention was drawn to a woman, a man, and a young boy who came walking slowly from an alley next to the station, and stopped right in front of my doorway, oblivious. Never before had I realized just how typically Russian my relatives looked, but now, not more than fifteen feet away, I saw a whittled down version of my own family tree.

The woman, the very image of my grandmother, had a scarf pulled tight over her head, and was wearing a blue, print dress and thick, quilted coat. At the top of the lavender socks that held her fat ankles together, a stripe of white, vein-crossed leg was showing. As a child I used to marvel at the lithe ballerina in the yellowed photographs from her youth, but by the time I came to know her, Grandma had acquired the same lumpy figure as all the older women I'd seen in every station since Ulan Bator, Mongolia. In the hard lines of her face I could see years of prayer and worry, and the pain of nine childbirths.

But that is retrospect; back then I knew only that being around Grandma filled me with a sadness that was never explained. The "conversations" we shared were brief, her English and my Russian being equally nonexistent, but whenever we'd drive the six hours to visit her, there'd always come a time when my mother would indicate that Grandma wanted to "talk" with me. Dutifully I would go into the big dining room crammed with old furniture and sit on the footstool next to her stuffed rocking chair. Light slanted in through the window, flooding the room, and in Grandma's pupils I could see my own face reflected in distorted miniature. She would look at me through clear gray blue eyes, and drill deep down into my soul, silently imparting her untranslatable sorrows.

"Braah-dee!"

She'd been washing dishes in the kitchen one day when I was still a baby. Her husband, Mihail, who had brought her to Pennsylvania in 1908, was up on the roof doing repairs. Maria, my grandmother, heard a sliding sound and looked out the window over the sink. Mihail sailed by, head first, upside down. For a brief instant she glimpsed the terror in his eyes, and then he was gone. His head hit the concrete sidewalk below.

"Braah-dee!"

"Yes, Gram-maw."

"Braah-dee, you be good boy!" It was the only English she ever said to me.

"I will, Gram-maw." I would hug her, kiss her old thick lips, and, feeling awkward, take the folded dollar she always had for me. Now, in Russia, as the woman on the sidewalk turned and spoke to the boy, I heard a voice from far away: "Braah-dee, you be good boy!"

The boy—blond bangs cut straight across his forehead—looked frighteningly like I had looked twenty years earlier. He listened to the babushka's gravelly voice, reached into the grocery sack he was carrying, pulled out a yellow rag, and handed it to the man they were standing with. Then, holding hands, boy and babushka walked down the platform, away from the station, and disappeared.

The man was wearing a blue suit (no tie), pale white Panama hat, and natty cream-colored shoes—a dead ringer for my Uncle George. My strongest recollection of Uncle George was that after a day spent running a coal mine, and after his dinner, he liked nothing more than to sit in his study overlooking the Monongahela River, and listen to Pittsburgh Pirates baseball games. I was allowed, if I was not too noisy, to sit on the rug next to the radio that was taller than I was, and parrot things like, "Mazeroski's on deck—he'll poke one." Or: "Big pitch comin'," when the count reached 3–2.

Now this man in the Panama hat walked over to a dark puddle, rolled up his pant legs, and calmly stepped in. Water rose to his ankles. He took the yellow rag, bent over, soaked it in the puddle, and rubbed it back and forth, cleaning dirt from his loafers.

I sensed a presence behind me—the Chinese conductor. He, too, had been watching. We looked at each other. He snorted and nodded out the window. I smiled back, pretending to have absolutely no connection with this station, with the unfortunates wandering the platform, and especially none with this man who had no more sense than to clean his shoes in half a foot of water.

He was done now. He climbed from the puddle, wadded up the yellow rag, balanced it on an iron fence post, unrolled his cuffs, and patted them down. He straightened his lapels and his hat. He put his hands behind his back and strolled toward the station. I could tell he was rehearsing the greeting he would deliver to his fellow idlers. *"Hello, comrades,"* I imagined him saying, while water squished between his toes. *"It would be nice day to go somewhere else, no?"*

The train whistle blew. The conductor moved away from the opening and shut the door. He pressed his hands together at his cheek and tilted his head. "Go sleep," he commanded.

I went back to my compartment and dreamed, strangely enough, of Amy.

58

O-LEEM-PEEK!
O-LEEM-PEEK!
LO SANG-A-LEEZ!

America has all that Russia has not. Russia has things that America has not. Why will America not reach out a hand to Russia, as I have given my hand?

—ISADORA DUNCAN
A speech, 1929

W HEN I AWOKE ON DAY FIVE and made my way to breakfast, it became apparent that a slight thaw was underway. Two Russian men in the middle cars surprised me with *"Dobre utro"*— *Good morning*—and in the dining car I found the frumpy waitress smiling at Tom the Australian while serving him a plate of sausage and eggs.

"She's not charging, either."

"What's going on?"

"Did you see her holding her jaw yistadie? I figured she had a toothache, so I gave her some pain pills. Now watch this."

As she passed our table, Tom stopped her and pointed to his cheek. She smiled and put her palm to her own face and spoke a paragraph sprinkled with the word *horosho—good.*

"Brad," Tom said, pointing at me. "Brad *horosho.*"

She put her hand on my shoulder and made a reasonable approximation.

"What's *your* name?" I asked.

She said something long and very unpronounceable.

"Call her 'Glad'," Tom said. "It's the short form."

"Glad."

"Da." She had a pretty smile. "Glad. Glad."

A moment later Glad came back with a bottle of apple juice, proud that she'd learned my "usual." After breakfast she passed out free candies to everyone who seemed to have any connection to Tom, and later, during her break, we saw her snuggling in a booth with one of the cooks, a meaty fellow with a Yasir Arafat beard.

"Springtoim in Soy-bih-yuh," Tom said.

It could have been the weather or the drugs, but I began to suspect that this little warming trend was a function of location. We were actually out of Siberia now, drawing closer to Moscow and Europe and the first weak pulse of capitalism. At each stop there were more and more things to spend our rubles on. Fresh raspberries—wrapped in sheets of *Pravda* newsprint, and peddled by toothless babushkas—appeared on the platforms. Other hawkers pushed flowers, tomatoes, cucumbers; the kiosks offered stamps, postcards, candies, and bottled drinks. Tom the Australian bummed a ruble from me, saying he needed to buy a toothbrush, but later I saw him dickering with a beer vendor.

Signs of industry multiplied. Smokestacks and warehouses became more prominent, a development accompanied by an increase in the size, number, and grimness of nearby apartment blocks. The cities always seemed to deliver something bizarre. In one town I saw an empty brown bus, the only vehicle in sight, careening repeatedly and inexplicably around and around an otherwise empty traffic island; at a station stop a haggard alcoholic screamed shaving instructions at me; and a gang of policemen stopped Terry the Longhair at machine gunpoint and removed the film from his camera. Russ the Mennonite created a short wave of concern by failing to return from one stop, but just as I was beginning to think I'd inherited his peanut butter, he showed up panting and clutching his camera.

"I went the long way around to avoid some policemen, and by the time . . . I got back to the tracks, the train was moving. I was running and screaming, and luckily one of the conductors saw me. . . . He lowered the steps and I just managed . . . to get on the last car."

But only a few of my memories deal with the cities. When I think of that part of my trip, I see myself standing in the hall, watching the infinite scenery go by, trading barbs with Bill from North Carolina, listening to the click of Russ's camera and the inevitable scream. I remember countless late-night games of "If-you-were-at-home-right-now-what-would-you-eat?" And I remember lying in my bunk reading *Islands in the Stream* and being washed in melancholy at Hemingway's final line: "You never understand anybody that loves you."

I paused there on my rocking bunk, pulled my sleeping bag up to my chin, and took stock of my life. I thought of my wife. What was she thinking? I still didn't know. I thought of Amy (Why, I now asked myself, didn't we sleep together?) and saw that my relationship with her was merely a condensed and sexless version of my marriage. Would my future relationships be nothing but reruns? What would the rest of my life hold? New marriage(s)? Kid(s)? Job(s)?

I spent a while thinking about all the people I knew: How had they messed up their lives? How had they messed up mine? How should they have done things differently? What was their most basic problem? If I wound up divorced, how would that affect my relationship with them? I scribbled a dozen postcards and told everyone I loved them. When I read them back to myself, I was struck by how good my life looked on paper. In the middle of Russia, I remember feeling halfway satisfied.

But what I mostly recall is the countryside. The Ural Mountains—covered with pines and riddled, I knew, with invisible missile silos—crept up gradually from the West. The tracks followed a clear river through these hills, and on its banks I caught glimpses of a populace that, like the Japanese, seemed ignorant of wars and aggressions: frolicking picnickers with heavy baskets of food and drink; winsome young ladies sunning in 1950's bikinis; a troop of uniformed Pioneer scouts double-timing along the river; bicyclists, backpackers, a concession stand with a fleet of blue rowboats to rent. Limestone cliffs rose from the river's edge, and atop them was a dreamy landscape of storybook farms and villages. The golden spires of ancient onion-domed churches became as commonplace as the pictures of Lain-een and cries of "'at's moin," from Tom the Australian.

"They've got really tiny houses," said Bill from North Carolina as we passed through a village of notched log homes. "It's a nation of toolsheds."

Bill was a constant source of amusement, one of those needling, jocular people around whom something intriguing is always happening. On our last afternoon on the train he came bursting into our compartment, slid the door shut as though a posse were close behind, flopped down on the bed, held his sides, and rocked with unedited laughter.

"I can't believe it! I fucking can't believe it! You know how those Russians haven't said a thing to us since we got on the train? Well, Terry just came down and asked if I had anything to sell. He's been selling stuff to them all morning! You know that baseball hat I had? It said 'USA' on the front, and had the Olympic rings and little golden arches? Somebody gave it to me for free in Beijing, and I just sold it for *fifty bucks!*" He rocked back and forth again, choking with glee. "It was a nice hat, but *fifty bucks!*"

"Dollars or rubles?" I asked him.

"Rubles. Forty-five rubles. Here, look ..." He pulled a wad of bills out of his shorts. "You got any old blue jeans? You can get sixty rubles for them. Terry just got sixty for a pair he was gonna throw out."

Neither Russ nor I had anything we wanted to sell, but we were both curious. "How do you do it?" Russ asked.

"You go down there with Terry. You walk into this one room, and there's all these Russian guys sitting around, nobody sayin' a thing. Then they shut the door, and all hell breaks loose. None of them speak English, and none of us speak Russian, so Terry writes prices on little pieces of paper and sticks them on anything that's for sale and just starts passing them around."

"How do you know what to charge?" I asked.

"Terry just makes it up. He asked me how much my hat was worth and I said probably five or ten bucks, so he whacks down a big 'sixty.' I said, 'Shit, nobody'll pay that!' But he said to let 'em make an offer. Man, it was crazy!" Bill began howling again at the memory. "They shut that door, and all of a sudden there was money and shoes and T-shirts and jeans and tapes and sunglasses and hats ... just flyin' around that room. People squabbling, and whackin' down offers and sayin', *Nyet! Nyet!*' Nobody wanted my hat, but then one guy saw the Olympic logo and the 'USA' and the McDonald's arches and started going, 'O-leem-peek! O-leem-peek! Lo Sang-a-leez!' Then everyone wanted it. This guy scratched out the sixty and wrote forty. I said, *Nyet! Nyet!*' and wrote fifty, and he wrote forty-five, and I said, 'You got a deal, sucker!'

"I'm tellin' you, it was crazy! Joe got fifty-five for a pair of running shoes he paid twelve bucks for in Australia. Any T-shirt with writing on the front goes for ten rubles. It could say *Fuck Russia!*, and you'd still get ten ... no, you'd probably get fifty for that one! A half-decent pair of blue jeans went for eighty! If you had something good to sell, no telling how much you could get. God, it was great! They bought every single thing we had! There were five of us and five of them in that tiny little place, and we were all laughin' and bumpin' into each other. Then, as soon as it was over, they opened the door and got real serious again. You should sell something just to see 'em go nuts! Next time you go to the dining car—watch! You'll see 'em all wearing blue jeans and T-shirts, and there'll be some fool wearin' my hat."

59
CHALLENGED

. . . the Intourist office keeps track of all travelers. There is no such thing as a foreigner arriving at a station or airport and going independently to a hotel of his choice.

—CHARLOTTE Y. SALISBURY
Russian Diary

L ATER, A COUPLE OF HOURS FROM MOSCOW, Bill and I found each other standing in the hall again, staring out the window, and started reminiscing about the trip. Things that had happened just a couple of days earlier had already acquired the aged texture of remembered childhoods. We exchanged addresses and life philosophies and promised to keep in touch.

Bill planned to be on the road for at least another year. After Berlin he would take the overland East Block route—Czechoslovakia, Hungary, Bulgaria, Romania—down to Istanbul. That, he figured, would burn up three months. He would go through Lebanon (if he couldn't get into Lebanon, he'd bypass it on a ship) to Israel, then Egypt, and up the Nile through Sudan to Kenya. "I want to climb Kilimanjaro." With the arrival of winter he planned to fly to New Delhi, and wander around Asia—India, Nepal, Burma, Thailand, Malaysia—and then see what came next.

"Good luck! I know a bowel-buster when I hear one."

"You got to do it while you can," he said. "Hey, are you stayin' in Moscow?"

"For two hours. That's all they give you, right?"

In Beijing we'd been given tickets to Moscow, plus vouchers, redeemable in Moscow, for tickets to Berlin. The lady at the Russian embassy had instructed me that two hours after our Trans-Siberian arrived in Moscow, another train would depart for Berlin, and I would be on it.

"Yeah, the old bitch told me the same thing. But look at this." He took out his passport and turned to his transit visa. "They tell you you're supposed to go right through, but if you look at the visa, it says we've got two extra days to get out of the country. Today's the seventeenth, right? But look here where it says how long it's good for." He pointed. "What's that say?"

232

I looked closely. "It looks like the nineteenth."

"That's what I think. I bet we don't have to be out of the country until the nineteenth. Look at yours, see if it says the same thing." It did. "I bet we could spend a couple of days in Moscow without anyone hassling us. I've got it figured. We came through in the summer and the weather was great and there were no problems, right?"

Right.

"But what if it had been winter? Maybe we'd have gotten stuck in a snowdrift for a few hours, or a whole day, or even two days. You know it's got to happen once in a while. And if we were late getting to Moscow, we'd miss our connection, and so would everyone else on the train, right?"

Right.

"So what are they gonna do? Arrest all of us because we couldn't get out of the country in time? Nah! They're not *that* stupid. They just build a couple extra days into the visa and don't tell you about it, and then if something goes wrong, they've got their asses covered. Whad'ya think?"

"Where would we stay?" I asked, unwittingly enrolling.

"Heck, I can always go one night without sleep. And I wouldn't mind sleeping in a park or the train station, just to have a couple of days in Moscow. You ever been there?"

"Three days once."

"I was there for a week last year. Great time. Moscow's so weird I think it's my favorite city. When we get there, I'm gonna see if these vouchers are good until the nineteenth, and if they are, I'm stayin'."

He looked at me and grinned. I looked out the window, pondering, and trying to figure out whether I'd just been informed, invited, or challenged.

60
HIT
THE PLATFORM
RUNNING

Whenever you are unhappy . . . go to Russia.
Anyone who has come to understand that country
well will find himself content to live anywhere else.

—MARQUIS DE CUSTINE
Russia in 1839

B ILL'S SUGGESTION WAS PERFECTLY TIMED. During the six and a half days on the train, I had recovered my health. I may not have divined all the answers to my life's questions or come up with a ten-year plan, but I was at least digesting food without incident, sleeping soundly at night, and feeling energetic by day.

But now I felt a need to make something good happen, something that would wipe out the memory of my Chinese collapse. In Japan, climbing onto my bicycle and attacking the unknown countryside had proved beneficial. *Sleeping in a Moscow park*—there's a ring to that. Maybe this North Carolinian was worth a listen.

"We'll get tickets to the ballet and the circus, and I know some great places to eat. We can rent a car and drive to Leningrad." By the time the train reached Moscow, he'd proposed so many scenarios that I felt I was watching a shell-game operator. "I know a guy at the American embassy—I'll give him a call, maybe he can pull a string or two for us. Last time I was here, he gave me tickets to the Bolshoi, and I ended up having dinner with the ambassador and his wife and then going to the ballet with them. Just the three of us."

What was the ambassador's name?

"I can't remember right now, but it's true."

 hen the train rolled into Yaroslavsky Station on the eastern edge of Moscow, Bill hit the platform running. "I've been here before," he had announced on Carriage Number Eight. "I know how to get to the other station."

Like the Pied Piper, he led me and a half-dozen other back-packers down into the Moscow subway system, where he handled the ticket machines with commuterlike familiarity, and then across town to Bellaruskaja Station, terminal for trains to Berlin. I stayed a few paces behind, watching, trying to decide how much faith to put in him. *Dinner with the ambassador!* Was he just an unstable keg of blond dynamite, or one of those people for whom miracles regularly occur? He was likable in a roguish way, and halfway convincing, but I was wary. Cards and conversation do not a travel partner make.

Ahead of me, he was sliding through the crowd with an enviable confidence, all business now, flicking his rucksack from shoulder to shoulder, darting around slower pedestrians. He was dressed for a day at the beach: rubber flip-flops, blue running shorts, and a T-shirt that had seen many better days. Of all of us, he was the lightest packer, and clearly our leader. I thought: Watch out—you're getting sucked into his wake.

Even during Tuesday evening rush hour, the hush of the tomb prevailed in Moscow's commuting corridors. The Russians were out in great mute numbers, shuffling through crowded intersections and riding quietly up and down the three-story escalators of their cathedral-subways. It was a summer evening; people were dressed casually, and in spite of their silence looked happy. Young women with the bulky, rounded breasts one forgets about in Asia were strolling singly or in pairs, wearing colorful frocks, light dresses, high heels, and clutching at one another in the casual European way.

"Isn't this great?" Bill called over his shoulder. "We're back in Moscow! Can you believe it?"

Weeks and months had passed since most of us had walked streets filled by people of our own race. We were part of the European masses now. As we crowded into a subway car, the sounds of our excited voices, spewing English, attracted curious glances; when we returned these looks, there was eye contact, nods of recognition, even a few tentative smiles.

A hunched older woman with faded blue eyes looked briefly at my face, then away, leaving me with a feeling of connectedness. Having visited Asia and the Middle East, I do not delude myself into thinking I know those people; the demons of the Japanese, the Chinese, the Indians, the Mongols, the Iranians, remain their private secrets. But this lady next to me was no stranger; somewhere in time past, her ancestors and mine had shared the same cave or castle or bomb shelter. When our eyes met, her demons mocked me. *You are known here. You are not foreign. You are home now.*

t Bellaruskaja Station Bill went right to work, marching up to various policemen and flashing his ticket voucher as though it were a KGB I.D. His theory on information gathering: "You just start asking questions until somebody gives you an answer." Eventually one of the policemen led Bill and his trailing entourage to the second floor and pointed to an obscure booth on the far side of the lobby. A woman imprisoned behind the window eyed our approach with an unconcealed scowl. Bill stomped up and addressed her as though he were her immediate superior.

"Dobre vecher." Good evening. "Do you speak English?"

"A lee-tool," she grunted.

I stood behind Bill, eavesdropping.

"I have a voucher for Berlin." He dropped it through the slot. "Can I get a ticket for tomorrow?"

"I haff teekets only for today! I cannot geef you teekets I haff not! You want teeket for tomorrow, you come back tomorrow."

"Is my voucher good for tomorrow?"

She picked it up and fingered the pages as though examining a feces. "Ees good today," she spat.

"I know it's good today." Bill scowled back. "Will it be good tomorrow?"

"You haff fisa?"

"Of course."

"Giff me." She drummed her fingers on the counter. Bill grumbled and forked over his passport. She turned to the visa page and studied it. "You cannot to stay een Moscow!" she trumpeted.

"I can until the nineteenth. Look again!"

She glanced up, surprised, as though seeing him for the first time. With passengers, she was used to being the bully, not the bull-ee. Petulantly she reexamined the visa.

"Yes, ees good until nineteenth, but ees only transeet fisa. You can not to stay een Moscow! For to stay een Moscow you need too-deest fisa. Ees summertime. Moscow full of too-deests. Effry room full. You haff resserfation? You no haff resserfation, you no haff room! Where will you stay?"

"Look, lady, if I come back tomorrow with this voucher, do I, or do I not, get a ticket to Berlin? Just tell me that! Just do your goddamn job!"

The frontal assault knocked the woman back; her scowl melted into uncertainty. Who could tell—maybe this guy knew somebody? A quiver of apology entered her voice: "Eef there ees room, I geef you teeket." She no longer hoped to intimidate Bill, just to get rid of him.

"And what about the next day? If I come back the next day, the nineteenth, will you give me a ticket?"

"Eef there ees room . . ."

"What if I come back on the twentieth?"

"I cannot geef teeket without fisa. Your fisa fee-neesh on nineteenth."

"Thanks a lot." Bill grabbed his voucher and passport and turned away from the window. Out the side of his mouth he muttered, "Told you."

61
AN OPENING IN THE KREMLIN WALL

The first Rome fell because of its heroics; the second Rome—Constantinople—fell victim to the Turks; but a new and third Rome—Moscow—has sprung up in the north, illuminating the universe more brightly than the sun. Two Romes have fallen, a third stands, a fourth shall not be.

—The monk PHILOTHEOS to Vasily III of Moscow in 1511

A GAPING HOLE LABELED "MOSCOW" had been suddenly blasted in the side of my trip. Since Beijing I had assumed the Russian capital would be but a blip in my afternoon, and before Bill from North Carolina mentioned his scheme, I had pictured my evening being spent in a cozy sleeping berth on the way to Berlin.

But now my chances of spending the night in a train station, a park, or a prison cell seemed about equal. The only thing that appeared certain was that I would not wind up in a hotel room. Our transit visas allowed us to move through the country, but not to linger. And even if we *had* had too-deest visas, the chances of finding a room in Moscow in July, height of the season, were nil. And *supposing* that we somehow managed the impossible and found one, neither of us was willing to pay the price; rooms for foreigners were exorbitant, we knew, and had to be paid for in "hard" (Western) currency. Hotel rooms were out.

Once he had confirmed it, Bill told several people from the train about the two-day grace period built into the visas, but only Bee the British Nurse and Joe the Bush Pilot elected to stay. The four of us stashed our backpacks in the station's storage room, and, not knowing what else to do, joined a taxi queue, intending to go to Red Square. But when we reached the head of the line, we were unable to communicate; no matter how we mangled or mispronounced "Kraim-lean" or "Rett Square," the drivers responded with shrugs and blank stares or accusatory bursts of Russian. Just like New York. Several times we were shunted aside in favor of the next party in line. Ten frustrating minutes passed. Suddenly Moscow felt immensely intimidating.

Bill fumed and stewed and cursed the "stupid" drivers, and regretted that he'd recruited such an inept group of followers. Bee and Joe looked impotently into the distance, as though hoping to spot a rescue party rounding a corner. The other people in line were of no assistance; they stepped around us and sped off in the waiting taxis.

Finally I had an inspiration. In my notebook I drew three soft ice-cream cones, side by side, with twisting tops, which I hoped would resemble onion-domed steeples. I showed this crude drawing to one of the drivers, who smiled, muttered something that sounded like "Saint Basil's," and waved us into his taxi. As the cab spun through the thoroughly Western, yet surprisingly empty streets, our anxieties vanished.

It was seven-thirty in the evening when the driver deposited us at Red Square; the changing of the guard in front of Lenin's tomb was only half an hour away. The late-afternoon sun distorted our bodies into long stripes on the gray bricks of the courtyard. Straight ahead of us, at the far end of the square, the domes of St. Basil's Cathedral—green and red and white and orange—swirled upward into a pale blue sky. One side of the courtyard was lined with the ornate façade of the GUM department store; opposite was the Kremlin Wall, and in front of the wall was the centerpiece of Soviet culture, a red granite bunker over the crypt of Vladimir Ilyich Lenin, whose preserved body lay in a viewing chamber several stories underground. At the door a pair of guards in ceremonial outfit were finishing off the last of their motionless three-hour shift. Flocks of hushed tourists were gathered for the guard change.

"Have you been inside Lenin's tomb?" Bill asked me.

I never had.

"It's a trip. His body's under glass, and you can walk right by it. It's the most interesting thing in Moscow. Maybe we'll do it in the morning."

There was a sprinkling of Westerners among the growing crowd, but mostly it was a Russian gathering. A man in a military uniform kept looking at my hiking shoes, wondering, no doubt, how much I'd want for them. A pair of teenage sweethearts looked on in awe as Bee, in search of a better view, clambered up onto Joe's shoulders, scissoring his neck between her thighs. But mostly we were ignored: the casual Westerner in Red Square goes unheeded.

The two soldiers were replaced by an identical pair, who goose-stepped through an opening in the Kremlin Wall and froze into position at the very stroke of eight o'clock. The crowd snapped a thousand pictures and then slowly scattered.

"We're going off on our own," Joe and Bee announced. "Any clue about where to stay tonight?"

Bill and I mentioned parks and the train station as possibilities, but nothing brilliant.

"Maybe we'll see you back at the station later," Joe said. We never saw them again.

Bill and I strolled across the Red Square courtyard and wandered among the halls and shops of the sprawling GUM. Empty shelves, crude wares, and the most basic of commodities screamed the plight of the Soviet consumer. The fact that sugar was now in stock was a big deal. In one main display window sacks and boxes of it were arranged in a pyramid shape around a sign announcing: SUGAR!!! Another window had COFFEE!!! A long queue had formed for ice-cream cones, but as I watched, the supply ran out. The vendor, a babushka, folded up her portable stand, and the fifty people stranded in midqueue melted away without a murmur.

Not having planned to stop in Moscow, I had spent all my rubles and now was hoping to meet a Russian Brother Thomas. At a splashing fountain inside GUM, three teenagers approached. "I need a pack, Amerika," one of them said, chuckling and pointing to my day pack.

"I need it, too!" I answered.

"In Amerika you get another. You get min-nay packs!"

"But America is very far away."

"You cap-ee-ta-leest . . ." he teased. "You have efferything. But I have no pack."

"That's life."

"Feefty rubles!" he said.

"No."

"A hundred!"

"Sorry pal." I thought: Have I ever called anyone "pal" before? I lingered with him a moment, hoping he would offer to change money, but he didn't, and I left him.

"I've got all these free rubles from selling my hat," said Bill. "I'll splash for dinner." We searched for a restaurant or cafeteria, but found none. Above a doorway in the distance we saw a sign with fork, knife, and spoon, but when we reached it, we discovered a cutlery shop.

We left GUM, walked the adjacent streets, and stopped at a row of vending machines that dispensed flavored mineral water. Atop each machine was an upturned glass from which all customers drank.

"Do you think they're safe?" I asked Bill.

"I used 'em last time, and I'm still alive. If this were China, I'd say 'no way,' but we're safe here. Come on, I'll splash." He began dropping coins into the machine.

We drank. But finding food was not so easy. The "great places to eat" that Bill knew of were in another part of Moscow, and our attempts to enter two nearby restaurants were repelled by blustering doormen who, instead of welcoming our business, shooed us away. "Ignorant fuckers," Bill muttered.

The crowds had thinned from the streets as we walked toward Moscow's unofficial tourist center, the Hotel Intourist—a skyscraper located less than two blocks from Red Square. "I know we can get something to eat there," said Bill. "They've got three restaurants."

But even though Bill changed from shorts to long pants in a rest room, getting into a restaurant was a struggle. At our first stop we were informed that the establishment was reserved exclusively for card-carrying hotel guests; at the second place, prices posted in the window started at twenty rubles—much more than we were willing to pay; at the third we were told we needed a reservation.

We'd been hungry when we arrived in Moscow, and now, several hours later, we were also irritated. "It's time to *push it!*" Bill said, as we regrouped in the hotel lobby. "There were empty tables in that last place. I'm going back in there and make 'em serve me. You coming?"

I had no better plan. Once more I followed. We walked through the front door, and straight past the *maître d',* who was busy shooing off other would-be diners, and sat down at one of several empty tables. A clean linen table-cloth and a lineup of fancy tableware awaited us. A red-jacketed waiter approached, and instead of challenging, greeted us, "Good evening, gentle-men. What can I get you?"

"Now that's more like it," said Bill.

The *maître d'* looked over. He tossed his hands once, and shrugged.

62

I'D BE
SO DAMN
JEALOUS

Russia is a hard country to visit, it is hard to relax and feel natural. Almost everything I did involved a struggle, whether ordering meals, getting a taxi, making plans to see the sights, go shopping— anything. The general atmosphere and mood is so rigid, so full of red tape, so stupid and unnecessary to any of us who are accustomed to being able to do what we want with a minimum of restrictions. It is all so frustrating.

—CHARLOTTE Y. SALISBURY
Russian Diary

DURING A LEISURELY DINNER of chicken, rice, spinach, cheese, brown bread, butter, vanilla ice cream, and coffee, Bill and I drank a bottle of wine and relaxed. Was this his usual manner? I asked him. Did he always barge into places and get what he wanted?

"Pretty much. I've learned that if you want to get something, you've got to *push it.* So I've practiced. I get sick of people who could give you a break, but don't. What skin off anybody's back would it have been to let us into one of those other restaurants? When I'm in a position to help somebody, I do what I can for 'em. But when you travel, you run into all sorts of dildos who've gotten a little bit of power, and all of a sudden think their job is to hassle you. I just want to be treated fair, the way I treat people at home. I don't take any shit anymore. There were people chasing me all over China trying to tell me I couldn't go here, couldn't go there, couldn't sleep here, had to sleep there, had to pay FEC. I ignored all of them. If someone told me I had to pay FEC, I whacked down people's money and told 'em if they didn't like it, they didn't have to take it, but it was all they were gettin' outa me."

I said I felt uncomfortable going against rules, however stupid, that people set up for their own country. "Shouldn't we leave behind as good an impression as possible?"

"Well, I guess somebody's got to be Mr. Congeniality, and somebody's got to *push it.* You be Mr. Congeniality."

As the level in the wine bottle dropped, we became more and more aware of how happy and how lucky we were—sitting in the Hotel Intourist, eating dinner while the world revolved around us. "I think about the people I went to school with and what they're doing right now, and I can't help but think that most of 'em would love to trade places with me. I may not know where I'm going to sleep tonight, but I can't think of any of *them* I'd trade with. You know—if I were still in North Carolina, and I heard about someone living the life I've been living for the last three years, I'd be so damn jealous."

When the meal was done and Bill had "splashed" for it, we began wondering what our next move would be. Where were we going to sleep? "You know," Bill said, "we should have a hotel room."

"That would be nice," I said, knowing full well it was impossible. "It seems funny to leave a fancy restaurant and go curl up in the train station or some park."

"It's impolite of them not to have a room waiting for us. Just for the hell of it, let's see if they've had a no-show here. I've got a Visa card I haven't used yet. If it's not a fuckin' fortune, I'll splash for a night."

"**D**o you have reservation?" Behind the registration counter was a friendly middle-aged Russian woman.

"No," said Bill. "But maybe someone has canceled?"

"We have nothing," she said apologetically. "All of these . . ."—she held up a two inch stack of papers—"all of these are people who have reservations, and I have no room for them. I am trying to find them room somewhere in Moscow, but everywhere is full. Even if you had reservation, I would not have room." She frowned sympathetically.

"Just out of curiosity," Mr. Congeniality asked, "if you did have a room, how much would it cost?"

"Cheapest room is seventy rubles. Hard currency." Eighty-five dollars.

"For two people?" I asked.

"One person, seventy rubles. Two people, one hundred forty rubles." One hundred seventy dollars—the price of a Beijing-to-Berlin train ride. "Much money. How much do you pay now?"

"Nothing," I said. "We can't find a room."

"Where do you stay?"

"The train station," said Bill.

"Train station?" The lady found this funny. "From where have you come?"

We were a duet: "Beijing."

"Beijing!" She whistled. "That is long ride! Why do you not have reservation?"

"We have transit visas," I told her.

"Ahh!" Her eyes flickered. Now she saw our predicament.

I lowered my voice. "If you were us, what would you do?"

The woman thought for a moment, and then looked up. "I think it will not work, but you might try Hotel Metropol, next to Red Square. They have some rooms there, tourist class, for twenty-six rubles."

"Per person?"

"No, for double room. But I think they, too, will be full. I am sorry." She hoisted her papers again. "I would help you if I could, but you can see ..."

63

NO RESSERFATIONS

If an ass goes travelling, he'll not come home a horse.

—THOMAS FULLER
Gnomologia

THE METROPOL IS ONE OF MOSCOW'S OLD BUILDINGS; the smell of history strolls its wide halls, oozes from the ornate woodwork, and waltzes the floor of the grand ballroom with the ghost of the Revolution clutched in its arms. But since the Russians consider the Metropol's shared showers, old light fixtures, and lack of air-conditioning less than contemporary, they house foreign tourists in the large, modern high rises sprouting on the city's edges.

"Let me handle this," Bill said as we marched up the hotel's front steps and across the vaulted lobby. Bristling, ready for action, preparing for another demonstration of *pushin' it,* Bill kept a pace ahead of me. We stopped at the registration counter; behind it were three unsmiling women. The stern fortyish one in the middle was flanked on either side by equally forbidding assistants, both in their twenties. I thought: Come on, smile.

Bill leaned his elbows on the counter and grinned at them. "Hello!" he said, with overdone enthusiasm.

No response.

"We want your cheapest room." He directed his words at the older one in the middle.

"We heff no rooms. We are phool."

Bill winked at me, then turned back to the counter. "Ahhh, come on. We know you got rooms here! Twenty-six rubles."

"No rooms! Phool!" She was writing in a thick ledger, acting for all the world as though we did not exist.

"Ah, get off it!" Bill reached across the counter and thumped his index finger up and down on her ledger. "We know you've got rooms. Twenty-six rubles! We know all about it." He smiled knowingly at the three stricken women, leaned all his weight on one elbow, and turned away from the counter. "Don't we, Brad?"

If this was *pushin' it,* I wanted no part of it. Bill was already beyond any standard of decency, and wasn't about to get any extra encouragement from me. As surprised as the women, I stood there dumbly, like a Russian or a Chinese, awaiting the inevitable arrest.

The women were slowly recovering. "Ooof!" breathed one of the younger ones. "Americans!" They muttered among themselves in Russian. I thought I understood one snatch of their conversation: *Natasha! You call the police.*

Bill turned back to the counter. "One room—twenty-six rubles. We know you've got it. Just give it to us."

"Do you heff resserfation?" trilled the lady in the middle, finding her tongue.

"No, but we know you've got a room for us, don't you?" He reached out again, grinning all the while, and thumped the ledger. "You've got plenty of 'em. Twenty-six rubles."

"No resserfations! How ken we heff room for you? Eet ees summertime. There are thousands too-deests en Moscow! Effry room iss phool! Who do you think you are? Heff you no respect? . . ."

While she harangued, Bill looked away, occasionally turning to smile at her. "Come on, lady. You can't fool us. We know you've got rooms."

Loud enough so that they could hear him, Bill turned to me and said, "Ain't this a crockashit? You know they're lyin'! They've got rooms. I can tell. And we're gonna get one. I'm going to stand here until we do! Their job is to take care of tourists, not hassle them. These are the kind of people I was tellin' you about."

Alone, I would have accepted the first rejection—thanked the women for their trouble, excused myself, slunk back into the street to look for a bushy park. These women had a phool hotel. How could they put us, who weren't even supposed to be here, in rooms they did not heff? It was their country, their system, they made the rules. Who were we to argue? I was poised on the brink of intervention, ready to mutter a quick apology and drag Bill out to the street if things took a bad turn. If the manager appeared, or if the women mentioned something more about police, I would bolt. Instructed to be on a train to Berlin, here we were, brave from wine, bothering three innocent desk clerks in the middle of the night, just two blocks from KGB headquarters. If Bill were to persist, we might see Siberia again.

But persist he did. While the older woman admonished our thoughtless and decadent manners, Bill stood directly in front of her, three feet away, mimicking her facial movements, moving his lips in synch with hers. While she preached on in her high shrill voice ("We heff order here! We heff plans! You ken not come een and . . .") Bill mirrored her stiff posture and flapping hands; he bobbed his head back and forth, eyebrows raised stiffly, lips popping soundlessly. The height of mockery.

After a moment he turned to one of the younger women. "We know you've got rooms. Shut this dame up and give us one!"

"Ooof!"

The doorman and the elevator man—two swollen, older men with hands clasped officiously behind their backs—ambled over to see what the racket was all about. Bill was leaning back against the counter again, both elbows jammed up under his armpits, relaxed and smiling. The two men asked a question of the older woman, who unleashed a torrent of cluckings.

"Don't worry," Bill told the men. "In about two more minutes she's gonna give us a room. Twenty-six rubles. Then everything'll quiet down."

The men shook their heads, returned to their posts, and entered immediately into trances that shut out the world. It was not their problem. It did not exist.

I looked at the three women. The younger ones were watching Bill—thumping the book, "Twenty-six rubles. Come on, now!"—with disbelief. Something was about to give: something always does. The older lady was going to scream at the top of her lungs, the KGB were going to burst through the front entrance, guns drawn and blazing, and I was going to use Bill's riddled body to shield my retreat.

But it was the thing I least expected that suddenly came to pass. I noticed one of the younger women suppressing a smile. In a moment her lips twisted into a smirk. In another moment she dropped her head and stared at the papers in front of her, lest she burst right out and laugh. She was getting a kick out of Bill!

"Right about now ..." he said softly out of the side of his mouth. He was still leaning back against the counter, the Metropol's brand-new owner dropping by after a late-night poker game to survey his winnings.

Next there was a lull—"I think we're in," Bill said—then animated jabbering. The older one shuffled some papers and turned a page in the very ledger Bill had been thumping. My chest tightened.

"We heff one last room." Her voice was calm, even. "Eet was reserffed for someone else, but we ken not hold foreffer. You may heff. Twenty-six rubles."

"I knew it." Bill spun to face the three women. "It's about time."

Trying to control my elation, I thanked the women a thousand times, but now they were laughing, the hurt faces and harsh words of a moment before forgotten. It had all been an act, and I was the only one fooled.

"You had it all along," Bill accused them. "There's no reservation, is there?"

"I tell you the truth," said the older woman. *Tha troot!* But the younger ones were smiling.

"How min-nay nights?" she asked.

"Two," I said.

"At least," said Bill.

"Puss-parts." We threw down credit cards and passports. The woman studied our visas. A look of horror returned to her face. "But you heff only transeet visas. You are not to be een Moscow!"

She looked up. In front of her, only three feet away, there was Bill, leaning his face over the counter, grinning, saying nothing.

"Ooof," she said, and tossed a key on the counter. "Rrroom Four-oh-seffen."

64
WHACK.
SPLASH.
PUSH IT.

*I have no sense of guilt. I look upon myself as
a prisoner of war. I am under no moral obligation
to conform to, or in any way accept, the sentence
imposed upon me.
. . . I am what you call a hooligan!*

—EMMELINE PANKHURST
Quoted in *The Fighting Pankhursts,*
by David Mitchell

ROOM 407 WAS A GOOD DREAM—not quite the opposite of a nightmare, but a pleasant hallucination, nonetheless: high ceilings, parquet floors, and a red Persian rug; single beds with firm mattresses and clean white sheets; behind a partition near the door, a mirror and sink; by the window, an armchair and small desk with telephone; and down the hall, a shared toilet and a shower that, while we were there, ran only cold water.

The room was on the fourth floor in the front of the building, and for entertainment Dr. Push It and I could both sit in the window well and watch the view.

By day, office workers marched on the sidewalk below with all the enthusiasm of death-row inmates; drivers stood on the pavement next to their cabs, smoking cigarettes; various idlers leaned against the wall of the hotel, watching. "KGB," Bill assured me. At night, to our right, we could see the lit figurines in the cornicework atop the Bolshoi Ballet building; to our left, the lights of Red Square.

The morning after we arrived, a bus full of young blacks pulled up to the front entrance, unloaded a collection of long sculling oars, and carried them into the hotel. Emblazoned in red on the backs of their flashy black sweat suits was one word: CUBA.

"God, this is interesting," I told Bill. "Too bad we've got to leave tomorrow."

"Who says?" It was his motto. "Tell me. If you could have it any way you wanted, wouldn't you stay here a while?"

"I'd stay a week."

"Then why give up without a fight? Let's go try to get our visas extended. If it doesn't work, it doesn't work, but let's at least try. You saw how they were bluffing at the desk. I bet the whole country's bluffing."

henever I describe the events of that day to people with experience in Moscow, I am always assured that what we did— or rather what *Bill* did, with minor help from me—is not actually possible. Playing good cop/bad cop, the two of us cajoled, wheedled, threatened, and pleaded with the Russian bureaucracy, and in the end wound up, I am told, in some sort of reality warp where things moved at the speed of diplomatic light.

We started at the Metropol's registration desk, where now there was only one woman, a different one.

"We were in four-oh-seven last night," Bill told her. "Instead of two nights, we're gonna stay a week."

"Passports."

A concerned look came into her eyes as she studied our visas. She stopped and leafed through her ledger, then through our passports again. Ledger. Passports. Ledger. Finally she looked up. "You have no visas. How do you have room here?"

Bill dropped his credit-card receipt on the desk. "We already got permission to stay, and we've paid for two nights. What we need you to do is reserve our room for the whole week."

"Eem-po-see-bull. Nobody stays without visa. And you have only transit visas that expire tomorrow."

"We're going to get them extended today."

"To change even tourist visa is eem-po-see-bull, but transit visa ... Pfft! What is that?"

Mr. Congeniality stepped forward. "We've ridden six days on the train all the way from Beijing. The woman last night was kind enough to give us a room. This morning we see how wonderful the view is, and we think it would be a pity to leave so soon. We can't go home and say we were in the world's most beautiful city and stayed only two nights. If you were us, what would you do?"

She was quiet a moment. "Eleven years I work here. I know if I give you room without visa, my superior will know before one hour. Police will come to your room. My mother, if she asks me this question, I tell her same thing: Eem-po-see-bull. Maybe you go to Intourist and maybe you ask them to extend your visa and maybe miracle happens, but I think not."

A friendly woman at the Intourist office in the Metropol lobby listened to our plan, then laughed out loud. "Maybe for circus I can find you tickets; and if I am quite lucky, maybe ballet; but visa extensions—impossible.

"If I were you? Difficult to say. Since you have not even reservations for train ride out, your situation is not only impossible, but doubly impossible. If you at least had reservations, then maybe I would send you to another office that handles visa problems of foreign students. You are truly dreaming about staying here a week. I know one person who had an emergency and was permitted to stay one extra day. But that was in winter, when it is easier to get train reservation. And without train reservation, everything else is waste of time."

"For day after tomorrow?"

The color drained from the face of the very young man behind the train-reservations window. "July is height of tourist season. Also, university has just finished. From January every train is booked full. These other people you see here make reservations for September, October. Besides, you should not be in Moscow. It says this on your visa. I cannot help you."

"If you were us, what would you do?"

"I would go to train station this minute. Today some seats are reserved for people from Beijing train. Tomorrow there will be no seats. You will have trouble. Big trouble. You should not be here."

Bill stepped forward. "But we *are* here, pal. We've waited in that line an hour just to talk to you, and we're going to stand right here until we get reservations for the day after tomorrow. There's no way we're leaving without 'em. No way."

"Train is full."

"You're lying, pal. I can tell."

Pal looked at Bill. Then at me. Then at Bill. Then at me. Then at Bill. Then at the thirty people in line behind us. Then at his ledger. At Bill. At me. At the line. Back to his ledger. He shook his head, spoke to himself in muttered Russian, opened his desk and took out two forms.

"Attaboy."

B y now it was noon, and the visa office was closed for lunch. We'd had a late breakfast but were ready for ice cream. At the Hotel Intourist we found a crowded restaurant where a group of foreign tourists were finishing up a luncheon. Dishes of vanilla ice cream were being brought out of the kitchen and passed out to everyone. I asked an American tourist how he had gotten served. "I don't think the restaurant's open for normal business. We're all part of a tour group, and this meal's included."

I was ready to leave, but Bill spotted an unoccupied table, strewn with dirty dishes, and sat down. I joined him. Several waiters marched by with ice-cream trays, ignoring us.

"Okay, Brad. It's your turn to *push it.*"

He had commandeered the hotel room and was engineering the visa extensions; the least I could do was get us some ice cream. I flicked a hand at a passing waiter. He looked away, kept walking.

"That's pathetic. You've got to really whack it out there." *Whack. Splash. Push it.*

"Relax. He saw me. He'll be back in a minute."

Several minutes passed. Another waiter went by, towing a cart full of ice-cream dishes. I waved at him. He shook his head, lowered his eyes, kept going.

"Oh, man. Where'd you learn *that?*" Bill was roaring. "You call that *pushin' it?*"

We watched the waiter serve all the other tables. When finally Bill could take it no longer, he slid his chair back, stood up, walked across the room, lifted two ice creams off an untended cart, and stomped back gripping one in either hand as though they were heads severed in battle. A waiter leaning against a nearby ledge, chin propped in his palms, watched the whole thing, uncaring.

Bill plunked the dishes down on our table. "Now *that's* how you push it for ice cream."

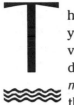his guy didn't know the meaning of *"Nyet! Nyet!"* During three years of fighting snarls of red tape on four continents, he'd developed a total and apparently fearless disdain for authority. He disputed every charge, bristled when told to wait, and viewed a *maître d'*, a conductor, a secretary, or any low-level diplomat with the same chop-licking spirit with which large dogs regard mailmen.

In the six hours we spent shuttling around Moscow in taxis, I saw him commit several brazen acts I might have fantasized, but would never have had the audacity to actually *do.*

A lobby guard at the visa office told us the building was closed; Bill waited three seconds and bolted past him, up the stairs. The guard, face swelling, shook his right index finger an inch from my nose, then turned and sprinted after Bill. A moment later the two of them reappeared at the top of the stairs. The guard had a scowl, Bill a smile, and a new name for me. "Mr. Granola, you can come up now. The secretary says it's okay."

After sitting for ten minutes outside the door of "Commissioner Bukovsky"—who, we were told, was busy in a meeting—Bill stepped past the secretary, knocked once, opened Commissioner Bukovsky's door (he was alone), and introduced himself.

The commissioner told us he was sorry that our request was impossible to grant, and then that, oh, yes, maybe if he were us, there *was* one thing he might try. "If you go to your embassy and get from them a piece of paper saying that you have met an emergency, maybe we can allow you one more day."

66 can't believe you," I told Bill in the taxi on the way to the embassy. "I thought that guard was going to kill us. You eat this up, don't you?"

"Wouldn't have it any other way. How many tourists do you think have seen Commissioner Bukovsky's office? If a travel agent had set us up here, we'd be missing all this. We'd be in some hotel on the edge of Moscow paying a bundle of money and stuck with KGB guides. But we're meeting real Russians. They don't give a shit what country we're from. They just want to get through the day so they can go home and kick back with a vodka."

"They'll need one after you."

"You shoulda seen me at the Super Bowl in Tampa! Raiders and Redskins. I paid two-hundred-fifty bucks for my ticket, and when the gate opened, I was the first one in the stadium. I got my banner set up, and went down to the field and saw the teams come in. I saw what's-his-name for the Raiders—Lester Hayes—and I was screaming, 'LESTER! YOU SUCK! YOU SUCK!' I gave it to Plunkett and Flores and Marcus Allen. They weren't gettin' an inch from me."

"So you're the jerk! I've seen you on TV about a million times."

"I'm the guy."

"Is Max Musser in?"

"I'm sorry," said the American college student working the embassy's front desk. "Mr. Musser is in Stockholm all this week. Maybe someone else can help you?"

Fifteen minutes later we left—Bill waving an official embassy request that our case be given special attention, me reconsidering his dinner-with-the-ambassador story. By late afternoon we strutted back into the Metropol carrying confirmed train reservations, one-day visa extensions, and official permission to stay a third night in the Hotel Metropol.

The woman at the reservation desk: "Eleven years. Never I have seen this."

The Intourist ticket woman was just as surprised, and she had something for us—ballet tickets. "And I can get circus tickets for tomorrow." The city that had pretended not to want us was proving very hospitable.

"Bill, how about if I splash for dinner?"

"Yeah, in the fancy dining room. It's the least you could do. But give me half an hour. I need a shower."

Half an hour later I was waiting at the ballroom door, when Bill came striding across the lobby wearing his shorts and flip-flops. The doorman saw him coming, closed the door, blocked it with his body, and pointed at Bill's bare legs. *"Nyet, nyet!"*

"Bill, go on up and change, and I'll go order for us." It's amazing what you can forget in thirty minutes.

"Fuck, no! It's hot. Who says I can't eat in there?"

A party of semiformal diners was coming out of the restaurant. The doorman pointed his chin toward them: *There! That's how my people dress.*

But following them through the door was a young foreign woman wearing shorts. Bill's eyes desocketed. The doorman's face sagged.

"Piss off!" Bill told him, and brushed past.

The doorman followed us inside and stood next to our table, beet-faced, lecturing.

"Piss off, buddy!" Bill studied his menu until a waiter descended from his elevated position on the pecking order and drove the doorman away.

"See! He was just hassling me! If you travel, you can't let anyone screw you around. You got to *push it.*"

65

ON THE FLOOR
OF MY HOTEL ROOM

*It is during a trip's final stage, the mopping-up
stage, that the traveler is likely to become irritated
by his surroundings, annoyed by new customs and
attitudes that earlier he might have found quaint
and cute. A Peace Corps volunteer told me that
upon entering the mopping-up stage of her tour
she started thinking: "Why do I have to be so
culturally sensitive all the time? Why can't they be
sensitive to me once in a while? Huh?"*

—LANCE FREE
The Art of Tripping

From my notebook:

I AM SITTING BENEATH A SHADE TREE in the small square
in front of the Bolshoi Ballet building. It is midafternoon. In the center of the square a fountain with
twenty-five nozzles is spraying a jet of water into the
air. The park is rimmed by green shrubs and beds of
red and yellow tulips. Stuck in the grass are small
signs that say, in Russian, STAY OFF. Every seat on every
bench is taken, but no one has set foot on the grass.

Thank God Bill's not here. He'd just *have* to step over the
little wire fence and lie down with his feet propped on the
sign. He's back in the room napping—dreaming, no doubt,
of attacking the visa bureau in Prague. Who is he, anyway,
and will it be possible, later, to forgive myself for having
hooked up with him? Certainly my trip is richer for having
met him, and I'm wiser for having learned the slash-and-
burn theory of travel, but what's left in our wake for the
next guy? What does the shop owner find the day after the
looters have their fun?

At my back are Red Square, St. Basil's Cathedral, and the
Kremlin complex. Last night, in the Kremlin Palace Theatre,
I saw *The Nutcracker*—the first live ballet performance of
my life—and I have vowed never to see another: it would

255

surely be a letdown. Throughout this country there is a heavy overtone of drabness and mediocrity, but there was nothing drab, ordinary, or second-rate about last night. It seemed the Russians had saved up the best of everything and packed it into that one performance. The theater was new and first-rate—plush seating, perfect acoustics, and a football field of a stage. The background scenes were vivid bursts of red and blue and green and orange and gold stretching from floor to vaulted ceiling and dwarfing the dancers, who were anything but dwarfs. Often there were fifty or sixty hard, springy bodies, in masterful shape, whirling across the set—a dazzling display of grace, coordination, and the human spirit. And, after two months of nothing but scratchy Asian tape players, I was overwhelmed by the clear and melodic strains of the orchestra. If I were keeping score, the Russians would get a huge plus in their column for last night.

The Hotel Metropol is behind me and to the right, just a block away. Further down the street, Prospect Karl Marxa, is the yellowed façade of Lubyanka Prison, headquarters of the KGB. The Russian who answers a middle-of-the-night knock on the door stands a good chance, sometime during his ordeal, of winding up at Lubyanka. It was stop number one for many of the 20 million Russians purged by Stalin. Twenty million! The Russians get a big double minus in their column for that one.

While I was writing the above, the two people next to me rose and departed, and their places were immediately taken by two Russian students. Like college kids everywhere, these two were enthusiastic and hip, but in a clumsy, Russian sort of way. The one closest to me, the more confident one, was tall and blond and spoke serviceable English. The other was short and dark and had a timid, scared look about him, as though he'd been beaten—not regularly, but enough to have a permanent scare thrown into him.

"*Sprechen Sie Doitch?*" the closest one asked, jiggling a cigarette pack at me.

"No," I said, and shook off the cigarette. "English."

"Amerika?"

"Yes."

"Ahh, good. Amerika is good."

"Yes," I said. "Russia is good, too."

"Do you like Moscow?"

"I love it."

"Ahh!" He flashed a thumbs-up. His partner, who knew hardly any English, asked what I had said, and the two of them spoke in Russian for a moment.

"What do you like in Moscow?" asked the spokesman.

"Everything. The streets are clean. The weather is nice. The food is good. . . ."

"Better than Amerika?"

"No. But better than China. I have just come from China." They did not understand. "Beijing," I said.

"Ahh, Beijing!" They talked excitedly between themselves. "You come all the way on train?"

"Yes. Russia is a beautiful country."

"Someday we ride train to Beijing," the spokesman told me.

"You will like it," I assured him.

"What else you like in Moscow?"

"The prices are cheap. The people are nice. The women are pretty. . . ."

"Ah, yes. Moscow women very pretty women, yes?" He laughed and translated for his friend, who leered, massaged an invisible hourglass suspended in the air in front of him, and then whispered in the spokesman's ear.

"Do you have blue jeans to sell?"

"No. I have nothing to sell. Next time," I promised, "I will bring a suitcase full of blue jeans."

"Trade shoes with me." He pointed at my Nike hiking shoes.

"No. They're my only ones."

"I give you mine plus twenty rubles." He raised his foot to show a red Jox running shoe that I wouldn't have taken for free.

"No. I like my shoes. And besides, yours would be too small." We compared feet, placing them side by side. Mine were at least two inches longer.

"Feefty rubles!"

"No. A thousand rubles, no!"

"Okay, okay," he said, and shrank back.

"Why would you want shoes you can't wear?" I asked, trying to keep the conversation alive.

"I sell them. I get maybe one hundred rubles. For blue jeans, new blue jeans, I give you two hundred rubles. For Jor-dish, two hundred-feefty!"

"I have nothing to sell. Nothing. Forgive me."

"Okay, okay . . ."

"Are you a student?" I asked.

"Yes."

"What do you study?"

"Engineering."

"Will you build missiles?"

He looked at me sideways. "No. Dams, buildings. I do not like war. I like women and music. Do you have records? Tapes to sell?"

"No."

"Walkman?"

"No. I am sorry." I should have bought one of everything in Hong Kong.

The second guy said something to the spokesman, who listened and then turned to me. "Do you need rubles?"

"No. I already changed money."

"How much?"

"Twenty dollars—sixty rubles," I said. "Was that good?"

"Is okay. Maybe you get eighty or ninety rubles, but seexty is okay. Where you changed?"

"Hotel Intourist. With a Russian man in the bar."

"That is dangerous place!" he said. "Maybe police. KGB!"

"The bank is even more dangerous. Twenty dollars, only sixteen rubles."

He laughed. "The bank is stupid."

His friend said something. "Okay. We go now," said the spokesman. They stood, shook hands with me, and left. And now I am alone.

Well, not exactly alone. There are probably two hundred Russians in this park with me. Children are leaning into the fountain, splashing hands in the water. On the benches around me, several people are reading this morning's Pravda. One man is carefully wiping the lens of his camera. The man on my left is biting a pastry that smells strongly of potato. Uniformed military men, chests adangle with medals, are parading their families. I have noticed a peculiarity about the way strolling Russian mothers hold the hands of their young ones: they grasp them at the wrist, creating the impression that the children of Moscow are under collective arrest.

I have been stunned by the women here. After Japan and China, where the women hide all (well, *nearly* all) signs of emotion or desire, these Russian women seem incredibly forward. They have fiery eyes, meaty bodies, flimsy clothes. In the lobby of the Hotel Intourist I was approached by a woman, heavily made-up, who must have been a prostitute or KGB or both. Or possibly she just wanted a ticket out. She asked first for a match and then if I'd buy her a drink. Twice I said no. But if I see her again, who knows...? I have had visions of grabbing a cute young one and spiriting her away to America to feed her fruit and vegetables and save her from the obvious horrors of being middle-aged in Russia. Nearly every person over thirty—especially any woman over thirty—appears soft, lumpy, out-of-shape. A lifetime of meat, potatoes, bread, and vodka takes a toll.

A young woman on the next bench has been watching me. Her hair is dark, her eyes light blue. Her dress, soft and red, would make a very small pile on the floor of my hotel room were she to step from it and let it fall. I smile and nod to her. She looks away. I go back to jotting notes. Soon she is watching me again. Later she stands and without looking back walks away across the square, accompanied by an older lady. Mother and daughter. Mother's hair is dyed red, almost orange, as if a terrible accident occurred at the hairdresser's or, more likely, at the kitchen sink. Mother's clothes, were she to step from them, would make a very big pile on the floor of my hotel room.

Now I'm sitting at the desk in room 407. It's my last night in Moscow, and just a moment ago, scanning back through my notebook, I was struck by the darkness of the images I've recorded since entering Russia: the POW scene at the border; out the train's window, sluggish workers and scolding policemen; inside, a frumpy waitress and dour passengers who turn into frothing consumers at the sight of a baseball hat the rest of the world takes for granted; and now Moscow, full of "ignorant fuckers" blocking us from restaurants and hotels, and children being marched around by the wrist.

Is this lopsided view accurate? Or am I seeing, possibly, only what I came to see—images I've been trained to expect, or maybe even to *project,* by American TV, newspapers, politics? Am I recording a halfway valid view of Russia, or just Red-bashing? Am I an insightful traveler or whining tourist? And is it naive to hope that a Trans-Sib rider can know Russia any better than a flat stone, skipped from bank to bank, can know a stream?

"Stay a week, write a book," a friend who spent two years in Moscow once told me, "stay a month, write an article; stay a year, write nothing." At the time, I supposed he was saying that it takes a year to see through the rough façade to catch a glimpse of the true Russian character—enduring, endearing, noble, beautiful, he promised—and that along with the glimpse would come the realization that Russia is describable only by its own prolific natives.

But I'm not buying that anymore. I want my own glimpse and I want it now. I haven't got a year; I've got one more day, and what I've seen so far leaves me very unconvinced that there's any layer of gold under all this permafrost. Sure, the frumpy waitress *did* loosen up after a while, and, yes, the ladies at the Metropol *did* in the end give us a room, but that's not enough. If the smiling babushka and the amazing ballet are this country's true soul, I want to *know* that.

I challenge you, dear Russia. Don't send me home without a sign. If you're hiding, show yourself.

66

IN RUSSIA WE HAVE TO GET PERMISSION

I suggested to our Intourist guide that the Russian people thought of Lenin as a god, worshiped him as if he were holy, revered his body the way Catholics do the bones and hair and scraps of flesh of saints. Our guide objected furiously to my observations, and denounced such blasphemy, but of course, it's true. Communism is a faith as much as Christianity or Buddhism . . . but no one could tolerate my suggestion that an atheistic society seems to need a substitute for what it has thrown out.

—CHARLOTTE Y. SALISBURY
Russian Diary

FROM THE WINDOW OF ROOM 407 I could see in the distance the long line of Lain-een spotters waiting to glimpse the sixty-year-old corpse. No matter that the morning sky was overcast and promised rain; the line—six, seven, and even ten people abreast in places—spilled out of Red Square like a wide speckled sash, wrapped around the Kremlin Wall, stretched past the Tomb of the Unknown Soldier, and disappeared out of sight in the trees beyond. Seven-thirty A.M.

"They must've started lining up at six!" I called.

Bill, fresh back from the shower, stood in the middle of the room toweling himself. "They probably camped there! But don't worry. We'll get in somehow."

"I'm not worried." Three days with Bill would fix any skeptic.

It was our last morning in Moscow. Our train to Warsaw, Berlin, and points beyond would leave Bellaruskaja Station at twelve-thirty. We had five hours to eat, pack up, catch a cab; the only other thing on our list was Lenin's mausoleum.

"His body's not that big a deal," Bill told me. "It's like any other dead one. He's wearing a suit and looks just like all the posters. If he hadn't been there so long, you'd think he was napping. But just being in there's a trip, and it's worth the wait. They've got guards out front that look you in the eye and check you out to make sure you're not carrying anything. An ugly guy like you, they'll frisk."

He looked at me.

I ignored it.

"Inside they've got guards every two feet. Seriously! Nobody's saying a word. You walk past old Lenin as slow as you can, and if you're too slow, they poke you and tell you to speed up. You get about thirty seconds, and then you're out again. What kills me is that they're all so into it—nobody's joking or clowning around—like they're scared of Stalin's ghost. *His* body was there, too, until a few years ago. When they ditched him, they had to change all the postcards. Now Lenin's their only religion. Weird! Can you imagine us having Washington's body in the Smithsonian and it being the most important thing in our country? More important than Dillinger's dick!"

Hard to imagine, I admitted.

"Well, Lenin's their biggest tourist attraction. He's Russia's Grand Canyon. We've got to get in there. You can't miss this."

While he dressed, I went down to the coffee shop to start the process of getting breakfast, an ordeal much like applying for a job. First I had to wave my hands for several minutes until a frowning waitress arrived at my table. Like all waitresses in the Metropol, she had the look of a spinster librarian peering disapprovingly over bifocals that had slid down her nose; but she wore no glasses, only the frown.

"Foucher!" she demanded, towering above my table. On the first morning this belligerence had been confusing, but by now I recognized it as meaningless ritual, and I knew the correct responses.

"No voucher."

Her frown deepened. "Ruum cart!"

I laid my room card on the table. She grabbed it and studied it as though it might be counterfeit.

"Ooof!" She tossed it back; it landed on my lap. "You mosst haff Rrroshian rrru-pulls."

I patted my hip pocket. "I'm loaded."

"Ooof!" Her worst fear had come to pass; she had to serve me. She grimaced and took out a pen. I ordered double servings of bread, butter, jam, cheese, soft-boiled eggs, the fruit dish ("Ni froot!!" she sang happily), coffee, milk, and sugar. She clucked at every request, shook her head, scribbled on her pad, and finally stormed away drooling muttered oaths down the bib of her uniform. By the third morning I'd become accustomed to this horrible treatment. In fact, I'd grown to respect it: these waitresses were acting out every waitress's fantasy.

While I was playing with my white linen napkin, inventing stories about the waitresses and the other diners and admiring the brooding murals on the ceiling, Bill arrived. "I had to go back up and change. I couldn't get by him with shorts today. I needed a girl to come walking out wearing 'em. That was key."

"Hey!" I said, remembering something. "I'll be back in a couple of minutes. Don't eat my food."

"Where you going?"

"You'll see."

"**D**obre utro," I said.

The Intourist ticket lady looked up from her work. "Good morning!" she replied, motioning me to the chair by her desk. "How was the show?"

We talked about how great last night's circus had been, and I thanked her for having unearthed our tickets.

"And today you must leave?" she asked sadly. During the three days of our stay, we had developed a genuine fondness for each other.

"Yes," I said. "We'll miss Moscow. And you, too. You've been a great help."

"To help tourists—that is my job."

"Well, you're very good at it."

"Thank you." She accepted the compliment with a shrug and a half-grin.

"And now I have one last favor to ask."

She sighed. "What is that?"

"We would like to see Lenin's tomb, but our train leaves at twelve-thirty. We'll miss it if we stand in that line."

"Yes. The line is very long and very slow."

"Maybe you can write a note in Russian for us on Intourist stationery." The guidebooks, other tourists, and the main Intourist office had all hinted that the rules at the tomb are sometimes bent for foreigners. "Just something simple, like: *In the interest of peace and international harmony, please let these two young men, who have a train to catch, go to the front of the line.*"

"Oh, but I cannot!" Fear bordering on panic crept into her eyes. "I am not official! I am just teeck-et lady." In her excitement, her English deteriorated.

I was surprised. She'd been so helpful with all our other requests, and to me this one seemed harmless. "You wouldn't want us to go back to America without seeing Lenin!"

She was quiet a moment. "Sometimes, at eleven o'clock, the police permit foreign tourists to go ahead of the line. Maybe today this will happen. If you take your passports to the police lines, maybe they will let you go through."

"How often does that happen?" I thought: She's trying to get rid of me.

"I do not know."

"Wouldn't it be better if we had a note from Intourist?"

"Yes. But I cannot write this note. I am afraid for my job. I am just little person. I am not big boss."

"You're as good as any big boss. Probably better."

She liked that, but she was scared. "Nobody has given me permission for that."

"I will give you permission."

She laughed, and then the fearful look returned. "I'm sorry. I cannot."

I sat there for a minute, trying to understand her fears. I was leaving Moscow in a few hours, but she would have to stay and live with whatever consequences such a note would produce. It wouldn't be right to pressure her.

"I'm sorry. I didn't realize what it was like for you."

There was a silence during which she looked at me with empty, vitality drained eyes. I regretted having asked.

"Well . . ." I stood to go. "Thanks again for everything you did for us. You made our stay here just terrific. I've had more fun in Moscow than anywhere else on my trip." I stretched my hand over the desk, and she took it.

"I am sorry," she repeated, her voice remorseful, sad. She let go of my hand. "America is different. In America you would write the note for me, yes?"

"Yes."

"But here it is not done. In Russia it is different. In Russia we have to get permission."

She really wanted to do it. Something, maybe Bill's influence, came over me. I dropped to one knee in front of her desk and flung my arms out like one of the circus clowns. "But you *can* do it!" I used my fear-melting smile. "I've already given you permission."

"Stop!" She was trying not to laugh.

But I didn't stop. "You can do anything. You're a representative of Intourist. For me, you *are* Intourist! You've got a desk, and stationery, and a pen. . . . Surely you can write a simple note. You've already done more difficult things for us. At the last minute you found tickets for the circus"—a flicker of life came to her eyes—"and *The Nutcracker,* and you told us how to get our visas extended.... You're probably the best Intourist worker there is. You're efficient and helpful, and you are the nicest and ... and ... and just about the prettiest lady in all of Moscow!"

I began to blush.

She began to blush.

I smiled.

She smiled.

I laughed.

She laughed.

She pursed her lips, shook her head in mock disgust, reached into her drawer, pulled out a piece of paper, and started writing.

We remember a line for canned meat that stretched out for several blocks. It was a gray winter day, and, as everyone watched, a woman dashing across the street to get in line was run over by a streetcar. She screamed, the line twitched with the shock, and the people in it screamed in turn. But no one left his place to go and help her—no one but those at the very end of the line, who had nothing to lose.

—VLADIMIR SOLOVYOV and ELENA KLEPIKOVA
"Where Does the Waiting Line Lead?"
Christian Science Monitor, November 17, 1986

"LET ME DO THE TALKING," BILL SAID.

We were walking over toward the line, which was even longer now and moving at a snail's pace.

"Here. This makes up for the ice cream." I gave him the ticket lady's note and told my story.

"Hey, not bad. You *pushed it!*"

The area around Red Square had been blocked off by metal crowd-control barriers. On their near side was a gathering of several hundred people; immediately on the other side were scores of soldiers and policemen spaced at ten-foot intervals, some armed, all unsmiling. We shouldered to the front and Bill offered the note to several different guards, but it only seemed to antagonize them. Over the next half hour probably two dozen soldiers or policemen read it. *"Nyet, nyet!"* they would growl and gesture toward the end of the line.

The crowd was full of other foreigners, all wanting the same thing we wanted. With Russian phrase books they were trying to impress the guards

265

with the urgency of their desires and their great fondness for Russia and Lenin. All of us received equal treatment: *"Nyet, nyet!"*

Beyond these soldiers was a no-man's-land, seventy-five yards wide, and beyond that, parallel to the barricades, was the world's longest and most completely hushed line of people. I tried to overlook it, but it was obvious— the scene looked like old concentration-camp film footage. Some of the prisoners—those in the line—were being separated and led off to some supposedly preferential treatment, leaving the rest of us behind for extermination.

Bill was angry, of course. "You'd think there'd be one decent guy among all these fuckin' jerks. All we need is *one* guy!" Already we'd tried most of the guards, but none would be bothered.

And then, after all the rejections, one of the soldiers read our note and didn't scream, *"Nyet, nyet!"* Nor did he wave us off. A soft look came into his eyes. He held his hand out flat, palm down, patting the air gently—*Stay put!* He couldn't just shove aside the barricade and let the entire crowd through, but maybe, just maybe, he could figure out a way to help two guys with a note written in Russian on Intourist letterhead.

"All right," Bill breathed quietly. "He's our man."

"Our Man" turned his back to us and surveyed the scene. Across seventy-five yards of gray cobblestone was the line—moving, but barely. It extended off to the right, stretching so far that individual faces were indistinguishable. Clearly the line was impossible, its end not even visible.

Standing behind the guard with Bill and me, there were now over five hundred people who for one reason or another had elected not to join the line. Some had the built-in excuse of being foreigners; others were Russians waiting for friends who had the patience for the line, and others, it seemed, had just come to watch. There was a feeling of importance in the air, as though something of life-and-death significance were taking place. I was reminded of the crowd that gathered across from the White House the day Nixon resigned—a quiet and subdued group, no one joking.

Our Man turned back to us. "I go chief," he said very quietly. We watched his progress as he walked unhurriedly down the barricades, strode across the no-man's-land, and approached a burly soldier standing—legs spread wide, hands gripped behind his back—in the middle of the open area. With the Kremlin Wall towering in the background, and St. Basil's Kool-Aid-colored domes (lime, orange, raspberry) looming at the far end of Red Square, we saw Our Man offer up the note. "Chief" grabbed it roughly, read it quickly, and had the same reaction as all the others. Even at seventy-five yards, I could read his lips: *"Nyet, nyet, nyet!"* We watched Our Man retrace his steps.

"Thanks for trying," Bill told him when he arrived back, tail dragging.

Our Man nodded, shrugged, and motioned Bill to lean close. "Maybe bus," he said softly. He pointed down the barricades to where tour buses full of Russians were lined up, awaiting permission to pass through.

"Let's try it," Bill said to me. "Maybe we can get on one of them." We thanked Our Man for his efforts—he poked his lower lip out two millimeters and nodded once—and then walked toward the buses.

Surprisingly, when Bill banged on the door of the first bus in line and showed our note to the Russian guide, we were welcomed aboard. We stood in the aisle of the packed bus and said *"Dobre utro"* to a few smiling tourists. The proletariat were conspiring with the foreign agents. They would sneak us through the barricades, and together we would outwit the system....

But suddenly there was loud thumping on the door of the bus. The guide who had allowed us to board opened the door and was tongue-whipped by a blue-uniformed policeman.

"I'm sorry," she said to Bill and me. "They saw. You must go." We were expelled back into the masses. The policeman shook a finger at us—*"Nyet, nyet!"*—and stormed away.

"Ignorant fucker."

We stood in the crowd for a few moments, empty of inspiration.

"We should go check out of the hotel," I suggested, "and come back at eleven."

"Yeah, maybe, but let's try Our Man one more time."

We walked back.

"I see you," he said, grinning, touching his eyes. He had watched us get tossed off the bus. He shrugged helplessly. While we stood there, I studied the soldier. He had posture that was straight but not stiff, and a good face, a kind face—the face of a man who would never push the Button. He was clean-shaven, with a small cleft in his chin, delicate pink lips, and black eyebrows. Smidgens of sideburn crept down from his ears. His eyes showed no hint of redness; the irises were a hard, dark black. I imagined that his grandfather had been killed during the Revolution, his father had died fighting World War II, and that somewhere he had a wife and ten-year-old daughter.

"Now what?" Bill asked him.

"May-be ..." he said, in thickly accented English. He held up his wrist and pointed at the eleven on his watch face. "May-be ..." Maybe it would be a day when tourists would be allowed to cut line at eleven o'clock. This remote possibility was becoming our last hope; already it was quarter after ten, and we'd tried every trick we knew. What choice did we have?

"Eleven o'clock?" Bill pointed at the ground. "You? Here?"

Our Man nodded. He pointed at the ground, at his watch, at us, and then at himself. "May-be," he said, and shrugged.

68

NOTHING SO GROUNDING

Never answer a telephone that rings before breakfast. It is sure to be one of three types of persons that is calling: a strange man in Minneapolis who has been up all night and is phoning collect; a salesman who wants to come over and demonstrate a new, patented combination Dictaphone and music box that also cleans rugs; or a woman out of one's past.

—JAMES THURBER
Lanterns and Lances

W E TROTTED BACK TO THE METROPOL and packed, a five-minute task. "You go on down," I told Bill. "I want to try calling one more time." After three days of busy signals—long-distance line unavailable—my call went right through.

"Hello ..."

There is nothing quite so immediate, so clear, so grounding, as the voice of one's wife. Since I'd last heard it, I'd been through China, Amy, dysentery, Mongolia, and across Siberia, had drifted into so many different worlds that I'd come to believe I'd never again be able to relate to my old one. But even from halfway around the world, a simple "hello" erased all that. Suddenly I was no longer a globe-trotting adventurer, but once again no more, no less than the best friend and enemy of the woman who'd taken my last name.

"Hi—it's me."

Expensive silence.

"Remember me?"

"Sure," she said. "Sorry. It's a shock. How are you? Where are you?"

"Moscow."

"Idaho?"

I laughed. "Russia."

"Is Amy there?"

"No, Amy's not here."

"Where is she?"

"I last saw her in Beijing."

"You're not with her anymore?"

"No. It was just for a while."

"Oh," she said.

Another expensive silence.

"Well, I just wanted to check in with you," I told her. "It's been a while, huh?"

"Yeah. Sometimes I forget you exist. I have to keep reminding myself."

"I know the feeling. Sometimes I forget I exist, too!"

She laughed.

"When are you coming home?"

"Soon."

"When?"

"About five weeks. I'm going to hang out in Europe a while, go some places I've never been, and then visit Mom and Dad in Virginia. But I'll be back by our anniversary."

"Oh."

"How do you feel about seeing me?" I asked.

"I don't know."

"Do you want to see me?"

"Yes ... but not right away. Five weeks sounds about right."

"Yeah," I said, "that feels right to me, too."

"How's the trip going?"

"I got sick in China. . . ."

"Ohhh ... Bad?"

"Well, it was only the splats, and I'm fine now, but it sort of ruined China for me." I thought: China boils down to two sentences. "But Russia's been great."

"Has the trip been everything you hoped for?"

"I can't remember what I hoped for."

"You wanted a good tan and to forget me."

"Oh, yeah. Well, oh-for-two so far."

"Good."

We laughed.

"But this *has* been good for me. When I left, I may have acted like I knew what I was doing, but I really didn't have a clue what I was doing or where I was going. . . ."

"Me either. Nobody really does. Do they?"

Bill came to mind, but he was too much to explain. "Nobody I've met. You go looking for a desert island, and you wake up in a hotel room in Moscow, no tan, promising your wife you'll be home for your anniversary."

"Life's a trip," she said, chuckling. Then: "What do you think about *us* these days?"

"I don't know, but thank God I've gotten to where I can sometimes *not* think about us. Now I know I'll be able to live with whatever happens."

"Yes," she said, "the distance has been good, but it'll be good to see you again, too."

Silence.

"Well . . . I just called to let you know I was alive."

"Thanks."

Silence.

"I'll see you next month," I said.

"Yeah . . . See you next month. Thanks for calling."

"Sure. Good-bye."

"G'bye."

Pause.

"I love you," I said.

"I love you, too."

Click.

Click.

69

SEVENTEEN MINUTES AFTER ELEVEN

I like to believe that people in the long run are going to do more to promote peace than our governments.

Indeed, I think that people want peace so much that one of these days governments had better get out of the way and let them have it.

—DWIGHT D. EISENHOWER
In a broadcast with Prime Minister Harold
Macmillan of England, August 31, 1959

T HE FOREIGNERS BEHIND THE BARRICADES were anxious. "It's eleven o'clock!" they screamed, holding up watches and waving passports. The guards ignored them or hurled hard little *nyet*'s back across the barricades. By five after eleven it was obvious: this wasn't one of those days when foreigners would cut line. The crowd was fuming. For a while I feared a riot, but the guards glared and stonewalled, and soon the hush returned to Red Square.

Bill and I had been standing by Our Man, not saying anything. He had acknowledged our return by lifing his eyebrows and nodding slightly. Now, with occasional pats of the air, he indicated that we should keep waiting. But the clock was ticking; if something didn't happen soon, we might as well forget it. At ten after eleven, Bill tapped Our Man's shoulder and pointed to the "12:30" on our note. Our Man glanced at it, nodded, shrugged, patted the air. *Be patient.*

Now there really was no hope. We had to leave for the station within twenty minutes, half an hour at the absolute most. It was going to take a miracle.

The guard turned to us. His face had a new tenseness. His jaw was clenched. "Bus." Down the line we could see the barricades being moved aside for a bus to come through. He pointed at Chief—still guarding the middle of the courtyard—and made a motion with his hand as though the bus would run Chief over.

"What?" said Bill.

The guard shielded his eyes with the palm of his hand, like a horse's blinder.

"Ah." Bill nodded and turned to me. "The bus is gonna block Chief's view for a moment."

The guard was nodding now and motioning to the barrier between us.

"He's going to slide this thing back for us." Bill was whispering so the foreigners around us wouldn't hear.

Inverting the "V" of his middle and index fingers, the guard made walking motions in the air, marching his hand toward the distant line.

Bill nodded. "We'll walk."

The guard speeded his fingers up, and shook his head.

"We won't run."

My heart was jumping. Seventy-five yards of cobblestone spread before us like the Pacific. When the bus screened off Our Man's boss, Bill and I would walk right through the barrier and the line of armed guards. For several dozen seconds we would be unprotected, isolated from the throng— two blond boys strolling across a Red Square no-man's-land as though we knew what we were doing. By the time Chief saw us, it would be too late. That was the theory.

Our Man was watching the bus. It was in position now, ready to come through the barrier. A squad of soldiers with rifles was moving over to guard against hangers-on. *Great Escape* images flickered across my mental screen. We were about to ride out with the laundry, scale the fence while the guards broke up a fake fight, dash for the woods.

Our Man brushed the shoulder of his uniform as though gold braid were perched there.

"Chief . . ." Bill guessed.

Our Man nodded and pointed at his eyes.

"If Chief sees this . . ."

Our Man nodded and dropped his hands down low. He clenched his fists lightly by his thighs, bent his elbows at a right angle, made two jerking pelvic motions, and then pointed at himself.

"If Chief sees this, you're gonna get fucked."

Our Man nodded gravely. His ass was on the line. If this didn't work, we were all in big trouble. Him, us, maybe even the Intourist ticket lady. Our Man made his fingers walk the air again; they moved rapidly, but they didn't run.

"We're cool," Bill told him.

He gave us a last look.

The bus was revving its engine.

Our Man was opening the barricade a crack.

The bus was pulling into the courtyard.

Suddenly my feet were moving.

We were past the line of soldiers.

The barricade scraped back into place behind us. In English someone in the crowd moaned, "Hey, look at those guys!" We were in no-man's-land now, walking side by side across the cobblestones, eyes down. I glanced to our right. Chief was still screened off. Anyone else watching us might logically assume we had official permission. Or, just as logically, they might shoot us.

"Are you looking like you know what you're doing?" I asked Bill out of the side of my mouth.

"It should be obvious by now. I always know what I'm doing."

We were halfway across. I felt the eyes of the crowd on my back, sharp as bayonets. Ahead, I saw the faces of people in line turning to watch us, and began wondering how to accomplish a smooth entrance into their ranks.

"No way we're stoppin' here!" said Bill, clairvoyant. "Won't do us any good. We've got to get up near the front."

My instinct was to find a place to hide, but Bill was right. If we joined the line at this point, we'd still miss our train. Ahead we could see the line snaking through Red Square for three hundred yards, right to the entrance of the mausoleum. Pairs of policemen were stationed at spots along the way. We reached the line but kept five yards away, marching parallel to it, on toward the napping Lenin. A few feet to our right the funereal masses eyed us without comment.

"Got your passport out?" Bill asked.

It was already in my hand. In his hand I saw the blue of passport and the white of Intourist letterhead.

"What'd your wife say?"

" 'Don't get shot.' "

"If you do, anything I should tell her?"

"She missed a great trip."

I matched my steps to Bill's. Five steps from the first pair of guards, as though we'd practiced, we both raised our passports at the same instant. The guards eyed us coldly, but stepped aside.

"They've heard of me," Bill said.

We were within two hundred yards of the mausoleum now. Another set of guards stepped aside, let us pass.

"If no one stops us, I'm gonna walk on into the Kremlin and have tea with Chernenko. You comin'?"

"Where you go, I go."

The last checkpoint was only a hundred yards from the entrance of the tomb. This time the guard held up his hand and blocked our path. We stopped and presented our passports. He looked at us for a moment with a "vut-dah-hell?" expression, and head-jerked us into the line. The Russians moved aside to absorb us. No one—us, them, or the guard—had said a word. The line had tapered down to two abreast by this point and was moving right along. A clock on the Kremlin tower said seventeen minutes after eleven.

70
ISN'T EVERYONE WRITING A BOOK?

He wrote and it seemed good; read and it seemed vile; corrected and tore up; cut out; put in; was in ecstasy; in despair; had his good nights and bad mornings; snatched at ideas and lost them; saw his book plain before him and it vanished; acted his people's parts as he ate; mouthed them as he walked; now cried; now laughed; vacillated between this style and that; now preferred the heroic and pompous; next the plain and simple; now the vales of Tempe; then the fields of Kent or Cornwall; and could not decide whether he was the divinest genius or the greatest fool in the world.

—VIRGINIA WOOLF
Orlando

I T WAS GOOD TO BE ON A TRAIN AGAIN, to be sitting across from Bill in the dining car with a bottle of muddy-brown apple juice and a pastry in front of me, letting the whirlpool of Moscow settle. I was looking forward to a day in transit, a day without demands, a day to sit and think and watch more of the world drift past.

Two happy Africans from the next table, fluent in English and Russian, helped Bill order a meal of pork chops, potatoes, and peas. "Lay-tor you will hoff to hovv a dreenk with oss in our car," one of them said in a rich Afro-British accent. "We are zay-la-brating."

"Celebrating what?" Bill asked.

"We will tell you lay-tor," he said with a strong, toothy grin. The beer bottles on their table said the zay-la-bration was already under way.

Bill ate. I wrote.

> This trip's over. The rest is filler. Ever since that lady looked at me on the subway three days ago, life has been familiar again. I'm with my own tribe. No longer do I hallucinate buffalo herds or dream of jumping the train. No longer are there days and days to fritter carelessly away; no longer does life seem infinite. Warsaw is only nineteen hours away; a dozen hours beyond Warsaw lies Berlin; a stone's throw from Berlin one finds Amsterdam and London and . . .
>
> So what's it all mean? Am I fit again? Maybe. My marriage is still a toss-up, but I feel stronger for not being immobile while the coin spins through the air. Does travel heal? If not, it's at least a morphine injection. Maybe the greater truth is that *time* heals, and the personal truth is that travel's just the way I choose to spend my time.

"What are you writing all the time?" Bill asked, after many kilometers and many pages.

I slid my notebook across the table. He spun it around so that it was right side up, and hunched over it. He read:

> Trips are like quilts. On the quilt of this trip there is a filing-for-divorce square, a baptism square, a bike-trip square, a Fuji square, a Hiroshima square, an Amy square, a dysentery square, a Beijing square, a Trans-Siberian square, a Bill square, a Red Square, and a "who-knows-what's-next?" square.
>
> When I've got the squares all sewn together, I'll border them, add a backing, and have something to cuddle with on those dreary days when the world seems ordinary and repetitive.

"You know, I'm keeping a journal, too," Bill said, with uncharacteristic shyness. "I've been thinking of writing a book of my own."

What would his be about?

"My trip. What else? Isn't everyone writing a book about their trip? When I started out, I thought I could write something different. I had lots of clever thoughts I wanted to put in it, but that was three years ago. My thoughts have changed. I don't think the way I did when I was in college or when I was in Paris, or when I was yelling, 'You suck! You suck!' at the Super Bowl. I don't even think the way I did in China. My thoughts change so fast it seems ridiculous to write them down. When I read last year's journal—stuff I thought was pretty good when I wrote it—it's just embarrassing. Now I hardly ever write thoughts. Now all I write about is where I went, what I saw and ate, how much it cost, and whether it made me throw up or not." He laughed. "So what've you written about me?"

I grinned.

"Come on, show me some."

I took my notebook and thumbed through it. "Here, read about this morning."

Bill read the story of Lenin's tomb—"I come off pretty good here"—and then the postscript:

> We went back and thanked Our Man. He was all smiles now—pantomiming with his fingers our march to the front of the line, smacking his forehead in disbelief. He hadn't thought we'd do *that*.
>
> We ran back to the Metropol. Bill stopped to buy a huge bouquet of flowers, and we took them to the ticket lady. "It was nothing," she said, blushing while her co-workers hooted.
>
> We got our packs from the doorman, the same guy who hadn't liked Bill's shorts. Now he laughed and led us to a taxi. "Bellaruskaja," he told the driver. I think it translates: "Get 'em outa here."

Bill looked up, smiling, closed the notebook, and pushed it back to me. "Those Russians. They're decent folks if you push 'em hard enough."

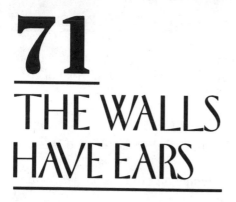

71
THE WALLS HAVE EARS

We will put our fingers around a glass together. We will put our hands in yours to shake in friendship. But we will not put our fingers on the ink pad.

—NIKOLAY BULGANIN, Russian premier, condemning the fingerprinting of applicants for U.S. visas, news reports May 28, 1956

WHEN WE LEFT THE DINING ROOM, Bill stopped off at the bathroom, and I continued on toward the compartment he and I were sharing with a Russian soldier who spoke no English and a student from Sierra Leone. The student, a woman, had just finished seven years of medical study in Moscow, and was going to London for a last gulp of Western decadence before returning home to a job in a public hospital. She would have some stories to tell, and I looked forward to hearing them.

But it was several hours before I made it back to our compartment. I was within two doors of it when one of the Africans from the dining car reached from a doorway and grabbed my arm.

"Now you will sit and talk with oss."

I protested, but lacking a good antisocial excuse, I yielded, and mentally surrendered my vague plans for the afternoon.

"You are American. Am I right?" He was smiling broadly. "I am from Ghana. I have bean in Musk-o for nine months and now I am going home. That is the coss for zay-la-bration. And what is your good name?"

I told him.

"Nice to meet you, Brohd. I am Akosi." He ushered me into his four-person compartment, where six other men were sitting knee-to-knee on the two lower bunks. "This is Brohd. He is an American, and he loves Stoli."

There was a giggle from the other occupants. Standing like icons on the car's fold-down table were two half-full bottles of Stolichnaya vodka—the stuff boycotted in America when the Korean jet was shot down. Next to them were two bottles of beer and one Pepsi. By the window there was a sliver of bunk space, and I stepped over all the knees and ducked through layers of cigarette smoke to get to it. Akosi followed, and somehow squeezed in beside me. "Are you cohm-fort-able?" He looked around, smiling hugely at everyone. "We are freeeee!"

When I asked what we were free from, the car exploded in guffaws. "What did I say?" I asked Akosi.

"Where hovv you josst bean?"

"Moscow."

"And how long were you there?"

"Three days."

More snickering.

Akosi pointed at a black man, another Ghanaian, seated across from us. "This is Christian." Christian and I shook hands and said how do you do, and there was a pause for more introductions. We were a checkerboard: three Ghanaians, one Ethiopian, two Poles, one Moroccan—four black faces, four white ones.

When we were done, Akosi called out, "Christian, how long have you bean in Musk-o?"

Christian had been there for two years, the others anywhere from nine months, like Akosi, to four years, without once leaving. "And now we are freeee!" Akosi rejoiced.

"Nawt josst yait," said Christian.

"But soon," said Akosi. His features, their impact multiplied by their nearness, were enormous. He had large ivory-colored teeth and later, while I cringed, he used them to pop the caps off the Pepsi and beer bottles.

"Have some Stoli, Brohd," he commanded, laughing.

I pleaded weak stomach, aversion to hard liquor, recent illness.

"You have had Stoli, yes? Then you know it leaves no hon-gover."

"I know nothing of the sort."

He dropped some ice cubes into a cup and began unscrewing the bottle top.

"Well, hell, then. Let me pour my own." I filled the cup with ice and dumped a slurp of vodka over top.

There were cries of protest. "More!" cried the More-occan and the Poles and the Ghanaians.

"Lay-tor," I said.

"American boys are very small drinkers," said Samuel, the third Ghanaian. His own cup was very full, and would be kept that way for the next several hours.

"Eight bottles of Stoli," Akosi whistled. "We had ten this morning, but now there are eight. We thought we would sell them in Poland, but instead we are zay-la-brating."

Did they drink like this in Moscow?

"Only sometimes," said Akosi. "We study very hard. But sometimes it is too much and we go crazy. Can you believe that before I went to Musk-o, like all students from Ghana I was tee-totaler. I drank nothing. The first few times I got very sick, but now I can drink a lawt."

I had a hunch that these Ghanaians would know the answer to a question I'd been wanting to ask someone: "Do people in Moscow ever smoke marijuana—"

I was going to finish my question with "or hashish?," but I didn't get the chance. Akosi's eyes widened; he grabbed my left biceps and stuck a finger to his lips. Samuel shut the door.

"The walls hovv ears!" Akosi hissed, lips an inch from my ear. He rapped lightly on the wall behind us.

"But . . ."

"The walls hovv ears!"

"But surely you can talk?"

Christian leaned over. "You are American. You are used to saying whatever you want. But you are not in America. Some of us have to go back to Musk-o. We have learned not to talk. When we are in Germany, or if you come to Ghana, you can ask us anything. But here," and he nodded at Akosi, "the . . . walls . . . hovv . . . ears."

Akosi, in a hushed voice: "We have seen friends deported for saying the wrong thing to the wrong person. And we have seen our Russian friends disappear. In the night they disappear. The . . . walls . . . hovv . . . ears."

To them I conceded: "The walls have ears." And to myself: People in Moscow sometimes smoke marijuana.

Samuel slid the door open, and as though nothing had happened, the conversation resumed. I asked Akosi if he thought he was better off as a teetotaler, or had learning to drink made him more complete? He became thoughtful. His eyes strayed out the window at a bank of yellow flowers blurring past. I glanced at the rest of the car; boisterous conversations, in Russian, were again flying back and forth between the bunks.

"I think I was better off as tee-totaler," Akosi said after reflection. "Drink makes monn stupid. But to live in Musk-o without drink makes a monn even more stupid. In Musk-o drink is nee-cess-ee-tee."

Would he drink when he went back to Ghana?

"A little, I sah-pose, but I will have much work to do. In Ghana we have many problems. We cannot feed all our people. We cannot educate ourselves. And we *need* education. We need many things. It is a very special privilege to go to Russia, to learn, to study, to become aware of the world. My cone-tree is expecting many things of me."

72
OUR COMMON LAP

Thank you all from the bottom of my heart for your hospitality and, as we say in Russia, for your bread and salt. Let us have more and more uses for the short American word "O.K."

—NIKITA KHRUSHCHEV
concluding first U.S. visit, 1959

O
VER THE NEXT HOUR OR SO, while I nursed my vodka and Akosi fleshed out his résumé, the rest of the car drained the first two bottles and initiated a third. They poured tall glasses, one after the other, and toasted like sailors.

"You mosst onderstond," said Akosi, eyes wide, happy, "we have earned this zay-la-bration. Stay in Musk-o more than three days, and you have earned something."

Suddenly Bill, whom I'd almost forgotten, was pulled in through the door and plopped down in a space across from me, next to the Moroccan. "They got me." I introduced him around and filled him in on what was happening. Samuel, whom I would see crawling on his hands and knees in the hall the next morning, splashed a big slug of vodka into a cup and ordered Bill to drink. Bill sipped.

When the Russians showed up, the car's descending level of sobriety went into an open tailspin. First there was Andrei, a tall blond with a beard, who seated himself next to the door. The Africans began laughing and pointing at the two of us, lookalikes from opposite ends of the political spectrum, now sitting like bookends on opposite ends of the bunk, sandwiching two Ghanaians and a Pole.

"Americanski, Russki," they laughed. "Brohd, Andrei." Andrei looked at me and I at him. We shrugged and reached across to shake hands. The car cheered. A large glass of vodka was passed to Andrei, another slurp added to mine.

Christian, who had not been drinking, quieted the car and made a speech, in Russian, which Akosi translated simultaneously for Bill and me. "It is silly for Americans and Russians to be wasting the resources of the entire world on buhmbs. In our cone-tree we have people who die because they cannot eat. And now we have bean to Musk-o and we know that Musk-o, too, has pruhblems." Everyone looked at Andrei, who nodded gravely. "And we know that America has pruhblems." The eyes of the car shifted to Bill and me; we nodded. "The whole world has pruhblems. But if we take the spirit of goodwill and friendship that is here, and take it back to our own cone-trees, to those who are not lucky enough to come here, then everything is po-see-bull."

Akosi took my hand and pulled it to the middle of the car. He reached over and grabbed Andrei's hand and pulled it toward mine. He held them together and put his own over top. Samuel and Christian and the Poles and Bill and the Moroccan and the Ethiopian and an Italian who had wandered in all threw their hands to the middle. Chocolate-colored hands, tan hands, white hands, rose in a knotted stack.

"Let us all promise," said Christian, while Akosi translated, "that we will go back to our homes and spread peeze among our peoples. And that we will make the superpowers talk to each other. If people can get together like this and talk, then we can have peeze."

The Russian conductor—a young man, under thirty, with the blue eyes of a mountain lake and a sharp, charcoal-colored uniform—chose this moment to poke his head into the compartment. The Poles at the door grabbed him by the wrists and yanked him into our midst. The stack of hands disappeared. Samuel passed a bottle to the newcomer, who put it to his mouth, chugged several times, gasped, and smacked his lips. He was shoved down into a spot next to Bill, across from Akosi and myself. Glasses were filled all around.

The conductor made the first toast, Akosi translated: "To peeze." Everyone else in the car clinked and drained their glasses; Bill and I sipped.

Next the Poles had a toast that needed no translation: "Solidarnosc!" The Africans screamed; the Russians rocked easily in their seats, absorbing this ribbing good-naturedly. The walls and their ears didn't give a damn about Solidarnosc.

A white-coated kitchen worker, a teenage Russian, stopped in the hall and stuck his head through the open door. The Africans greeted him like a long lost brother, but there was absolutely no room for him in the car. He stood in the doorway while the Africans introduced Bill and me to him. We were a novelty, a prize catch, two Americans come down from the summit to mingle among Poles and Russians and Africans, and they liked showing us off. The kitchen worker pointed to me and said something in Russian.

"He says you look like Andrei's braw-thar," Akosi told me.

I yelled across the compartment, "I am Andrei Sakharov!"

This was great humor. The car rocked with laughter, and I heard my own cackle above it all.

"Ah, Andrei Sakharov!" The kitchen worker stepped into the car, extended his hand to me, and pumped out a fifteen-second handshake. Akosi passed a bottle, half-full, the sixth or seventh of the afternoon, and right before our eyes the kitchen worker tipped it upright, drained it down his throat, smiled sickly, bowed once, and disappeared down the hall. During the afternoon he passed our door several times, and each time he would stop and point in at me. "Andrei Sakharov!" he would scream.

Every new act, every statement, every joke, every toast, produced a new round of laughter. Soon irritated banging erupted from the next compartment. "Maybe they will complain to the cone-doctor," Akosi said in Russian, and again no interpretation was needed. The conductor screamed maniacally and slammed back on the wall.

The Moroccan toasted Bill, who was seated next to him. Bill toasted back. A moment later I noticed the Moroccan, whose name was pronounced "Eight," whisper something in Bill's ear. Bill shook his head, but the Moroccan persisted.

"Brad," Bill called out, shock showing, "he says he wants to 'blow' me."

"Eight likes boys," Akosi said. "He means nahthing."

"I should kick his balls in!"

"No, no . . . ! He is paying you cohm-plee-ment."

Eight leaned over, whispering again. "In Warsaw," Bill cried, "he wants to get a hotel room with me! I'm gettin' outa here." He rose, clambered over the legs to the door, and vanished. Eight shrugged.

"Beel is focked op," Akosi squealed.

"American boys are very small dreenkers," said Samuel, who was beginning to look sick. Next to him, the conductor had removed his jacket and tie and unbuttoned his shirt. He and I looked at each other and smiled, but could not speak.

"Will you translate for me?" I asked Akosi.

"Of course."

"Ask him if he will talk with me person-to-person."

Akosi rattled off a couple of sentences, the conductor nodded.

"Tell him this. Tell him that in America there are many people who want peace, but that we sometimes act like we do not want peace, because really we are afraid of the Russians. Tell him that."

Akosi translated; the Russian nodded at Akosi and then at me.

"Tell him this, too. Tell him that I am an American, that I would like to have peace with the Russians, that that is one of the reasons I have come here, to tell him and his people that I am a normal American who wants peace, but that I, too, am often scared. I am afraid of Russians. Tell him."

Akosi told him. The Russian accepted this, and looked at me with soft eyes made softer by drunkenness.

"Now ask if he himself is ever afraid of Americans." While Akosi translated, I studied the conductor's open, vulnerable face, as pleasant a face as ever there was. I knew he would answer in the affirmative: of course he was sometimes afraid of Americans.

But the instant he perceived the thrust of my question, the conductor jerked his eyes from Akosi to me. Immediately they hardened. *"Nyet!"* he spat, clamping his jaw. He rattled in Russian.

"He says he is not afraid," Akosi told me "and that the Russians are not afraid, but you can see in his eyes—he is afraid."

I looked across at the conductor. His response had sobered me. I had met him halfway (actually much *more* than halfway), had admitted my fears and my feelings. But he had not budged. His face was still set, his jaw firm. Imagining himself invincible, he was a political cartoon.

"Yours is the American way to peeze," Akosi said to me. "You want to talk and say nice things. But now we must also try the Russian way." He passed the bottle to the conductor, who filled both our glasses. "To peeze." He chugged his in one gulp. I nibbled at mine. He smiled at me as though we'd settled everything, then stood, grabbed his coat, said a smiley, drunken good-bye, and lurched out into the hall. (Early the next morning, before I was out of bed, he came to my compartment with a cup of hot tea. "Peeze," he said, and smiled.)

With the conductor gone and with Bill gone and with Samuel beginning to nod away, the mood in the car tapered off. Only Akosi and I were still going. "I know," he was saying to me, "that all anybody wants is to be able to eat and learn and have families and have good things, but we are all afraid, so we pretend. The cone-doctor—you saw him—he is afraid. And if everyone stays only in their own cone-trees, the world will always be that way. If I had never bean away from Ghana, I would still be a silly person, ignorant of the world. That is why it is good for people to go to other cone-trees. People cannot leave Russia or Africa so easily. But it is easy for Americans. Americans see other places, and then they are not so afraid. Like you."

I promised that I had fears of my own.

"But what is there for you to be afraid of?"

I told him I was spending all my money, my wife wanted to divorce me, I had no idea what I would do with my life when I got back to my cone-tree.

"I tell you what you do. You go back and tell everyone you see that you have bean to Musk-o, you have bean around the world, and that everywhere you meet people like me who want only peeze. Tell them that it is possible for three Russians and three Ghanaians and two Poles and one Ethiopian and two Americans and one crazy Moroccan who likes boys to ride together in a railroad car peeze-vo-lee. Tell them to come and see for themselves.

Tell them to come and visit me in Ghana, or to come and visit me in Musk-o nexx jeer. Tell them josst like thet."

He stopped and looked directly at me with those wide white eyes, starting to show just a tinge of red. In the silence I became aware of the train's jiggling motion, of the poles flying by the window, of my own body, of the bodies of everyone else in the compartment, and I began wondering just how long Akosi and I'd been sitting like that, with our hands—his brown, mine pale—clasped together, fingers laced, resting in our common lap.

"Will you tell them that?" he begged me.

PART
FIVE

CURTAIN CALL

How much a dunce that has been sent to roam
Excels a dunce that has been kept at home!

—WILLIAM COWPER
The Progress of Error

AIL TRICKLED IN FOR MONTHS.

David and Heidi, the Canadians who sold me the bicycle in Japan, wrote to say they were on their way to Brazil.

Terry the Longhair was back in Madison, Wisconsin, "working for the fucking post office. How's your book coming?"

Walter from Okubo House reported that he was passing through New York, "traveling with a French teacher of mathematics with another diploma in law. Very down to earth, and as sharp as a tack, with a delicious wit."

Daniel Davidson, the Zen enthusiast and avant-garde artist, checked in from Chicago:

> My studio is set up and I've finished a few good paintings. But mostly I'm waiting for my fiancée, a Chinese girl, to rejoin me here and marry. A happy marriage has eluded me so far, yet now, and this seems strange even to me after so much disappointment, I've fallen in love, in the most classic, most innocent manner possible. There's no fool like a middle-aged lover, unless it be God's fool.

Russ the Mennonite wrote from Kansas:

> I've begun farming with my dad, and am thoroughly enjoying it. Fortunately, I've been able to work for a neighbor off and on doing some concrete and carpentry work, which brings in some cash until wheat harvest. Most of my pictures

turned out pretty good—except for the ah . . . pole shots.
How did you and Bill ever do without visas?

Bill sent a string of letters and postcards—Budapest, Istanbul, Jerusalem,
Bangladesh, and later Koh Samui, an island in the Gulf of Siam:

> The Man 100 Miles Up would be pretty upset with me. I've
> been sitting on my butt for a month, resting up for Tibet,
> but I'm still whipped from all this moving around. I've got a
> hut on the beach, and a new routine—I spend half the day
> thinking about what I'm going to think about the rest of the
> day.

Amy wrote:

> . . . The day after you left I went to the Beijing Hotel early
> for my expected rendezvous with the mythical (?) Dylan. By
> 1:00 in the afternoon I gave up in *FRUSTRATION.* Even re-
> turned the next morning . . . you know, he could have missed
> his train . . . Nope, he wasn't there. Midafternoon I returned
> to my hotel, was packing some things, and guess who
> walked in? Yum-yum . . .
> The black-market scam . . . I got exactly what I deserved—
> NOTHING!! It seems so stupid now. A long story—but in
> essence, on the Trans-Sib, the Russians confiscated $1100
> from Dylan because it wasn't declared on entry—he was
> passed out from champagne crossing the Mongolia/Russia
> border and didn't fill out a declaration form. An even longer
> story . . . I'm not going to create any more Dylan types in
> my life!!!

I feared that mail from me might cause trouble for Shi—the young Chinese
man who had never heard of Jesus—so I waited a long time before writing
to him, but I never heard back.

Letters I sent to Akosi and Christian also went unanswered, but San Francisco's city clerk was more responsive. Two months after my return, he
received an envelope from my wife and me—stuffed with official papers,
signed and countersigned. Within days he sent final confirmation.

It turned out to be one of those amicable "modern" divorces. We still
loved each other, but we had moved apart. She had a new job and a circle
of new friends, who knew me not as a friend but as one of my wife's problems.
And after years of moving around, she'd now been settled in San Francisco
for three straight years; I was still footloose, unrooted, flush from a trip
around the world.

I got my own apartment (no view of the Golden Gate Bridge, dammit), bought a word processor and a lighted globe, and stayed in one place—the right place, no doubt—just long enough to translate my notebooks.

The very day I finished, this arrived:

Kumemoto, Japan

Dear Mr. Brad Newshu,

How are you doing?

It is one year since we met you in Hiroshima when we went on school excursion.

We are sorry for not to write a letter soon.

We became the 9th grade in April.

We promised one another that we'll do our best in studying, sports, and so on.

We met you in Hiroshima when we went on school excursion.

We have enclosed a picture we took there. We hope you will like it.

from
All the girls in our class

ABOUT
THE AUTHOR

BRAD NEWSHAM believes that the reason none of his careers—underground miner, newspaper reporter, waiter, bank secretary, and San Francisco cab driver—has lasted more than a couple of years has something to do with the fact that he wandered into Afghanistan when he was twenty-two years old and very green. He says that his expectation for this book, his first, is that it "will bring a few letters to my mailbox."